P9-DZO-151

Android™ Tablets

FOR DUMMIES®

A Wiley Brand

3rd Edition

Android™ Tablets

FOR DUMMIES®

A Wiley Brand

3rd Edition

by Dan Gookin

FOR DUMMIES
A Wiley Brand

LONGWOOD PUBLIC LIBRARY

Android™ Tablets For Dummies® 3rd Edition

Published by: **John Wiley & Sons, Inc.,** 111 River Street, Hoboken, NJ 07030-5774, `www.wiley.com`

Copyright © 2015 by John Wiley & Sons, Inc., Hoboken, New Jersey

Published simultaneously in Canada

No part of this publication may be reproduced, stored in a retrieval system or transmitted in any form or by any means, electronic, mechanical, photocopying, recording, scanning or otherwise, except as permitted under Sections 107 or 108 of the 1976 United States Copyright Act, without the prior written permission of the Publisher. Requests to the Publisher for permission should be addressed to the Permissions Department, John Wiley & Sons, Inc., 111 River Street, Hoboken, NJ 07030, (201) 748-6011, fax (201) 748-6008, or online at `http://www.wiley.com/go/permissions`.

Trademarks: Wiley, For Dummies, the Dummies Man logo, Dummies.com, Making Everything Easier, and related trade dress are trademarks or registered trademarks of John Wiley & Sons, Inc. and may not be used without written permission. Android is a trademark of Google, Inc. All other trademarks are the property of their respective owners. John Wiley & Sons, Inc. is not associated with any product or vendor mentioned in this book.

LIMIT OF LIABILITY/DISCLAIMER OF WARRANTY: THE PUBLISHER AND THE AUTHOR MAKE NO REPRESENTATIONS OR WARRANTIES WITH RESPECT TO THE ACCURACY OR COMPLETENESS OF THE CONTENTS OF THIS WORK AND SPECIFICALLY DISCLAIM ALL WARRANTIES, INCLUDING WITHOUT LIMITATION WARRANTIES OF FITNESS FOR A PARTICULAR PURPOSE. NO WARRANTY MAY BE CREATED OR EXTENDED BY SALES OR PROMOTIONAL MATERIALS. THE ADVICE AND STRATEGIES CONTAINED HEREIN MAY NOT BE SUITABLE FOR EVERY SITUATION. THIS WORK IS SOLD WITH THE UNDERSTANDING THAT THE PUBLISHER IS NOT ENGAGED IN RENDERING LEGAL, ACCOUNTING, OR OTHER PROFESSIONAL SERVICES. IF PROFESSIONAL ASSISTANCE IS REQUIRED, THE SERVICES OF A COMPETENT PROFESSIONAL PERSON SHOULD BE SOUGHT. NEITHER THE PUBLISHER NOR THE AUTHOR SHALL BE LIABLE FOR DAMAGES ARISING HEREFROM. THE FACT THAT AN ORGANIZATION OR WEBSITE IS REFERRED TO IN THIS WORK AS A CITATION AND/OR A POTENTIAL SOURCE OF FURTHER INFORMATION DOES NOT MEAN THAT THE AUTHOR OR THE PUBLISHER ENDORSES THE INFORMATION THE ORGANIZATION OR WEBSITE MAY PROVIDE OR RECOMMENDATIONS IT MAY MAKE. FURTHER, READERS SHOULD BE AWARE THAT INTERNET WEBSITES LISTED IN THIS WORK MAY HAVE CHANGED OR DISAPPEARED BETWEEN WHEN THIS WORK WAS WRITTEN AND WHEN IT IS READ.

For general information on our other products and services, please contact our Customer Care Department within the U.S. at 877-762-2974, outside the U.S. at 317-572-3993, or fax 317-572-4002. For technical support, please visit `www.wiley.com/techsupport`.

Wiley publishes in a variety of print and electronic formats and by print-on-demand. Some material included with standard print versions of this book may not be included in e-books or in print-on-demand. If this book refers to media such as a CD or DVD that is not included in the version you purchased, you may download this material at `http://booksupport.wiley.com`. For more information about Wiley products, visit `www.wiley.com`.

Library of Congress Control Number: 2015943534

ISBN: 978-1-119-12602-7; 978-1-119-12604-1 (ebk); 978-1-119-12605-8 (ebk)

Manufactured in the United States of America

10 9 8 7 6 5 4 3 2 1

Contents at a Glance

Table of Contents

Introduction

S omewhere filling the void between the smartphone and the computer lies the premiere device of the 21st century. It's probably something you've never used but will soon be unable to live without. It's the tablet — specifically, an Android tablet.

The Android tablet is a gizmo that could fully replace your computer, as well as several other pieces of electronics you may tote around. It's an all-in-one, lightweight, battery-powered, long-lasting, fully mobile, telecommunications, information, and entertainment gizmo.

Oh, but I do go on.

As an Android tablet owner, or someone who's interested in purchasing such a device, you obviously want to get the most from your technology. Perhaps you've attempted to educate yourself using that flimsy *Getting Started* leaflet that comes with the thing. Now you're turning to this book, a wise choice.

New technology can be intimidating. Frustrating. No matter what, your experience can be made better by leisurely reading this delightful, informative, and occasionally entertaining book.

About This Book

Please don't read this book from cover to cover. This book is a reference. It's designed to be used as you need it. Look up a topic in the table of contents or the index. Find something about your tablet that vexes you or something you're curious about. Look up the answer, and get on with your life.

The overall idea for this book is to show how things are done on the Android tablet and to help you enjoy the device without overwhelming you with information or intimidating you into despair.

Sample sections in this book include

- Unlocking the tablet
- Activating voice input
- Importing contacts from your computer

✔ Adding more email accounts

✔ Running Facebook on your tablet

✔ Placing a Hangouts phone call

✔ Helping others find your location

✔ Renting or purchasing movies and TV shows

✔ Flying with an Android tablet

You have nothing to memorize, no sacred utterances or animal sacrifices, and definitely no PowerPoint presentations. Instead, every section explains a topic as though it's the first thing you've read in this book. Nothing is assumed, and everything is cross-referenced. Technical terms and topics, when they come up, are neatly shoved to the side, where they're easily avoided. The idea here isn't to learn anything. My philosophy while writing this book was to help you look it up, figure it out, and get on with your life.

How to Use This Book

This book follows a few conventions for using an Android tablet. First of all, no matter what name your tablet has, whether it's a manufacturer's name or a pet name you've devised on your own, this book refers to your tablet as an *Android tablet* or, often, just *tablet*.

The way you interact with the Android tablet is by using its *touchscreen* — the glassy part of the device as it's facing you. The device also has some physical buttons, as well as some holes and connectors. All these items are described in Chapter 1.

The various ways to touch the screen are explained and named in Chapter 3.

Chapter 4 covers text input on an Android tablet, which involves using an onscreen keyboard. You can also input text by speaking to the Android tablet, which is also found in Chapter 4.

This book directs you to do things by following numbered steps. Each step involves a specific activity, such as touching something on the screen; for example:

3. Tap the Apps icon.

This step directs you to tap or touch the graphical Apps icon on the screen. When a button is shown as text, the command reads:

3. Tap the Download button.

You might also be directed to *choose* an item, which means to tap it on the screen.

Various settings can be turned off or on, as indicated by a box with a mark in it, similar to the one shown in the margin. By tapping the box on the screen, you add or remove the check mark. When the check mark appears, the option is on; otherwise, it's off.

Some settings feature the Master Control icon. Tap the icon or slide the icon to the right to activate the switch, as shown in the margin. Tap the icon or slide the button to the left to disable the feature. Unlike check boxes, which control options, master controls activate or deactivate major tablet features.

Foolish Assumptions

Even though this book is written with the gentle handholding required by anyone who is just starting out, or who is easily intimidated, I've made a few assumptions. For example, I assume that you're a human being and not a colony creature from the planet Zontar.

My biggest assumption: You have or desire to own a tablet that uses Google's Android operating system. Your tablet might be an LTE tablet (one that uses the mobile data network) or a Wi-Fi–only model. This book covers both.

The Android operating system comes in versions, or flavors. This book covers Android version numbers 4.3, 4.4, and 5.0. These versions are known by the flavors Jelly Bean, Kit Kat, and Lollipop, respectively. To confirm which Android version your tablet has, follow these steps:

1. At the Home screen, tap the Apps icon.

Refer to Chapter 3 for a description of the Apps icon.

2. Open the Settings app.

3. Choose About Tablet.

This item might be named About Device. If you're using a Samsung Galactic tablet, find this item by first tapping the General tab atop the screen.

4. Look at the item titled Android Version.

The number that's shown indicates the Android operating system version.

Don't fret if these steps confuse you: Review Part I of this book, and then come back here. (I'll wait.)

More assumptions:

You don't need to own a computer to use your Android tablet. If you have a computer, great. The Android tablet works well with both PC and Mac. When directions are specific to a PC or Mac, the book says so.

Programs that run on your Android tablet are *apps*, which is short for *applications*. A single program is an app.

Finally, this book assumes that you have a Google account, but if you don't, Chapter 2 explains how to configure one. Do so. Having a Google account opens up a slew of useful features, information, and programs that make using your tablet more productive.

How This Book Is Organized

This book is divided into five parts, which for your convenience are organized sequentially. Each part covers a certain aspect of the Android tablet or how it's used.

Part I: Getting Started with Android Tablets

Part I covers setup and orientation, to familiarize you with how the device works. It's a good place to start if you're new to the concept of tablet computing, mobile devices, or the Android operating system.

Part II: Stay in Touch

In Part II, you can read about various ways that an Android tablet can electronically communicate with your online friends. Topics include working with the tablet's address book, sending and receiving email, browsing the web, chatting and texting with friends, making phone calls (don't tell the Phone Company), and exploring social networking.

Part III: Omni Tablet

This part explores the Android tablet's limitless potential: It's an eBook reader, a map, a navigator, a photo album, a portable music player, a calendar, a calculator, and, potentially, much more.

Part IV: Nuts and Bolts

Part IV covers a lot of different topics, from wireless networking to sharing information and from customizing the tablet to troubleshooting it. Also included is information on using the tablet aloft or overseas.

Part V: The Part of Tens

I wrap things up with the traditional *For Dummies* Part of Tens. Chapters in this part cover tips, tricks, suggestions, and important things to remember.

Icons Used in This Book

This icon flags useful, helpful tips or shortcuts.

This icon marks a friendly reminder to do something.

This icon marks a friendly reminder not to do something.

This icon alerts you to overly nerdy information and technical discussions of the topic at hand. Reading the information is optional, though it may win you the Daily Double on *Jeopardy!*

Where to Go from Here

Start reading! Observe the table of contents and find something that interests you. Or look up your puzzle in the index. When these suggestions don't cut it, just start reading Chapter 1.

My email address is dgookin@wambooli.com. Yes, that's my real address. I reply to every email I receive, and more quickly when you keep your question short and specific to this book. Although I enjoy saying Hi, I cannot answer technical support questions, resolve billing issues, or help you troubleshoot your tablet. Thanks for understanding.

My website is www.wambooli.com. This book has its own page on that site, which you can check for updates, new information, and all sorts of fun stuff. Visit often:

www.wambooli.com/help/android/tablets

The publisher also offers its own helpful site, which contains official updates and bonus information. Visit the publisher's official support page at

www.dummies.com/extras/androidtablets

You can also find this book's online Cheat Sheet at

www.dummies.com/cheatsheet/androidtablets

Enjoy this book and your Android tablet!

Part I
Getting Started with Android Tablets

Visit www.dummies.com for great Dummies content online.

In this part . . .

- ✔ Get this-and-that set up on your new Android tablet.

- ✔ Toil through activation and initial tablet configuration.

- ✔ Learn how to turn a tablet on and off and how to lock and unlock the screen.

- ✔ Discover the many sensual ways you can manipulate the touchscreen.

- ✔ Explore the onscreen keyboard and use dictation to create text.

That Out-of-the-Box Experience

*Y*our Android tablet adventure begins by opening the device's box. Sure, you've probably already done that. I don't blame you; I had already opened the box that my Android tablet came in before I read this chapter. No problem. So, to help you recall the ordeal, or to get you oriented if you found the process daunting, or just to prepare you for that out-of-the-box experience yet to come, this chapter provides you with a gentle introduction to your new Android tablet.

Initial Procedures

If you've purchased a cellular or LTE tablet, the folks who sold it to you may have already done some configuration before you left the store. That's great because an LTE tablet requires some extra setup before you can use the device. That duty is explained in Chapter 2. For now, all tablet owners — LTE and Wi-Fi — need to perform two basic tablet activities, described in this section.

Liberating the tablet from the box

Thanks to an excess of funds, your federal government has conducted numerous studies on how people use electronic devices. Men and women wearing white lab coats and safety goggles, and wielding clipboards, drew

Android tablet purchasing tips

The major things to look for when purchasing an Android tablet are the screen size and whether you want an LTE or a Wi-Fi–only device.

Larger screens are more visible and easier to read, but a larger tablet requires two hands to operate. A smaller size tablet might be more convenient. The only way to know which size works best for you is to manhandle an Android tablet at the store before you buy.

LTE tablets use the mobile data network to access the Internet, just like a smartphone. That ability comes with a monthly bill, but if you need Internet access anywhere, it's worth the price. Both LTE and Wi-Fi–only tablets can access Wi-Fi networks.

Some tablets feature removable storage in the form of a MicroSD card. This feature allows you to expand the device's storage and more easily share files with a computer.

Ensure that the tablet has both front and rear cameras. The camera resolution isn't vital, but if your tablet is going to be your only digital camera, getting a high-resolution rear camera is a plus. Also confirm that the rear camera has a flash.

Beyond these basic items, most Android tablets are the same, with only subtle software differences. Do ensure, however, that your tablet uses the Android operating system and can access and use the Google Play Store. Some low-price, bargain tablets restrict your purchases to the manufacturer's own app store. I don't see that limitation as a positive thing.

solid conclusions by thoroughly examining hundreds of Android tablets. The results were unanimous: An Android tablet works better when you first remove it from its box. Thank you, federal grant!

I assume that you're pretty good at the box-opening thing, so I probably don't need to detail that procedure. I can affirm, however, that it's perfectly okay to remove and throw away those protective plastic sheets clinging to the front, back, and sides of the tablet. And don't be embarrassed when, three weeks from now, you find yet another plastic sheet you haven't removed. Feel free to remove and throw away the plastic sheets.

Along with the tablet, you'll find the following items in the box:

- ✐ **USB cable:** You can use it to connect the tablet to a computer or a wall charger.
- ✐ **Power adapter:** Use this thing (and the USB cable) to charge the tablet's battery. The adapter may come in two pieces, both of which must be assembled.
- ✐ **Power charger and cable:** These are included with some tablets that don't use the USB cable to charge the battery.

 ✒ **Useless pamphlets:** If your tablet is like mine, you'll find that the safety and warranty information is far more extensive than the flimsy setup guide. That shows the priority our culture places on lawyers versus technology writers.

 ✒ **The 4G SIM card holder:** For an LTE tablet, you need a 4G SIM card. If you purchased your tablet at a phone store, someone there may have tossed the SIM card holder into the box as well. You can throw it out.

Keep the box for as long as you own your Android tablet. If you ever need to return the thing, or ship it anywhere, the original box is the ideal container. You can shove all those useless pamphlets and papers back into the box as well.

Charging the battery

The very first thing that I recommend you do with your tablet is give it a full charge.

Assemble the charging cord: Attach the wall adapter to the USB cable. Plug the cable into the tablet and the adapter into a wall socket. Wait.

Some tablets use their own charging cord, not the USB cable. If you own such a tablet, ensure that you're using that cord and not the USB cable; directions buried somewhere in the box explain how charging works.

Upon success, a large "battery charging" type of icon might appear on the tablet's touchscreen. This icon lets you know that the tablet is functioning properly — but don't be alarmed if the battery icon fails to appear.

If a Welcome screen or Setup screen appears when you charge the tablet, you can proceed with configuration. That process is covered in Chapter 2.

 ✒ Some tablets feature an HDMI connector, which looks similar to the USB or power connector. Don't jam the USB cable into that hole.

 ✒ Even if your Android tablet comes fully charged from the factory, I still recommend giving it an initial charge, to at least familiarize yourself with the process.

 ✒ The USB cable is also used for connecting the tablet to a computer to share information, exchange files, or use the tablet as a modem. The latter process, called *tethering,* is covered in Chapter 23.

 ✒ You can also charge the tablet by connecting it to a computer's USB port. As long as the computer is on, the tablet charges.

 ✒ Feel free to use the tablet while the battery is charging. And you don't have to wait for a full charge, either.

✔ When the battery is dead or just very low, you can't turn on the tablet. Just wait until the thing gets charged an eensie bit, and then it will turn on.

✔ The battery charges more efficiently if you plug it into a wall, as opposed to charging it from a computer's USB port.

✔ Most Android tablets I've seen don't feature a removable battery, so the battery cannot be replaced if it's defective. If the battery doesn't charge or keep a charge, you should return the tablet for a refund or replacement.

Tablet Exploration

Everyone loves a good game of hide-and-seek — except when it comes to technology. It's important that you know where certain key items are found on your Android tablet. The problem is that the location of these items isn't consistent, even when two tablets are made by the same manufacturer.

Finding things on the tablet

Take heed of Figure 1-1, which is my attempt at illustrating a generic Android tablet's hardware features. Use this figure as a guide as you follow along on your own tablet to locate some key features.

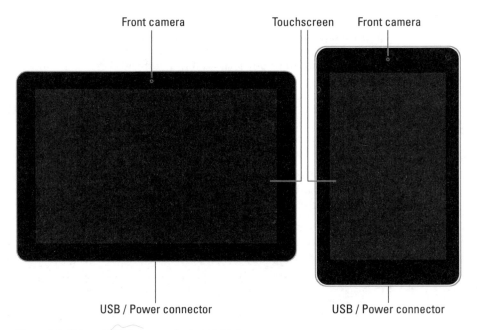

Figure 1-1: Things to find on your Android tablet.

Important items you'll find on the front of the tablet include the items in this list:

Touchscreen display: The biggest part of the tablet is its touchscreen display, which occupies almost all the territory on the front of the device. The touchscreen display is a look-touch gizmo: You look at it but also touch it with your fingers to control the tablet.

Front camera: The Android tablet's front-facing camera is found above the touchscreen. On larger tablets, the camera is on top when the tablet is oriented horizontally (refer to the left side of Figure 1-1). On small-format tablets, the camera is on top when the tablet is oriented vertically (refer to the right side of Figure 1-1).

Navigation icons: The bottom of the touchscreen shows the Android navigation icons. On some tablets, these icons are physical buttons found below the touchscreen. Refer to Chapter 3 for information on the navigation icons.

Important items found on the tablet's edges include the ones in this list:

Power/Lock key: This button, or key, turns the tablet on or off, or locks or unlocks the device. Directions for performing these activities are found in Chapter 2.

Volume key: The tablet's volume control is two buttons in one. Press one side of the key to set the volume higher or the other side to set the volume lower. This key is often found next to the Power/Lock key. It's the larger of the two.

USB/Power connector: This slot is where you connect the USB cable, which is used both to charge the battery and to connect your Android tablet to a computer. The slot is also where the tablet connects to the dock, should one of those be available. See the later section "Optional Accessories."

External storage slot: The tablet's external storage is added by inserting a memory card into the external storage slot. Details on using this feature are covered in the next section.

SIM card cover: This spot is used to access an LTE tablet's SIM card, which is inserted into a slot beneath the cover.

Headphone jack: This hole is where you can connect standard headphones.

Speaker(s): Stereo speakers are found left and right on the tablet, although smaller-format tablets may have their speakers on the back.

Microphone: A miniscule, circular opening serves as the device's microphone. Some tablets may feature two microphone holes. Don't worry if you can't find them; they're there.

The typical Android also has a back side. It's not shown earlier, in Figure 1-1, because the censors won't let me do an illustration but also because the back is boring: On it you may find the tablet's main camera and LED flash. That's it.

✔ Samsung tablets feature the Home button directly below the touchscreen. This physical button serves the same purpose as the Home icon on other Android tablets.

✔ Samsung tablets also feature touch-sensitive Recent and Back buttons. A Menu button is found instead of the Recent button on older tablets.

✔ Be careful not to confuse the SIM card slot with the external storage slot. They're not the same thing. You'll rarely, if ever, access the SIM card.

✔ SIM stands for Subscriber Identity Module. The SIM card is used by a cellular provider to identify your tablet and keep track of the amount of data transmitted over the mobile data network. Yep, that's so you can be billed properly. The SIM also gives your LTE tablet a phone number, though that number is merely an account and not something you can dial into or use for sending a text message.

✔ Don't stick anything into the microphone hole. Yes, it's tempting, but don't. Only stick things into your tablet that you're supposed to, such as the USB cable, headphones, memory card, or SIM card.

Inserting a MicroSD card

Removable storage is available on some Android tablets in the form of a *MicroSD card*. It can be used to store photos, videos, music, evil plans, and so on.

The MicroSD card is teensy. (That's a scientific description.) The card fits into a slot on the edge of your tablet but can also be inserted into your computer and read like any removable media card.

The card can be inserted into your tablet whether the device is on or off. Heed these directions:

1. **Locate the MicroSD card hatch on the tablet's edge.**

   Figure 1-2 illustrates the hatch's appearance, although it may look subtly different on your tablet. The card may be labeled *MicroSD*. Do not confuse it with the SIM card cover.

Lift here.

Figure 1-2: Opening the memory card hatch.

2. **Poke your fingernail into the slot on the teensy hatch that covers the MicroSD slot, and then flip up the hatch.**

   When pressure is applied to the slot, the hatch pops up and kind of flops over to the side. The cover may not come off completely.

3. **Orient the MicroSD card so that the printed side faces up and the teeny triangle on the card points toward the open slot.**

4. **Use your fingernail or a paperclip to gently shove the card all the way into the slot.**

   The card makes a faint clicking sound when it's fully inserted.

   If the card keeps popping out, you're not shoving it in far enough.

5. **Close the hatch covering the MicroSD card slot.**

If the tablet is on (and has been configured), you may see an onscreen prompt. If so, ignore the prompt and just tap the OK button on the tablet's touchscreen.

- ✔ Not every Android tablet features external storage. If you can't find a MicroSD card slot on the tablet's edge, that feature isn't available to your tablet.

- ✔ The tablet works with or without a MicroSD card installed.

- ✔ The MicroSD card is a purchase you must make in addition to your Android tablet. Check the tablet's documentation (on the box) to see which capacities are compatible with your tablet.

- ✔ MicroSD card capacity is in gigabytes (billions of bytes), abbreviated GB or just G. Common capacities include 16GB, 32GB, and 64GB. The higher the capacity, the more stuff you can store but also the more expensive the card.

- ✔ To use a MicroSD card with a computer, you need an SD card adapter. Insert the MicroSD card into the adapter, and then plug the SD card adapter into the computer. The adapter is an extra purchase, although some MicroSD cards come with such an adapter.

- ✔ SD stands for Secure Digital. It is but one of about a zillion media card standards.

> ✔ In addition to the MicroSD card, your Android tablet features internal storage. That storage is used for the programs you install on the tablet, as well as for the tablet's operating system and other control programs.
>
> ✔ Refer to Chapter 17 for more information on storage.

Removing the MicroSD card

Most of the time, the MicroSD card dwells contently inside your Android tablet. When the urge arises to remove it, heed these steps:

1. **Turn off your Android tablet.**

   You can damage the media card if you just yank it out of the tablet, which is why I recommend turning off the tablet first. Specific directions for turning off an Android tablet are found in Chapter 2.

2. **Open the itty-bitty hatch covering the MicroSD card slot.**

3. **Use your fingernail to press the MicroSD card inward a tad.**

   The MicroSD card is spring-loaded, so pressing it in eventually pops it outward.

4. **Pinch the MicroSD card between your fingers and remove it completely.**

The MicroSD card is too tiny to leave lying around. Put it into a MicroSD card adapter for use in your PC or another electronic device. Or store it inside a miniature box that you can label with a miniature pen in miniature letters: "MicroSD Card Inside." Don't lose it!

It's possible to remove the MicroSD card without turning off the tablet. To do that, you need to *unmount* the card while the tablet is running. This technical procedure is explained in Chapter 17.

Optional Accessories

Your credit card company will be thrilled when you discover that an assortment of handy Android tablet accessories are available for purchase. You can find them at the place where you purchased your tablet, online, or in the real world. Here are just a few of the items that you can consider getting to complete your tablet experience:

Earphones: You can use any standard cell phone or portable media player earphones with an Android tablet. Simply plug the earphones into the headphone jack at the top of the tablet and you're ready to go.

Covers, pouches, and sleeves: Answering the question "Where do I put this thing?" is the handy Android tablet pouch or sleeve accessory. Special pouches that double as covers or tablet stands are also available. Try to get one designed for your tablet. If not, check the size before you buy. Not every 10-inch tablet fits into the same 10-inch pouch.

Screen protectors: These plastic, clingy things are affixed to the front of the tablet, right over the touchscreen. They help defend the touchscreen glass from finger smudges and sneeze globs while still allowing you to use the touchscreen.

Vehicle charger: You can charge the Android tablet in your car if you buy a vehicle charger. It's an adapter that plugs into your car's 12-volt power supply, in the receptacle that was once known as a cigarette lighter. The vehicle charger is a must if you plan on using the Android tablet's navigation features in your auto or when you need a charge on the road.

Docks, various and sundry: Most people manhandle their tablets. Tsk, tsk. You can be more refined and get your Android tablet a dock. There are several kinds, from the simple prop-dock that holds up the tablet at a pleasant viewing angle to docks that contain keyboards to multimedia docks that feature USB ports.

Keyboard: Some docking stands double as tablet keyboards, but you can also obtain any Bluetooth keyboard for use with your Android tablet. See Chapter 16, which covers the Bluetooth connection.

USB Adapter: This USB adapter isn't the same thing as the USB cable that comes with your tablet. It's a dongle that plugs into the tablet's power/USB jack to allow the tablet to host a USB device, such as a keyboard, mouse, or modem, or an external storage device (hard drive or optical drive).

Other exciting and nifty accessories might be available for your tablet. Check frequently for new garnishes and frills at the location where you bought your tablet.

- ✔ None of this extra stuff is essential to using your tablet.

- ✔ You can use Bluetooth earphones or a cell phone Bluetooth headset with any Android tablet.

- ✔ If the earphones feature a microphone, you can use that microphone for dictation, recording, and even chatting online with friends.

- ✔ If the earphones feature a button, you can use the button to pause and play music. Press the button once to pause, and again to play.

- ✔ Android tablets generally don't recognize more than one earphones button. For example, if you use earphones that feature a Volume button or Mute button, pressing that extra button does nothing.

- ✔ Another useful accessory to get is a microfiber cloth to help clean the tablet's screen, plus a special cleaning-solution wipe. See Chapter 22 for more information about cleaning an Android tablet's screen.

Where to Keep Your Tablet

Like your car keys, glasses, wallet, and phaser pistol, your Android tablet should be kept in a safe, easy-to-find, always handy place, whether you're at home, at work, on the road, or orbiting the Klingon home world.

Making a home for the tablet

I recommend returning your Android tablet to the same spot whenever you finish using it. If you have a computer, my first suggestion is to make a spot right by the computer. Keep the charging cord handy, or just plug the cord into the computer's USB port so that you can synchronize information with your computer on a regular basis, not to mention keep the tablet charged.

Another handy place to keep the tablet is on your nightstand. That makes sense because, in addition to using the tablet for nighttime reading or video watching, it can serve as an alarm clock (see Chapter 14).

If you have a docking stand, plug your tablet into it whenever you're not toting it about.

Above all, avoid putting the tablet in a place where someone can sit on it, step on it, or otherwise damage it. For example, don't leave the tablet on a table or counter under a stack of newspapers, where it might get accidentally tossed out or put in the recycle bin.

Never leave the tablet on a chair!

As long as you remember to return the tablet to the same spot when you're done with it, you'll always know where it is.

Taking the Android tablet with you

If you're like me, you probably carry the Android tablet around with you to or from the office, at the airport, in the air, or in your car. I hope you're not using the tablet while you're driving. Regardless, it's best to have a portable place to store your tablet while you're on the road.

The ideal place for the tablet is a specially designed pouch or sleeve. The pouch keeps the device from being dinged, scratched, or even unexpectedly turned on while it's in your backpack, purse, or carry-on luggage or wherever you put the tablet when you're not using it.

Also see Chapter 21 for information on using an Android tablet on the road.

2

Android Tablet On and Off

In This Chapter

▶ Turning on an Android tablet

▶ Unlocking the screen

▶ Configuring the tablet

▶ Adding more accounts

▶ Locking the screen

▶ Shutting down the tablet

*T*he bestselling *Pencils For Dummies* has no chapter describing how to turn on a pencil. *Pens For Dummies* does have the chapter "Enabling the Pen to Write," but that's not really an on–off thing, and the author of that book describes in great detail how awkward an On-Off switch or power button would be on a pen. Aren't you and I lucky to live in an age when such things are carefully described?

Your Android tablet is far more complex than a pen or a pencil, and, often, it's more useful. As such an advanced piece of technology, your tablet features not an On–Off button but, rather, a Power/Lock key. That button does more than just turn the Android tablet on or off, which is why this book has an entire chapter devoted to the subject.

Greetings, Android Tablet

The first time you turn on an Android tablet — the very first time — it prompts you to complete the setup process. This step is necessary, and it may have already been completed for you by the cheerful people at the Phone Store who sold you an

LTE tablet. Whether or not that's the case, better read this section, just to be sure.

✔ Initial tablet setup works best when you already have a Google, or Gmail, account. If you lack a Google account, you're prompted to create an account in the setup process; see the next section.

✔ The tablet will not start unless the battery is charged. Or unless you plug it in. See Chapter 1.

Turning on your Android tablet for the first time

The very, very first time you turn on your Android tablet, you're required to work through the setup process. It's a must, but it needs to be done only once. If your tablet has already been set up, skip to the next section, "Turning on the tablet."

The specifics of the setup-and-configuration process differ from tablet to tablet. For example, some tablets may prompt you to sign in to services like Dropbox. Tablets on certain mobile data networks may require you to run specific setup apps, which you'll read about during the configuration process. Generally speaking, however, the process is similar on all Android tablets, which is what I've documented in this section.

I recommend reading through these steps first, and then turning on the tablet and working through them afterward — the process goes kind of fast, and the screen may dim if you spend too much time waiting between steps:

1. **Turn on the tablet by pressing the Power/Lock key.**

   You may have to press the button longer than you think; when you see the tablet's logo appear on the screen, the tablet has started.

   It's okay to turn on the tablet while it's plugged in and charging.

2. **Answer the questions that are presented.**

   You're asked to select options for some, if not all, of these items:

   • Select your language

   • Activate an LTE tablet on the mobile data network

   • Choose a Wi-Fi network (can be done later)

   • Set the time zone

   • Accept terms and conditions

   • Sign in to your Google account

   • Add other online accounts

   • Set location information

When in doubt, just accept the standard options as presented to you during the setup process.

To fill in text fields, use the onscreen keyboard. See Chapter 4 for keyboard information.

Other sections in this chapter, as well as throughout this book, offer information and advice on these settings. You can't screw up anything at this point; any selection you make can be changed later.

3. **After each choice, tap the Next button, or large triangle icon.**

   The Next button might appear on the screen, labeled with the text *Next,* or it might appear as a triangle icon, shown in the margin.

4. **Tap the Finish button.**

   The Finish button appears on the last screen of the setup procedure.

You're done. From this point on, starting the tablet works as described in the next section.

After the initial setup, you're taken to the Home screen. Chapter 3 offers more Home screen information, which you should probably read right away, before the temptation to play with your new tablet becomes unbearable.

✔ You may find yourself asked various questions or prompted to try various tricks when you first start to use the tablet. Some of those prompts are helpful, but it's okay to skip some. To do so, tap the OK I Got It button or select the Do Not Show Again check box.

✔ Additional information on connecting your tablet to a Wi-Fi network is found in Chapter 16.

✔ Location settings relate to how the tablet knows its position on Planet Earth. I recommend keeping all these items activated to get the most from your Android tablet.

✔ It's important to have a Google account on an Android tablet. If you don't have one, sign up during the setup process.

✔ By setting up your Google account, you coordinate with your new Android tablet whatever information you have on the Internet. This information includes your email messages and contacts on Gmail, appointments on Google Calendar, and information and data from other Google Internet applications.

✔ It isn't necessary to use any specific software provided by the tablet's manufacturer or the cellular provider. For example, if you don't want a Samsung account, you don't need to sign up for one; skip that step.

✔ See the later sidebar "Who is this Android person?" for more information about the Android operating system.

Turning on the tablet

To turn on your Android tablet, press and hold the Power/Lock button. After a few seconds, you see the tablet's start-up logo, enjoy some hypnotic animation, and maybe even hear a tune. Release the Power/Lock key; the device is starting.

Eventually, you see the unlock screen. See the later section "Working the screen lock" for information on what to do next.

Unlocking the tablet

You'll probably leave your Android tablet on all the time. That's great! Tablets are designed that way, and the battery supports keeping it on for lengthy periods. When your tablet is bored, or when you've ignored it for a while, it locks itself similarly to a computer entering Sleep mode. After the tablet is locked, the touchscreen turns off to save power.

To unlock the tablet, press the Power/Lock key. Unlike turning on the tablet, a quick press is all that's needed.

After unlocking the tablet, you see the lock screen. Work the lock as described in the next section, and then you can start using the device.

- On Samsung tablets, you can press the Home button to unlock the tablet. The Home button is centered below the touchscreen.
- On the Samsung Galaxy Note, you can unlock the tablet by removing the S Pen.
- If your tablet features a cover, opening the cover unlocks the device.
- Android tablets don't snore while sleeping, but they can dream. See Chapter 23.

Working the screen lock

The swipe lock isn't a difficult lock to pick. In fact, it's known as the No Security screen lock on some tablets. If you've added more security, you might see any one of several different screen locks on your tablet. Here are the common Android screen locks:

Swipe: It's the standard screen lock. Swipe your finger on the screen to unlock the device, as illustrated in Figure 2-1. If a more secure lock is set, you'll need to work it next.

Lock screen notifications

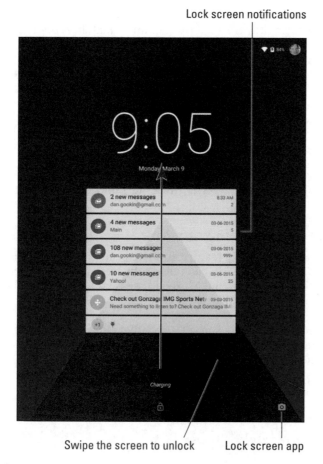

Swipe the screen to unlock   Lock screen app

Figure 2-1: The lock screen, featuring the swipe lock.

Pattern: Trace a preset pattern over the nine dots on the screen.

PIN: Type a number to unlock the device.

Password: Type a password, which can include letters, numbers, and symbols.

Some tablets provide additional, fancy screen locks. Among the variety are the following:

Face Unlock: Look at the tablet. In a few moments, your visage is recognized and the tablet unlocks.

Fingerprint: Rub your finger or thumb over the sensor, such as the Home button on a Samsung Galaxy Tab S, to unlock the device.

Signature: The Samsung Galaxy Note line of tablets lets you sign your name on the screen by using the S Pen. If the signature matches, the tablet unlocks.

Finally, some tablets provide the None option for the screen lock. When this option is selected, the device lacks a screen lock and you can use the tablet immediately.

The PIN and password locks are considered the most secure. To use certain tablet features, you must choose either the PIN or password screen lock. Other locks offer moderate security, and may require a PIN or password as a backup. The swipe and None locks are the least secure.

See Chapter 20 for information on setting your tablet's screen lock.

Unlocking and running an app

Your tablet's lock screen may feature app icons, such as the Camera icon, shown earlier, in Figure 2-1. You can unlock the tablet *and* run a given app: Drag the app icon across the touchscreen. The tablet unlocks, and the chosen app starts automatically.

✔ When a secure screen lock is set, the tablet isn't actually unlocked when the app runs. To do anything else on the tablet, you must eventually work the screen lock.

✔ Refer to Chapter 3 for details on performing the drag operation.

Who is this Android person?

Just like a computer, your Android tablet has an operating system. It's the main program in charge of all the software (apps) inside the tablet. Unlike a computer, however, Android is a mobile device operating system, designed primarily for use in tablets and cell phones.

Android is based on the Linux operating system, which is also a computer operating system, though it's much more stable and bug-free than Windows, so it's not as popular. Google owns, maintains, and develops Android, which is why your online Google information is synced with your tablet.

The Android mascot, shown here, often appears on Android apps or hardware. He has no official name, though most folks call him Andy.

More Accounts

Your Android tablet can serve as home to your various online incarnations. That includes your email accounts, online services, subscriptions, and other digital personas. I recommended adding those accounts to your tablet to continue the setup-and-configuration process.

With your tablet on and unlocked, follow these steps:

1. **Tap the Apps icon.**

   The Apps icon is found at the bottom of the Home screen. It looks similar to the icon shown in the margin, although it has many variations. See Chapter 3 for the variety.

   When you tap the Apps icon, you view the Apps drawer, which lists all apps available on your tablet.

2. **Open the Settings app.**

   You may have to swipe the Apps drawer screen left or right a few times, paging through the various icons, to find the Settings app.

   After you tap the Settings icon, the Settings app runs. It shows commands for configuring and setting tablet options.

3. **Choose the Accounts category.**

   On some Samsung tablets, tap the General tab atop the Settings app screen to find the Accounts category.

   Some tablets may name the item Accounts and Sync.

   Upon success, you see all existing accounts on your tablet, similar to the ones shown in Figure 2-2.

4. **Tap Add Account.**

   The Add Account item is illustrated in Figure 2-2, although it may appear as only a plus sign, shown in the margin.

5. **Choose an account from the list.**

   For example, to add a Facebook account, choose the Facebook app from the list.

   Don't worry if you don't see the exact type of account you want to add. You may have to add a specific app before an account appears. Chapter 15 covers adding apps.

6. **Follow the directions to sign in to your account.**

   The steps you take depend on the type of account you're adding. Generally speaking, you sign in by using an existing username and password.

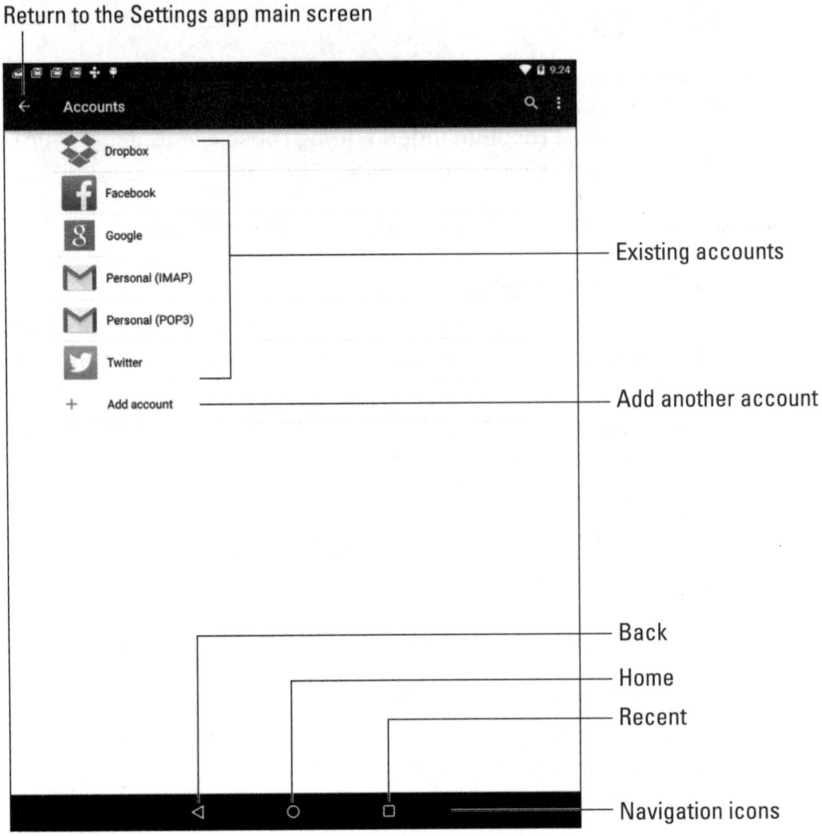

Return to the Settings app main screen

Accounts

Dropbox

Facebook

Google

Personal (IMAP)

Personal (POP3)

Twitter

+   Add account

Existing accounts

Add another account

Back

Home

Recent

Navigation icons

Figure 2-2: Accounts listed in the Settings app.

 You can continue adding accounts by repeating these steps. When you're done, tap the Home icon to return to the Home screen.

✔ See Chapter 6 for specific information on adding email accounts to your Android tablet.

✔ Chapter 9 covers social networking on your tablet. Refer there for specific information on adding Facebook, Twitter, and other social networking accounts.

✔ The accounts you add are your own. If you need to add another user to the tablet (who would have her own accounts), see Chapter 20 for information.

Transferring information from your old tablet

Here's one task you don't need to worry about: All the Google information associated with your old tablet — your current phone — is instantly transferred to your new Android tablet. This information includes contacts, Gmail, events, and other Googly account data. You can even install apps you've previously obtained (free or purchased).

As you add other accounts to your tablet, the information associated with those accounts is migrated as well. The only category not migrated is media installed on the old device. If you've synchronized the media with an online-sharing service, the information can easily be transferred. Otherwise, refer to Chapter 17 for information on moving over photos, videos, and music to your new Android tablet.

The End of Your Android Tablet Day

I know of three ways to say goodbye to your Android tablet; only one of them involves the application of high explosives. The other methods are documented in this section.

Locking the tablet

Locking the tablet is cinchy: Simply press and release the Power/Lock key. The display goes dark; your tablet is locked.

- Your Android tablet still works while locked; it receives email, can play music, and signals alerts. While it's locked, the tablet doesn't use as much power as it would with the display on.

- The tablet will probably spend most of its time locked.

- Locking doesn't turn off the tablet.

- Any timers or alarms you set still activate when your tablet is locked. See Chapter 14 for information on setting alarms.

- To unlock your tablet, press and release the Power/Lock key. See the section "Unlocking the tablet," earlier in this chapter.

- Refer to Chapter 19 for information on setting the automatic timeout value for locking the tablet.

Turning off your Android tablet

To turn off your tablet, heed these steps:

1. **Press and hold the Power/Lock key.**

   You see the Device Options menu, which may contain only one item: Power Off. Some tablets feature more items on this menu, such as the Samsung version of the Device Options menu, shown in Figure 2-3.

Figure 2-3: The Device Options menu.

If you chicken out and don't want to turn off your tablet, tap the Back icon to dismiss the Device Options menu.

2. **Tap the Power Off item.**

   If a confirmation message appears, tap the OK button. The Android tablet turns itself off.

The tablet doesn't run when it's off, so it doesn't remind you of appointments and doesn't collect email, nor do you hear any alarms you've set. The tablet isn't angry with you for turning it off, though you may sense some resentment when you turn it on again.

- ✔ Varieties of the Device Options menu on various Android tablets include the Restart command as well as commands to silence the speakers or control vibration. I've also seen a Kid Mode command on some tablets.

- ✔ Samsung tablets sport a Restart command on the Device Options menu. To restart other Android tablets, you need to turn the device off and then on again, as described in this chapter.

- ✔ The tablet can be charged while it's off.

- ✔ Keep your tablet in a safe place while it's turned off. Chapter 1 offers some suggestions.

How Android Tablets Work

*I*t used to be that you could judge how advanced something was by how many buttons it had. Starting with the dress shirt and progressing to the first computer, more buttons meant fancier technology. Your Android tablet tosses that rule right out the window. Beyond the Power/Lock key and the volume key, the device is shamefully bereft of buttons.

My point is that in order to use your tablet, you have to understand how a touchscreen works. That *touchscreen* is the tablet's main input device — the gizmo you use to do all sorts of wondrous and useful things. Using a touchscreen may be a new experience for you, so this chapter provides a general orientation to the touchscreen and how an Android tablet works.

Basic Operations

Your Android tablet's ability to frustrate you is only as powerful as your fear of the touchscreen and how it works. After you clear that hurdle, as well as understand some other basic operations, you'll be on your way toward mobile device contentment.

Touching the touchscreen

Minus any buttons and knobs, the way you control an Android tablet is to manipulate things on the touchscreen with one or two fingers. It doesn't matter which fingers you use, and you should feel free to experiment with other body parts as well, although I find fingers to be handy.

Here are some of the common ways to manipulate the touchscreen:

Tap: The basic touchscreen technique is to touch it. You tap an object, an icon, a control, a menu item, a doodad, and so on. The tap operation is similar to a mouse click on a computer. It may also be referred to as a *touch* or a *press*.

Double-tap: Tap the screen twice in the same location. Double-tapping can be used to zoom in on an image or a map, but it can also zoom out. Because of the double-tap's dual nature, I recommend using the pinch or spread operation to zoom.

Long-press: Tap part of the screen and keep your finger down. Depending on what you're doing, a pop-up menu may appear, or the item you're long-pressing may get "picked up" so that you can drag (move) it around. *Long-press* might also be referred to as *touch and hold*.

Swipe: To swipe, you tap your finger on one spot and then move your finger to another spot. Swipes can go up, down, left, or right; the touchscreen content moves in the direction in which you swipe your finger. A swipe can be fast or slow. It's also called a *flick* or *slide*.

Drag: A combination of long-press and then swipe, the drag operation moves items on the screen.

Pinch: A pinch involves two fingers, which start out separated and then are brought together. The effect is used to *zoom out,* to reduce the size of an image or to see more of a map.

Spread: The opposite of pinch is spread. You start out with your fingers together and then spread them. The spread is used to *zoom in,* to enlarge an image or see more detail on a map.

Rotate: A few apps let you rotate an image on the screen by touching with two fingers and twisting them around a center point. If you have trouble with this operation, pretend that you're turning the dial on a safe.

You can't manipulate the touchscreen while wearing gloves unless the gloves are specially designed for using electronic touchscreens, such as the gloves that Batman wears.

Using the navigation icons

Below the touchscreen dwell three icons. They can appear as part of the touchscreen itself; or, on some tablets, they may be part of the bezel or may even be physical buttons. These are the navigation icons, and they serve specific functions.

Traditionally, you find three navigation icons: Back, Home, and Recent. The appearance of these icons can vary, with the most common variations shown in Table 3-1. The Lollipop version of the navigation icons are used in this book's margins.

Table 3-1		Navigation Icon Varieties
Icon	*Lollipop*	*KitKat and Earlier*
Home	⬤	⌂
Back	◀	↩
Recent	◻	▱

 Back: The Back icon serves several purposes, all of which fit neatly under the concept of "back." Tap the icon once to return to a previous page, dismiss an onscreen menu, close a window, or hide the onscreen keyboard, for example.

 Home: No matter what you're doing on the tablet, tapping this icon displays the Home screen. When you're already viewing the Home screen, tapping the Home icon returns you to the main, or center, Home screen.

 Recent: Tapping the Recent icon displays the Overview, a list of recently opened or currently running apps. The list scrolls up and down, so when it's too tall for the screen, just swipe it with your finger to view all the apps. Choose an app from the list to switch to that app. To dismiss the Overview, tap the Back icon. See the later section "Switching between running apps" for more info.

 ✔ On Android tablets without the Recent icon, long-press the Home icon to see the Overview.

✔ Older Android tablets may sport the Menu icon or button instead of the Recent icon. Tap the Menu icon to display a pop-up menu from which you can choose commands.

✔ The three navigation icons may hide themselves when certain apps run. In most cases, the icons are still there — just invisible. Tap the screen to summon them. For some full-screen apps and games, swipe the screen from top to bottom to see the icons.

✔ The Back icon changes its orientation, shown in the margin. Tap this icon to hide the onscreen keyboard, dismiss dictation, or perform other actions similar to the Back navigation icon.

Setting the volume

There are times when the sound level is too loud. There are times when it's too soft. And, there are those rare times when it's just right. Finding that just-right level is the job of the volume key that clings to the side of your Android tablet.

When the volume key is on the tablet's side, press the top part of the key to make the volume louder; press the bottom of the key to make the volume softer. When the volume key is on the top edge of the tablet, press the left part to increase volume and the right part to decrease volume.

As you press the volume key, a graphic appears on the touchscreen to illustrate the relative volume level, similar to the one shown in Figure 3-1.

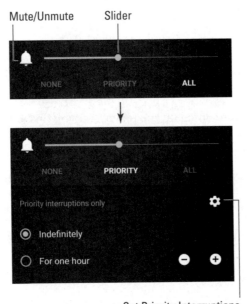

Figure 3-1: Setting the volume.

You can continue pressing the volume key, or use your finger to adjust the onscreen slider and set the volume.

Some tablets may display specific controls for certain noise-making activities, such as media (movies, music), games, system sounds, and notifications.

The onscreen volume control disappears after a few moments.

- ✔ When the volume is set all the way down, the tablet is silenced. In Figure 3-1, tapping the Bell icon mutes the tablet.

- ✔ Silencing the tablet by sliding down the volume level may place it into Vibration mode. Not every tablet features Vibration mode.

- ✔ The volume key works even when the tablet is locked. That means you don't need to unlock the tablet if you're playing music and you only need to adjust the volume.

- ✔ Refer to Chapter 19 for more details on setting the tablet's volume and Vibration mode.

Changing the orientation

Your Android tablet features a gizmo called an *accelerometer*. It determines in which direction the tablet is pointed or whether you've reoriented the device from an upright position to a horizontal one (or vice versa) or even upside down. That way, the information displayed on the tablet's screen always appears upright, no matter how you hold it.

To demonstrate how the tablet orients itself, rotate the tablet to the left or right. Most apps change their orientation to match however you've oriented the tablet, such as the Home screen, shown in Figure 3-2.

The rotation feature may not work for all apps, and it may not even work for the Home screen. In that case, open the web browser app to experiment with rotation.

- ✔ Most games present themselves in one orientation only.

- ✔ The onscreen keyboard is more usable when the tablet is in its horizontal orientation. Chapter 4 covers using the onscreen keyboard.

- ✔ You can lock the orientation if the rotating screen bothers you. See the section "Making Quick Settings," later in this chapter.

- ✔ A great application for demonstrating the Android tablet accelerometer is the game *Labyrinth*. You can purchase it at the Google Play Store or download the free version, *Labyrinth Lite*. See Chapter 15 for more information about the Google Play Store.

Vertical Orientation

Horizontal Orientation

Figure 3-2: Android tablet orientation.

There's No Place Like Home Screen

The main base from which you begin domination of your Android tablet is the *Home screen*. It's the first thing you see after unlocking the tablet, and it's the place you go to whenever you leave an app.

 To view the Home screen at any time, tap the Home icon found at the bottom of the touchscreen. Some tablets feature a physical Home button or key, which performs the same duties as the Home icon.

Touring the Home screen

The typical Android tablet Home screen is illustrated in Figure 3-3. Several fun and interesting things appear on the Home screen. Find these items on your own tablet's Home screen:

Status bar: This area at the top of the screen shows notification icons and status icons. The status bar may disappear, in which case a quick swipe of the screen from the top downward will redisplay it.

Notification icons: These icons come and go, depending on what happens in your digital life. For example, new icons appear whenever you receive a new email message or have a pending appointment.

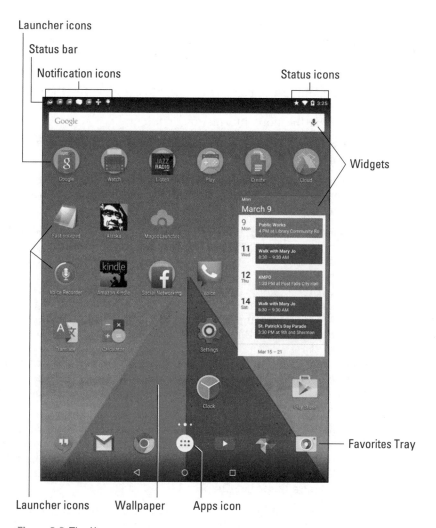

Launcher icons

Status bar

Notification icons

Status icons

Widgets

Launcher icons   Wallpaper   Apps icon

Figure 3-3: The Home screen.

The section "Reviewing notifications," later in this chapter, describes how to deal with notifications.

Status icons: These icons represent the tablet's current condition, such as the type of network to which it's connected, signal strength, and battery status, as well as whether the tablet is connected to a Wi-Fi network or is using Bluetooth, for example.

App launcher icons: The meat of the meal on the Home screen plate, app (application) launcher icons are where the action takes place. Tapping a launcher icon opens an app.

Widgets: A widget is a window through which you view information, control the tablet, access features, or do something purely amusing. A special widget is the Google Search widget, which lets you search the Internet or use the powerful Google Now feature.

Folders: Multiple apps can be stored in a folder. Tap the folder to see a pop-up window listing all the apps. Tap an app icon to start. See Chapter 18 for more information on folders.

Wallpaper: The background image you see on the Home screen is the wallpaper.

Favorites Tray: The lineup of icons near the bottom of the screen contains slots for popular launcher icons. The favorites tray shows the same icons at the bottom of every Home screen page.

Apps icon: Tap this icon to view the collection of apps and widgets available on your tablet. See the later section "Finding an app in the Apps drawer."

Ensure that you recognize the names of the various parts of the Home screen because these terms are used throughout this book and in whatever other scant Android tablet documentation exists. Directions for using the Home screen gizmos are found throughout this chapter.

✔ The Home screen is entirely customizable. You can add and remove icons from the Home screen, add widgets and shortcuts, and even change wallpaper (background) images. See Chapter 19 for more information.

✔ Touching a part of the Home screen that doesn't feature an icon or a control does nothing. That is, unless you're using the *live wallpaper* feature. In that case, touching the screen changes the wallpaper in some way, depending on the wallpaper that's selected. You can read more about live wallpaper in Chapter 19.

✔ You may see numbers affixed to certain Home screen icons. Those numbers indicate pending actions, such as unread email messages, indicated by the icon shown in the margin.

Accessing multiple Home screens

The Home screen is more than what you see. It's actually an entire street of Home screens, with only one Home screen *panel* displayed at a time.

To switch from one panel to another, swipe the Home screen left or right. There are pages to the left of the main Home screen page, and pages to the right. The number of panels depends on the tablet. Many tablets let you add or remove panels; see Chapter 19 for details.

Figure 3-4 illustrates the Home screen index, used on some tablets to help you determine which Home screen is displayed. You can swipe the index or tap one of the dots to zoom to a specific Home screen panel.

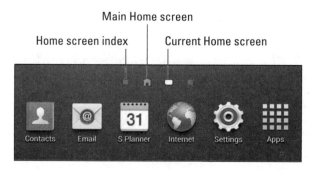

Figure 3-4: The Home screen panel index.

↙ When you tap the Home navigation icon, you return to the last Home screen page you viewed. To return to the main Home screen panel, tap the Home icon a second time.

↙ Some tablets reserve the far left Home screen panel for the Google Now app. See Chapter 14 for information on Google Now.

↙ The main Home screen is often the center Home screen panel, though some Android tablets let you choose any page as the main one.

Reviewing notifications

Notifications appear as icons at the top of the Home screen, as illustrated earlier, in Figure 3-3. To review them, you pull down the notifications drawer by dragging your finger from the top of the screen downward. The notifications drawer is illustrated in Figure 3-5.

Scroll through the list of notifications by swiping the drawer up and down. To peruse a specific notification, tap it. Choosing a notification displays more information, and it may also dismiss the notification.

You can dismiss a notification by sliding it left or right. To dismiss all notifications, tap the Clear Notifications icon, shown in the margin. You may need to slide the notification drawer up or down to locate the Clear button.

To hide the notifications drawer, tap the Back icon, swipe the screen upward, or tap anywhere else on the Home screen.

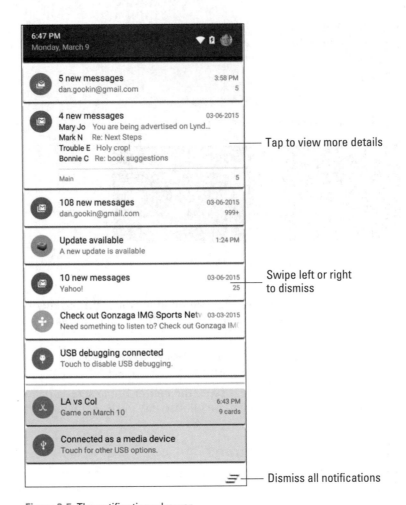

Figure 3-5: The notifications drawer.

- Some tablets require you to swipe the screen from the top-left edge to see the notifications drawer. When you swipe down from the top-right edge, you see the Quick Settings shade. See the next section.

- When more notifications are present than can be shown on the status bar, you see the More Notifications icon displayed, similar to the one shown in the margin.

- Dismissing some notifications doesn't prevent them from appearing again in the future. For example, notifications to update your apps continue to appear, as do calendar reminders.

- Ongoing notifications cannot be dismissed. They include items such as USB (refer to Figure 3-5), Bluetooth, and Wi-Fi connections.

✔ Some apps, such as Facebook and Twitter, don't display notifications unless you're logged in. See Chapter 9.

✔ Your Android tablet plays a notification ringtone whenever a new notification floats in. You can choose which sound plays; see Chapter 19 for more information.

Making Quick Settings

Many common settings for Android tablet features are found in the Quick Settings drawer, which sits atop the notifications drawer. The Quick Settings appear as large buttons, which either access popular features or turn settings on or off, such as Bluetooth, Wi-Fi, Airplane Mode, Auto Rotate, and more.

The stock Android method for accessing the Quick Settings depends on the Android operating system version. For Lollipop, swipe the screen from top to bottom twice; once to see the navigation drawer and again to view the Quick Settings, shown in Figure 3-6. For Android KitKat, swipe the screen from top to bottom but starting from the right side of the status bar.

Figure 3-6: The Quick Settings drawer.

Samsung tablets always show the Quick Settings atop the navigation drawer. Figure 3-7 illustrates how the icons may look. You can swipe them left or right to view more or tap the View All icon to see all available Quick Settings.

Adjust sound

Adjust brightness

View All Quick Settings

Quick Settings

Settings app

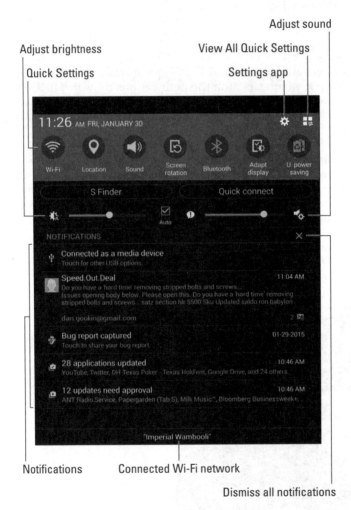

Notifications

Connected Wi-Fi network

Dismiss all notifications

Figure 3-7: A Samsung tablet's Quick Settings.

Dismiss the Quick Settings drawer by tapping either the Back or Home icons.

The World of Apps

You probably didn't purchase a tablet so that you could enjoy the thrill-a-minute punch that's packed by the Android operating system. No, an Android tablet's success lies with the apps you obtain. Knowing how to deal with apps is vital to being a successful, happy Android tablet user.

Starting an app

To start an app, tap its icon. The app starts.

Apps can be started from the Home screen: Tap a launcher icon to start the associated app. Apps can be started also from the Apps drawer, as described in the section "Finding an app in the Apps drawer."

You can also start an app found in a Home screen folder: Tap to open the folder, and then tap an icon to start that app.

Quitting an app

Unlike on a computer, you don't need to quit apps on your Android tablet. To leave an app, tap the Home icon to return to the Home screen. You can keep tapping the Back icon to back out of an app. Or you can tap the Recent icon to switch to another running app.

✔ Some apps feature a Quit command or an Exit command, but for the most part you don't quit an app on your tablet — not like you quit an app on a computer.

✔ If necessary, the Android operating system shuts down apps you haven't used in a while. You can directly stop apps run amok, which is described in Chapter 18.

Wonderful widgets

Like apps, widgets appear on the Home screen. To use a widget, tap it. What happens after that depends on the widget and what it does.

For example, the YouTube widget lets you peruse videos. The Calendar widget shows a preview of your upcoming schedule. A Twitter widget may display recent tweets. Other widgets do interesting things, display useful information, or give you access to the tablet's settings or features.

New widgets are obtained from the Google Play Store, just like apps. See Chapter 18 for information on working with widgets on the Home screen.

Finding an app in the Apps drawer

The launcher icons you see on the Home screen don't represent all the apps in your tablet. To view all installed apps, you must visit the Apps screen: Tap the Apps icon on the Home screen. This icon has a different look to it, depending on your tablet. Figure 3-8 illustrates various looks to the Apps icon, though more varieties may exist.

Figure 3-8: Apps icon varieties.

After you tap the Apps icon, you see the Apps drawer. Swipe through the icons left and right across the touchscreen.

To run an app, tap its icon. The app starts, taking over the screen and doing whatever magical thing that app does.

- ✔ As you add new apps to your tablet, they appear in the Apps drawer. See Chapter 15 for information on adding new apps.

- ✔ Some tablets allow you to create folders in the Apps drawer. These folders contain multiple apps, which helps keep things organized. To access apps in the folder, tap the folder icon.

- ✔ The Apps drawer displays apps alphabetically. On some tablets, you can switch to a non-alphabetical viewing grid. With that feature active, it's possible to rearrange the app icons in any order you like.

- ✔ For apps you use all the time, consider creating launcher icons on the Home screen. Chapter 18 describes how.

Switching between running apps

The apps you run on your tablet don't quit when you dismiss them from the screen. For the most part, they stay running. To switch between running apps, or to any app you've recently opened, tap the Recent icon. You see the Overview, similar to what's shown in Figure 3-9.

To switch to an app, choose it from the list.

- ✔ You can remove an app from the Overview by swiping it off the list, left or right, or up or down, depending on the tablet's orientation. Removing an app from the Overview is pretty much the same thing as quitting an app.

Dismiss an app

Recent icon   Recent apps

Figure 3-9: The Overview shows recently used apps.

✔ For tablets that lack the Recent icon, long-press the Home icon to see the Overview.

✔ The Android operating system may shut down apps that haven't received attention for a while. Don't be surprised if you see an app missing from the Overview. If so, just start it up again as you normally would.

Common Android Icons

In addition to the navigation icons, various other icons appear while you use your Android tablet. These icons serve common functions in apps as well as in the Android operating system. Table 3-2 lists the most common icons and their functions.

Table 3-2		Common Icons
Icon	*Name*	*What It Does*
	Action Bar	Displays a pop-up menu. This teensy icon appears in the lower-right corner of a button or an image, indicating that actions (commands) are attached.
	Add	Adds or creates a new item. The plus symbol (+) may be used in combination with other symbols, depending on the app.
	Close	Closes a window or clears text from an input field.
	Delete	Removes one or more items from a list or deletes a message.
	Dictation	Lets you use your voice to dictate text.
	Done	Dismisses an action bar, such as the text-editing action bar.
	Edit	Lets you edit an item, add text, or fill in fields.
	Favorite	Flags a favorite item, such as a contact or a web page.
	Overflow	Displays a menu or list of commands.
	Refresh	Fetches new information or reloads.
	Search	Searches the tablet or the Internet for a tidbit of information.

Icon	Name	What It Does
	Settings	Adjusts options for an app.
	Share	Shares information stored on the tablet via email, social networking, or other Internet services.

Various sections throughout this book give examples of using the icons. Their images appear in the book's margins where relevant.

✔ Other common symbols are used on icons in various apps. For example, the standard Play and Pause icons are used as well.

 ✔ Older tablets may use the Menu icon to display onscreen menus. This icon serves the same function as the Overflow icon, shown in Table 3-2. The icon is found as a button on the device.

✔ Some Samsung tablets use a MORE button in place of the Overflow icon.

 ✔ Another variation on the Settings icon is shown in the margin. It serves the same purpose as the Gear icon, shown in Table 3-2, although this older Settings icon is being phased out.

Creating and Editing Text

*Y*our Android tablet lacks a keyboard — a real one, at least. To sate the tablet's text-input desires, you use something called an *onscreen keyboard*. It works like a real keyboard, but with the added frustration that it lacks moveable keys. Don't fret! You can add a real keyboard to your tablet, and you can even forgo typing and just dictate your text. It's all covered here.

Behold the Onscreen Keyboard

The onscreen keyboard reveals itself on the bottom half of the tablet's touchscreen whenever text input is required. The stock Android keyboard, known as the Google Keyboard, is shown in Figure 4-1. Your tablet may use the same keyboard or some variation that looks subtly different. All onscreen keyboards are based on the traditional QWERTY layout and not something designed merely to tick you off.

In Figure 4-1, as well as on your tablet's touchscreen, you see keys from A through Z, albeit not in that order. You also see the Shift key for changing the letter case, and the Delete key, which backspaces and erases.

Your tablet may show more keys — such as Tab and Caps Lock — or it may
show fewer keys.

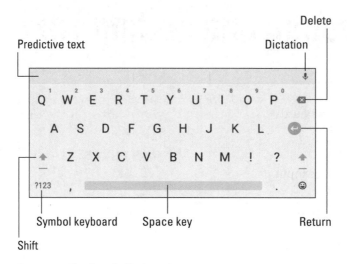

Figure 4-1: The Google Keyboard.

The Enter key changes its look, depending on what you're typing. Your keyboard may show these variations graphically or by labeling the key with text,
both of which are shown in Figure 4-2.

Figure 4-2: Enter key variations.

Here's what each key does:

> **Return:** Just like the Return or Enter key on a computer keyboard,
> this key ends a paragraph of text. It's used mostly when filling in long
> stretches of text or when multiline input is available.

> **Go:** This action key directs the app to proceed with a search, accept
> input, or perform another action.

Search: You see this key appear when you're searching for something on the tablet. Tapping the key starts the search.

Next: This key appears whenever you're typing information in multiple fields. Tap this key to switch from one field to the next, such as when typing a username and password.

Done: This key appears whenever you've finished typing text in the final field and you're ready to submit the form.

The large key at the bottom center of the onscreen keyboard is the Space key. It's flanked left and right by other keys that may change, depending on the context of what you're typing. For example, the / (slash) key or .com key may appear in order to assist in typing a web page or email address. Though these and other keys may change, the basic alphabetic keys remain the same.

- ✔ To display the onscreen keyboard, tap any text field or spot on the screen where typing is permitted.

- ✔ If you pine for a real keyboard, one that exists in the fourth dimension, you're not stuck. See the nearby sidebar, "A real keyboard?"

- ✔ To dismiss the onscreen keyboard, tap the Back icon. It may appear as the Hide icon, shown in the margin.

- ✔ Some onscreen keyboards feature a multifunction key. It may be labeled with the Settings (Gear) icon, a Microphone icon, or another icon. Long-press the multifunction key to view its options.

- ✔ The keyboard changes its width when you reorient the tablet. The keyboard's horizontal presentation is wider and easier for typing.

A real keyboard?

If typing is your thing and the onscreen keyboard doesn't do it for you, consider getting your Android tablet a real keyboard. You can do so in two ways. First, you can see whether your tablet features an optional *keyboard dock.* This docking stand props up the tablet at a good viewing angle and also provides a laptop-size keyboard.

When no docking station is available, you can obtain a Bluetooth keyboard for your tablet. The Bluetooth keyboard connects wirelessly, giving you not only a larger, full-action keyboard but also all the divine goodness that wireless brings. You can read more about Bluetooth in Chapter 16.

Everybody Was Touchscreen Typing

Typing should be a basic activity. It *should* be. Typing on a touchscreen keyboard can be, well, touchy. Use my advice in this section to get some basics and perhaps discover a few tricks.

Typing one character at a time

The onscreen keyboard is pretty easy to figure out: Tap a letter to produce the character. As you type, the key you touch is highlighted. The tablet may give a wee bit of feedback in the form of a faint click or vibration.

- To type in all caps, press the Shift key twice. The Shift key may appear highlighted, the shift symbol may change color, or a colored highlight may appear on the key, all of which indicate that Shift Lock is on. Tap the Shift key again to turn off Shift Lock.

- Above all, it helps to *type slowly* until you get used to the onscreen keyboard.

- A blinking cursor on the touchscreen shows where new text appears, which is similar to how typing text works on a computer.

- When you make a mistake, tap the Delete key to back up and erase.

- When you type a password, the character you type appears briefly, but for security reasons, it's then replaced by a black dot.

- See the later section "Text Editing and Correcting" for more details on editing your text so that you can fix those myriad typos and boo-boos.

Accessing special characters

You're not limited to typing only the symbols you see on the alphabetic keyboard. Tap the ?123 key to get access to additional keyboard layouts, samples of which are shown in Figure 4-3.

In Figure 4-3, the symbol keys are accessed by tapping the key labeled ~[<, although some tablets label that key as Sym (for *sym*bols).

Tablets with multiple sets of symbol keys let you page through them by tapping the 1/2 and 2/2 keys. Some tablets may have three sets of symbol keyboards, in which case the keys are labeled 1/3, 2/3, and 3/3.

To return to the standard alphabetic keyboard (refer to Figure 4-1), tap the ABC key.

Show alpha keyboard

Show symbol keyboard

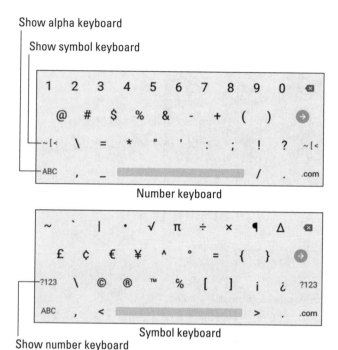

Number keyboard

Symbol keyboard

Show number keyboard

Figure 4-3: The number and symbol keyboards.

Some keys feature a pop-up palette from which you can choose variations on a character. The key is to long-press the key. Upon success, you see additional characters, similar to the ones shown for the A key in Figure 4-4.

Choose a character from the pop-up palette. If you choose the wrong character, tap the Delete key on the onscreen keyboard to erase the mistyped symbol.

You can use this long-press technique also to access the gray or tiny characters on the alphanumeric keyboard, such as the numeric keys shown on the top row in Figure 4-1.

Typing quickly by using predictive text

As you type, you may see a selection of word suggestions just above the keyboard. That's the tablet's *predictive text* feature. You can use this feature to greatly accelerate your typing.

Drag your finger over a character to select it.

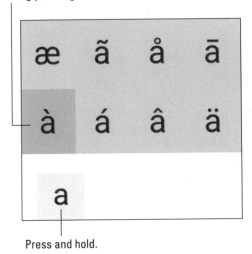

Press and hold.

Figure 4-4: Special-symbol pop-up palette-thing.

In Figure 4-5, I typed the word *I*. The keyboard has suggested the words *can*, *am*, and *just*. Each of those is a logical choice for the next word after *I*. Additional choices are viewed by long-pressing the center word, as called-out in the figure. Tap a word to insert it into your text.

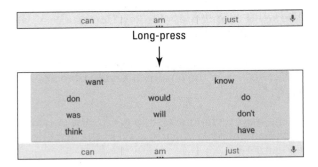

Figure 4-5: Predictive text in action.

When the desired word doesn't appear, continue typing: The predictive text feature begins making suggestions, based on what you've typed so far. Tap the correct word when it appears.

Predictive text should be active for the Google Keyboard. If not, see Chapter 19 for information.

Typing without lifting your finger

If you're really after typing speed, consider using gesture typing. It allows you to type words by swiping your finger over the onscreen keyboard, like mad scribbling but with a positive result.

Gesture typing works by dragging your fingers over letters on the keyboard. Figure 4-6 illustrates how the word *taco* would be typed in this manner.

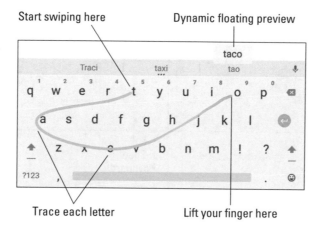

Figure 4-6: Using gesture typing to type *taco.*

The gesture typing feature may not be active when you need to type a password or for specific apps. When it doesn't work, type one letter at a time.

Also see Chapter 19 for information on activating this feature, which isn't on by default for certain Android tablets.

Android Tablet Dictation

The Android tablet has the amazing capability to interpret your dictation as text. It works almost as well as computer dictation in science fiction movies, though I can't seem to find the command to locate intelligent life.

The Dictation feature is officially known as Google Voice Typing. If you see the Microphone icon on your keyboard, Dictation is active and ready to use! If not, see Chapter 19 for information on enabling dictation.

Speaking instead of typing

Talking to your tablet really works, and works quite well, providing that you tap the Dictation key on the keyboard and you don't mumble.

After tapping the Dictation key, you see a special window at the bottom of the screen, similar to the one shown in Figure 4-7. When the text *Speak Now* appears, dictate your text, speaking directly at the tablet. Try not to spit.

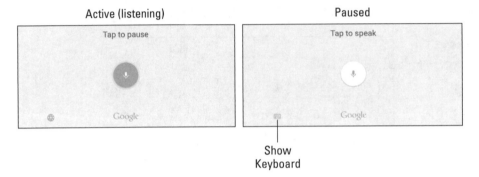

Figure 4-7: Google Voice Typing.

As you speak, a Microphone graphic flashes. The flashing doesn't mean that the Android tablet is embarrassed by what you're saying. No, the flashing merely indicates that the tablet is listening, detecting the volume of your voice.

As you blab, the tablet digests what you say, and the text you speak — or a close approximation — appears on the screen. It's magical and sometimes comical.

- ✔ The first time you try voice input, you might see a description displayed. Tap the OK button to continue.

- ✔ You can't use dictation to edit text, but you can edit text you dictate like any other text. See the section "Text Editing and Correcting," later in this chapter.

- ✔ If you don't like a word that's chosen by the dictation feature, tap the word on the screen. You see a pop-up list of alternatives from which to choose.

- ✔ Speak the punctuation in your text. For example, you would say, "I'm sorry comma and it won't happen again" to have the tablet produce the text *I'm sorry, and it won't happen again* or something close to that.

✔ Common punctuation you can dictate includes the comma, period, exclamation point, question mark, colon, and new line.

✔ You cannot dictate capital letters. If you're a stickler for such things, you have to go back and edit the text.

✔ Dictation may not work where no Internet connection exists.

Uttering s**** words

The Android tablet features a voice censor. It replaces those naughty words you might utter; the first letter appears on the screen, followed by the appropriate number of asterisks.

For example, if *spatula* were a blue word and you uttered *spatula* when dictating text, the dictation feature would place *s******* rather than the word *spatula* on the screen.

Yeah, I know: silly. Or should I say "s****."

The tablet knows a lot of blue terms, including George Carlin's infamous "Seven Words You Can Never Say on Television," but apparently the terms *crap* and *damn* are fine. Don't ask me how much time I spent researching this topic.

See Chapter 23 if you'd like to disable the dictation censor.

Text Editing and Correcting

You'll probably do more text editing on your Android tablet than you anticipated. That editing includes the basic stuff, such as spiffing up typos and adding a period here or there as well as complex editing involving cut, copy, and paste. The concepts are the same as you find on a computer, but the process can be daunting without a physical keyboard and a mouse. This section irons out the text-editing wrinkles.

Moving the cursor

The first part of editing text is to move the cursor to the right spot. The *cursor* is that blinking, vertical line where text appears. On a computer, you move the cursor by using a pointing device. The Android tablet has no pointing device, but you do: your finger.

Tap the spot on the text where you want the cursor to appear. To help your accuracy, a cursor tab appears below the text, similar to the one shown in the margin. You can move that tab with your finger to precisely locate the cursor in your text.

After you move the cursor, you can continue to type, use the Delete key to back up and erase, or paste text copied from elsewhere.

> ✔ You may see the Paste Command button appear above the cursor tab. This button is used to paste in text, as described in the later section "Cutting, copying, and pasting text."

> ✔ Some onscreen keyboards may feature cursor movement keys, appearing as left- and right-pointing triangles. Use those keys to move the cursor as well as the stab-your-finger-on-the-screen method.

Selecting text

Selecting text on an Android tablet works just like selecting text in a word processor: You mark the start and end of a block. That chunk of text appears highlighted on the screen. How you get there, however, can be a mystery — until now!

Text selection starts by long-pressing or double-tapping a chunk of text. Upon success you see a chunk of selected text, as shown in Figure 4-8.

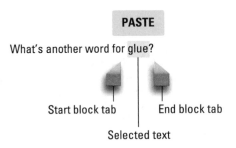

Figure 4-8: Android tablet text selection.

Drag the start and end markers around the touchscreen to define the block of selected text.

While text is selected, the Contextual action bar appears atop the screen, similar to what appears in Figure 4-9, although your tablet may sport a custom action bar. You use the action bar to deal with the selected text.

Close action bar and
un-select text

Select all   Copy

Cut   Paste

Figure 4-9: Text selection Contextual action bar.

In addition to the action bar, covered in the later section "Cutting, copying, and pasting text," you can delete a selected block of text by tapping the Delete key on the onscreen keyboard. You can replace the text by typing something new.

To cancel text selection, tap the Done button on the action bar, or just tap anywhere in the text outside the selected block.

 ✔ Selecting text on a web page works the same as selecting text in any other app. The difference is that text can only be copied from the web page, not cut or deleted.

 ✔ Seeing the onscreen keyboard is a good indication that you can edit and select text.

 ✔ The action bar's Select All command can be used to mark all text as a single block.

Cutting, copying, and pasting text

Selected text is primed for cutting or copying, which works just like it does in your favorite word processor. After you select the text, choose the proper command from the Contextual action bar. To copy the text, choose the Copy command. To cut the text, choose Cut.

Just like on a computer, cut or copied text on an Android tablet is stored on a clipboard. To paste any previously cut or copied text, move the cursor to the spot where you want the text pasted.

 ✔ A quick way to paste text is to look for the Paste command button above the cursor tab. To see that button, tap anywhere in the text. Tap the Paste command button to paste in the text.

 ✔ Some tablets feature a Clipboard app, which lets you peruse, review, and select previously cut or copied text or images. You might even find the Clipboard button on the action bar or onscreen keyboard.

 ✔ You can paste text only into locations where text is allowed. Odds are good that if you see the onscreen keyboard, you can paste text.

Dealing with spelling errrs

Similar to a word processor, your Android tablet may highlight misspelled words. A vicious red underline appears beneath the suspect spelling, drawing attention to the problem and general embarrassment to the typist.

To remedy the situation, tap the red-underlined word. You see a pop-up list of alternatives, similar to the one shown in Figure 4-10. Tap a replacement or, if the word is correctly spelled but unknown to the Android tablet, choose to add the word to a personal dictionary.

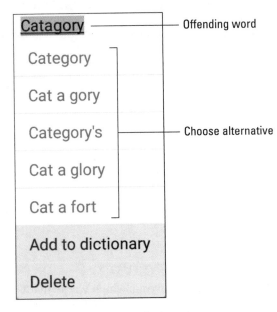

Figure 4-10: Fixing a misspelled word.

> ✓ Words may be autocorrected as you type them. To undo an autocorrection, tap the word again. Choose a replacement word from the predictive text list, or tap the Replace button to see more options.
>
> ✓ Yes! Your tablet has a personal dictionary. See Chapter 23 for details.

Part II
Stay in Touch

Have fun communicating by adding emojis to your Hangouts chats. Find out how at www.dummies.com/extras/androidtablets.

In this part . . .

- ✓ Organize your contacts in the tablet's address book, keeping them handy for email, social networking, voice chat, or video chat.

- ✓ Send and receive email using your tablet.

- ✓ Explore the web using the tablet's web browser or the Google Chrome app.

- ✓ Covertly turn your tablet into a phone using the Hangouts and Skype apps.

- ✓ Share your life using your Android tablet and various social networking apps.

All Your Friends

In This Chapter

▶ Exploring the tablet's address book

▶ Searching and sorting your contacts

▶ Creating a new contact

▶ Importing contacts

▶ Editing contacts

▶ Putting a picture on a contact

▶ Deleting contacts

To best use your tablet as a communications tool, you need to keep track of people. That means having their email information, website addresses, social networking info, and phone numbers because — and this isn't really a secret — it's possible to make phone calls with your tablet. That communication all starts with keeping all your friends' information in a single app.

The Tablet's Address Book

You most likely already have contacts in your Android tablet's address book because your Google account was synchronized with the tablet when you first set things up. All your Gmail contacts, as well as other types of contacts on the Internet, were duplicated on the tablet, so you already have a host of friends available. The place where you can access these folks is the tablet's address book.

    ✔ The tablet's address book app is named either Contacts or People. The stock Android name is Contacts, although the app has been called People in the past. For the sake of consistency, this chapter refers to the app as Contacts.

✔ Many apps use contact information from the Contacts app, including Gmail, Hangouts, as well as any app that lets you share information such as photographs or videos.

✔ Information from your social networking apps is also coordinated with the Contacts app. See Chapter 9 for more information on using the tablet as your social networking hub.

Using the address book

To peruse your Android tablet's address book, open the Contacts app. You may be blessed to find that app's icon on the Home screen. If not, tap the Apps icon to locate the Contacts app in the Apps drawer.

The address book app shows a list of all contacts in your Android tablet, organized alphabetically by first name. Figure 5-1 illustrates one way the Contacts app might look.

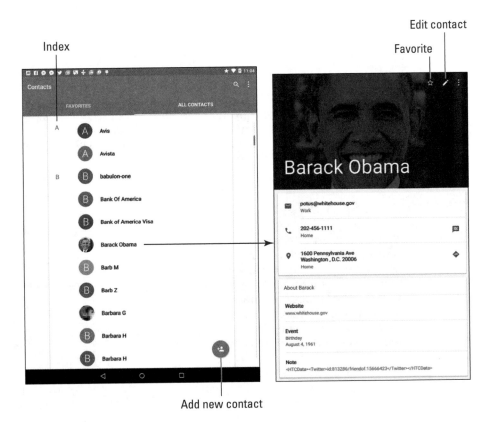

Figure 5-1: The Contacts app.

Scroll the list by swiping your finger on the touchscreen. Some versions of the app feature an index off to one side of the screen; use the index to help you quickly view an entry.

The list of activities you can do with a contact depends on the information shown and the apps installed on your tablet. Here are some common activities:

Place a phone call. No, an Android tablet isn't a phone, but when you install a phone-dialer app such as the Hangouts Dialer or Skype, tapping a contact's phone number activates that app and you can use the tablet to make a call. See Chapter 8 for details.

Send email. Tap the contact's email address to compose an email message. When the contact has more than one email address, you can choose to which one you want to send the message. Chapter 6 covers email.

View a social networking status. Some address book apps display social networking information on the contact's screen, such as a tweet or Facebook status update. See Chapter 9 for more information on social networking.

View an address on a map. When the contact has a home or business address, you can choose that item to view the address using the Maps app. When you choose the Maps app, you can then get directions, look at the place using the Street View tool, or do any of a number of interesting things, as covered in Chapter 10.

Some tidbits of information that show up for a contact don't have an associated action. For example, the tablet doesn't sing *Happy Birthday* whenever you tap a contact's birthday information.

- ✔ Some address book apps display contact information side-by-side with the contact index. In Figure 5-1, the contact's information appears on a card. Dismiss the card by tapping the Back navigation icon.

- ✔ Not every contact has a picture, and the picture can come from a number of sources (Gmail or Facebook, for example). See the later section "Adding a contact picture" for more information.

- ✔ Also see the section "Joining identical contacts" for information on how to deal with duplicate entries for the same person.

Sorting the address book

The tablet's address book displays contacts in a certain order. Most often, that order is alphabetically by first name. You can change this order if the existing arrangement drives you nuts. Here's how:

1. **Tap the Action Overflow icon on the Contacts app main screen.**

2. **Choose Settings.**

3. **Choose Sort By.**

4. **Choose First Name or Last Name, depending on how you want the contacts sorted.**

   The Contacts app normally sorts entries by first name.

5. **Choose Name Format.**

   This command might be titled Display Contacts By or View Contacts Names By.

6. **Choose First Name First or Last Name First.**

   This command specifies how the contacts appear in the list: first name first or last name first. The Contacts app normally lists entries first name first.

There's no right or wrong way to display your contacts — only the method you prefer.

Searching contacts

You might have a massive number of contacts. Although the address book app doesn't provide a running total, I'm certain that I have more than 250,000 contacts on my tablet. That's either because I know a lot of people or they just owe me money.

Rather than endlessly scroll the Contacts list and run the risk of rubbing your fingers down to nubs, you can employ the tablet's powerful Search command to quickly find a contact:

1. **Tap the Search icon.**

   Some versions of the Contacts app show a Search or Find Contacts text box. If so, tap that box.

2. **Type the name you want to locate.**

   The list of contacts narrows the more you type.

3. **Once you see the matching person, tap that entry.**

To clear a search, tap the X at the right side of the Search text box. To exit the search screen, tap the Back navigation icon.

No, there's no correlation between the number of contacts you have and how popular you are in real life.

Even More Friends

Having friends is great. Having more friends is better. Keeping all those friends as entries in the tablet's address book is best.

Building a contact from scratch

Sometimes it's necessary to create a contact when you actually meet another human being in the real world. Or maybe you finally got around to transferring information to the tablet from your old datebook. In either instance, you have information to input, and it starts like this:

1. **Tap the Add Contact icon in the Contacts app.**

   Refer to Figure 5-1 for what the icon may look like, although different address book apps use subtly different icons.

2. **Choose an account with which to associate the contact.**

   Tap the action bar or account item (it may say *Google Account*) to choose an account.

   I recommend choosing your Google account. That way, the contact is synchronized with the Internet and any other Android gizmos you may own. Or if you use Yahoo! or any another account as your primary account, choose it instead.

   Do not choose the Device category. When you do, the contact information is saved only on your Android tablet. It won't be synchronized with the Internet or any other Android devices.

3. **Fill in the contact's information as best you can.**

   Type text in the various boxes with the information you know. The more information you provide, the better.

   Tap the action bar to the right of a field to set more details, such as whether a phone number is Mobile, Home, Work, or so on.

   To add a second phone number, email, or location, tap the Add New button, which may look like a large Plus icon.

   At the bottom of the Add New Contact screen, you'll find the button Add Another Field. Use that button when you can add more details for the contact, such as a birthday or website address.

4. **Tap the Done or Save button to complete editing and add the new contact.**

If you followed my advice in Step 2, the new contact is automatically synched with your Google account. That's one beauty of the Android operating system: You have no need to duplicate your efforts; contacts you create on the tablet are instantly updated with your Google account on the Internet.

Creating a contact from an email message

Perhaps one of the easiest ways to build up the tablet's address book is to create a contact from an email message. Follow these general steps when you receive a message from someone not already in your Android tablet's address book:

1. **View the email message.**

   You can't add a contact from the inbox; tap the message to view its contents.

2. **Tap the icon by the contact's name.**

   The Gmail app uses a letter icon for unknown contacts, such as the H shown in Figure 5-2. The Email app uses a generic human icon, also shown in the figure.

3. **Tap the OK button to create the new contact, if prompted.**

   If you don't see the prompt, you may see a card, such as the one shown on the right in Figure 5-2. If so, tap the Create Contact button and fill in the blanks. Tap the Save button to save the contact.

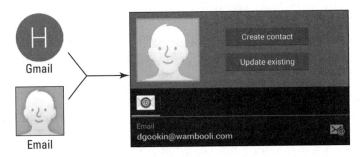

Figure 5-2: Adding a new email contact.

 These steps may vary, depending the tablet's incarnation of the Contacts app. You also may have to tap the Add New Contact icon, similar to the one shown in the margin. However you get there, complete creating the contact information as described in the preceding section. As a bonus, the contact's email address is already provided.

Sometimes you receive email from someone already in the address book, but who is using a new email address. If so, tap the Update Existing button, shown in Figure 5-2. Scroll through the address book to select the person, or the tablet may find the matching contact automatically. The new email address is added to that person's entry in the address book.

Importing contacts from a computer

Your computer's email program is doubtless a useful repository of contacts you've built up over the years. You can export these contacts from your computer's email program and then import them into your tablet. It's not simple, but it's possible.

The key is to save or export your computer email program's records in the *vCard* (vcf) file format. These records can then be imported by the Android tablet into the address book app. The method for exporting contacts varies, depending on the email program:

- ✓ **In the Windows Live Mail program,** choose Go⇨Contacts and then choose File⇨Export⇨Business Card (.VCF) to export the contacts.

- ✓ **In Windows Mail,** choose File⇨Export⇨Windows Contacts and then choose vCards (Folder of .VCF Files) from the Export Windows Contacts dialog box. Click the Export button.

- ✓ **On the Mac,** open the Address Book program and choose All Contacts. Then choose File⇨Export⇨Export vCard to save the vCards as a single file.

After the vCard files are created on your computer, connect the Android tablet to the computer and transfer them. Transferring files from your computer to the Android tablet is covered in Chapter 17.

With the vCard files stored on your tablet, follow these steps in the Address Book app to complete the process:

1. **Tap the Action Overflow icon.**

2. **Choose the Import/Export action.**

   If you can't find this action, look for a Settings command, and then choose Import/Export.

3. **Choose Import from Storage.**

   The action might instead read *Import from USB Storage* or *Import from SD Card.*

4. **Choose your Google account to save and synchronize the contacts.**

5. **Choose the Import All vCard Files option.**

6. **Tap the OK button.**

   The contacts are saved on your tablet and also synchronized to your Gmail account, which instantly creates a backup copy.

The importing process may create some duplicates. That's okay: You can join two entries for the same person in your tablet's address book. See the section "Joining identical contacts," later in this chapter.

Manage Your Friends

Don't let your friends just sit there, occupying valuable storage space inside your tablet! Put them to work. Actually, the tablet does the work; you just give the orders. This section lists some routine and common address book chores and activities.

Editing contact information

To make minor touch-ups on any contact, start by locating and displaying the contact's information. Tap the Edit icon, similar to the Pencil icon shown in the margin. When the Edit icon isn't visible, tap the Action Overflow icon and choose Edit.

Change or add information by tapping a field and then editing or adding new text.

Some contact information cannot be edited. For example, fields pulled in from social networking sites can be edited only by that account holder on the social networking site.

When you're finished editing, tap the Save button or Done button.

Adding a contact picture

Nothing can be more delicious than snapping an inappropriate picture of someone you know and using the picture as his contact picture on your tablet. Then, every time he contacts you, that embarrassing, potentially career-ending photo comes up.

I suppose you could use nice pictures as well, but what's the fun in that?

To use the tablet's camera to snap a contact picture, heed these directions:

1. **Locate and display the contact's information.**

2. **Tap the contact's picture.**

   If nothing happens after tapping the picture, tap the Edit icon, and then tap the picture.

3. **Choose the action Take New Photo, which might be titled Take Picture or something similar.**

4. **Use the tablet's camera to snap a picture.**

   Chapter 11 covers using the Camera app. Both the front and rear cameras can be used (but not both at the same time). Tap the Shutter icon to take the picture.

5. **Review the picture.**

   Nothing is set yet. If you want to try again, tap the Retry icon. Refer to Table 5-1 for definitions of the picture confirmation icons.

Table 5-1	**Picture Confirmation Icons**	
Icon	*Name*	*Function*
↰	Retry	Take another photo
✓	Done	Accept the photo and crop
✗	Cancel	Abandon your efforts

6. **Tap the Done icon to confirm the new image and prepare for cropping.**

7. **If you see a Complete Action Using card, tap Crop Picture and then tap the Always button. Tap OK to confirm.**

8. **Crop the image, as shown in Figure 5-3.**

   Adjust the cropping box so that it surrounds only the portion of the image you want to keep.

9. **Tap the Done button to crop and save the image.**

The image you took (refer to Step 4) now appears whenever the contact is referenced on your tablet.

To remove an image from a contact, you need to edit the contact as described in the preceding section. Tap the contact's picture while you're editing, and then choose the Remove Photo or similar command.

Portion discarded   Portion kept   Save the cropped image

Resize rectangle   Drag cropping rectangle

Figure 5-3: Cropping a contact's image.

You can also use any image stored on the tablet as a contact's picture. In Step 3, choose the Select New Photo command to view pictures stored or available on your tablet. Browse for and select an image, and then crop.

- ✔ For more information on the Complete Action Using prompt, see Chapter 18.
- ✔ See Chapter 12 for more information on photo management.

Making a favorite

A *favorite* contact is someone you stay in touch with most often. The person doesn't have to be someone you like — just someone you (perhaps unfortunately) contact often, such as your bookie.

 To make a contact a favorite, display the contact's information and tap the Favorite (star) icon by the contact's image, as shown in Figure 5-1. When the star is filled, the contact is one of your favorites and is stored in the Favorites group.

To remove a favorite, tap the contact's star again, and it loses its highlight.

The favorite contacts are all found by accessing the Favorites group. To view that group, tap the Favorites tab (refer to Figure 5-1). On some tablets, you may have to choose Favorites from an action bar on the Contacts app screen.

> ✏ Removing a favorite doesn't delete the contact, but instead removes it from the Favorites group.
>
> ✏ The Favorites group may be named the Starred group on some tablets.
>
> ✏ By the way, contacts have no idea whether they're among your favorites, so don't believe that you're hurting their feelings by not making them favorites.

Joining identical contacts

Your tablet pulls contacts from multiple sources, such as Gmail, Facebook, Yahoo!, and Skype. Because of that, you may discover duplicate contact entries in the tablet's address book. Rather than fuss over which entry to use, you can join the contacts. Here's how:

1. **Wildly scroll the address book until you locate a duplicate.**

   Well, maybe not wildly scroll, but locate a duplicated entry. Because the address book is sorted, the duplicates usually appear close together.

2. **Edit one of the duplicate contacts.**

   Tap the Edit icon to edit the contact.

   Editing may not be required for some versions of the Contacts app. So just go ahead and:

3. **Tap the Action Overflow icon and choose the Join action, which may be titled Link Contact on some tablets.**

   After choosing the action, you see a list of contacts that the tablet guesses might be identical. You also see the entire list of contacts, in case the guess is incorrect. Your job is to find the duplicate contact.

4. **Select a matching contact in the list to join the two contacts.**

   The contacts are merged, appearing as a single entry in the address book.

Joined contacts aren't flagged as such in the address book, but you can easily identify them: When looking at the contact's information, a joined contact appears as a single, long entry, often showing two sources or accounts from which the contact's information is pulled.

Separating contacts

The topic of separating contacts has little to do with parenting, although separating bickering children is the first step in avoiding a fight. Contacts in the address book might not be bickering, but occasionally the tablet may automatically join two contacts that aren't really the same person. When that happens, you can split them by following these steps:

1. **Display the improperly joined contact.**

   As an example, I'm a Facebook friend with other humans named Dan Gookin. My tablet accidentally joined my address book entry with another Dan Gookin.

2. **Tap the Action Overflow icon and choose the Separate action, which might also be called Separate Contacts.**

   The command might not be available, in which case you must first edit the contact, as described earlier in this chapter. At that point, tap the Action Overflow icon to choose Separate.

3. **Tap the OK button to confirm that you're splitting the contacts.**

You don't need to actively look for improperly joined contacts as much as you'll just stumble across them. When you do, feel free to separate them, especially if you detect any bickering.

Removing a contact

Every so often, consider reviewing your tablet's address book. Purge the folks whom you no longer recognize or you've forgotten. It's simple:

1. **Edit the forlorn contact.**

   Directions are offered earlier in this chapter.

2. **Tap the Action Overflow icon and choose Delete.**

   If you don't see the Delete item, the contact is brought in from another source, such as Facebook. You need to use that app to disassociate the contact.

3. **Tap the OK button to confirm.**

   Poof! They're gone.

 On some tablets, you may find a Delete icon (shown in the margin) directly on the contact's screen or on the Edit Contact screen. Tap that icon to remove it, and then tap the OK button to remove the contact.

- ✔ Because the Contacts list is synchronized with your Google account, the contact is also removed there — and on other Android devices.

- ✔ Removing a contact doesn't kill the person in real life.

You've Got Email

*T*he first email message was sent back in the early 1970s. Programmer Ray Tomlinson doesn't remember the exact text but guesses that it was probably something like "QWERTYUIOP." Although that's not as memorable as the first telegraph that was sent ("What hath God wrought?") or the first telephone message ("Mr. Watson, come here. I want you."), it's one for the history books.

Today, email has become far more functional and necessary, well beyond Mr. Tomlinson's early tests. Although you could impress your email buddies by sending them "QWERTYUIOP," you're likely to send and reply to more meaningful communications. Your Android tablet is happily up to the task.

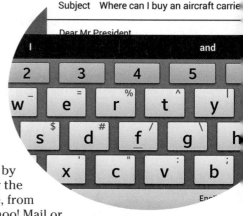

Android Tablet Email

Historically, Android tablets handled electronic mail by using two apps: Gmail and Email. Gmail handled only the Google email. The Email app handled everything else, from traditional ISP email to web-based email, such as Yahoo! Mail or Windows Live Mail, and even corporate email.

With the introduction of Android Lollipop, the Gmail app now handles all email. Even so, your tablet may come with the Email app as well. I cover both apps in this chapter and — as a bonus — both apps do tend to work the same.

✔ Both the Gmail and Email apps are located in the Apps drawer. You may also find launchers on the Home screen.

✔ The Gmail app is updated frequently. To review any changes since this book went to press, visit my website at

www.wambooli.com/help/android

✔ Although you can use your tablet's web browser to visit the Gmail website, you should use the Gmail app to pick up your Gmail. Likewise, you can use a web page to read most other email, but using the Email (or newer Gmail) app is preferred.

✔ If you forget your Gmail password, visit this web address:

www.google.com/accounts/ForgotPasswd

Setting up the first Email account

If your tablet uses the Email app, getting that first account set up works differently than when adding a second or third account. These steps apply only to the Email app. If you're using the Gmail app to add more email accounts, refer to the next section.

Adding your email account to your tablet's inventory of accounts is simple. Providing you know your email address and password, follow these steps:

1. **Start the Email app.**

   Look for it in the Apps drawer. If it's not there, use the Gmail app instead. See the next section.

   The first screen you see is Set Up Email. If you've already run the Email app, you're taken to the Email inbox and you can skip these steps. See the next section for information on adding additional accounts.

2. **Type the email address you use for the account.**

   For example, if you have a Comcast email account, use the onscreen keyboard to type your me@comcast.net email address in the Email Address box.

   You'll find a .com key on the onscreen keyboard, which you can use to more efficiently type your email address. Look for it in the lower-right corner of the screen.

3. **Type the account's password.**

4. **Tap the Next button on the screen or the Done button on the onscreen keyboard.**

   If you're lucky, everything is connected and you can move on to Step 5. Otherwise, you have to specify the details as provided by your ISP. See the later section "Adding an account manually."

5. **Review the items on the aptly named Account Options screen.**

   You might want to reset the Inbox Checking Frequency option to something other than 15 minutes.

   If the account will be your main email account, place a check mark next to the Send Email from This Account By Default option. Also see the later section "Setting the primary email account."

6. **Tap the Next button.**

7. **Give the account a name and confirm your own name.**

   The account is given the name of the mail server or your email address. That choice may not ring a bell when you receive your email. I name my ISP's email account Main because it's my main account.

   The Your Name field shows your name as it's applied to outgoing messages. So if your name is really, say, Cornelius the Magnificent and not wally78, you can make that change now.

8. **Tap the Done button.**

   You're done.

After configuring the account, messages are immediately synchronized with the tablet. You find those message in the inbox. See the later section "Message for You!" for what to do next.

If you use Yahoo! Mail, get the Yahoo! Mail app, which handles your Yahoo! mail far better than the Email app (or the Gmail app). The Yahoo! Mail app gives you access to other Yahoo! features you may use and enjoy. Obtain the Yahoo! Mail app from the Google Play Store. See Chapter 15.

Adding more email accounts

The Email app, as well as the newest version of Gmail, can be configured to pick up email from multiple sources. If you have a Windows Live account or maybe an evil corporate account in addition to your ISP's account, you can add them.

Both the Email and Gmail apps offer different ways to add a new email account. A more generic approach is to use the Settings app. Obey these directions:

1. **Open the Settings app.**

   It's found in the Apps drawer; tap the Apps icon on the Home screen to view the Apps drawer.

2. **Choose Accounts.**

   On Samsung tablets, tap the General tab to locate the Accounts item.

3. **Tap Add Account.**

   The three options for adding email accounts are:

   Exchange or *Microsoft Exchange ActiveSync.* For a corporate email account hosted by an Exchange Server (Outlook mail)

   Personal (IMAP). For web-based email accounts, such as Microsoft Live

   Personal (POP3). For traditional, ISP-email accounts, such as Comcast

   See the later section "Adding a corporate email account" for information on the Exchange option. The other two options work pretty much the same. In fact, on some tablets a single option, Email, may replace both.

4. **Choose the proper Personal email account type.**

5. **Type your email address and tap the Next button**

6. **Type the email account password and tap the Next button.**

7. **Continue working through the email setup as described in the preceding section.**

   Start with Step 5, where you review the account settings.

The only change between creating the first email account and adding more is that you will be asked whether the new account is the primary or default account. See the later section "Setting the primary email account" for details.

The new email account is synchronized immediately after it's added, and you see the inbox. See the later section "Checking the inbox."

Adding an account manually

If your email account isn't recognized, or some other booboo happens, you have to manually add the account. The steps in the preceding sections remain the same, but you need to provide more specific and technical details. This information includes tidbits such as the server name, port address, domain name, and other bothersome details.

My advice is to contact your ISP or email provider: Look on their website for specific directions on connecting an Android tablet to their email account. Contact them directly if you cannot locate specific information.

The good news is that manual setup is very rare these days. Most ISPs and webmail accounts are added painlessly, as described earlier in this chapter.

Adding a corporate email account

 The easiest way to set up your evil corporation's email on your tablet is to have the IT people do it for you. Or you may be fortunate and on the organization's intranet you'll find directions. I present this tip because configuring corporate email, also known as Exchange Service email, can be a difficult and terrifying ordeal.

It's possible to add the account on your own, but you still need detailed information. Specifically, you need to know the domain name, which may not be the same as the outfit's website domain. Other details may be required as well.

Above all, you need to apply a secure screen lock to your tablet to access Outlook email. This means you need to add a PIN or password to the device, which is covered in Chapter 20. You cannot access the Exchange Server without that added level of security.

And there's more!

You also need to grant Remote Security Administration privileges. This means your organization's IT gurus will have the power to remotely wipe all information your Android tablet. You must activate that feature, which is part of the setup process.

The bonus is that when you're done, you'll have full access to the Exchange Server info. That includes your email messages, as well as the corporate address book and calendar. Refer to Chapter 5 for information on the tablet's address book app; the Calendar app is covered in Chapter 14.

Message for You!

New email arrives into your tablet automatically, picked up according to the Gmail and Email apps' synchronization schedules. On newer tablets, use the Gmail app to read all your email. Otherwise, use the Email app to read non-Gmail email.

Getting a new message

The arrival of a new email epistle is heralded by a notification icon. Each email app generates its own version.

For a new Gmail message, the New Gmail notification, similar to the one shown in the margin, appears at the top of the touchscreen.

For a new email message, you see the New Email notification.

Conjure the notifications drawer to review the email notifications. Tap a notification to be whisked to an inbox for instant reading, as described in the next section.

Checking the inbox

To peruse your Gmail, start the Gmail app. The Gmail inbox is shown in Figure 6-1.

Choose non-Gmail accounts by tapping the account icon from the navigation drawer (refer to Figure 6-1). You can view only one account's inbox at a time.

If your tablet still uses the Email app, open it to view its inbox. You see a single account's inbox, or you can choose to view the universal inbox, shown as Combined view in Figure 6-2.

- Gmail doesn't show up in the Email app. Use the Gmail app to read your Google mail.

- The Gmail app lacks a combined inbox. To view specific inboxes, tap an account bubble on the navigation drawer, as illustrated in Figure 6-1.

- Multiple email accounts that are gathered in the Email app are color-coded. When you view the combined inbox, you see the color codes to the left of each message — as long as messages from multiple accounts are available.

- To view an individual account's inbox in the Email app, choose the account from the navigation drawer.

Reading email

To view a specific email message, tap its entry in the Inbox, as shown earlier in Figures 6-1 and 6-2. Or you can choose a new email notification. Reading and working with the message operate much the same whether you're using the Gmail or Email app:

- Swipe the message up or down by using your finger to read it.

- Browse between messages by swiping the screen left or right.

✓ Tap the left-pointing arrow or chevron at the top left corner of the screen to return to the inbox.

To work with the message, use the icons that appear above or below the message. These icons, which may not look exactly like those shown in the margin, cover common email actions:

Reply: Tap this icon to reply to a message. A new message window appears with the To and Subject fields reflecting the original sender(s) and subject.

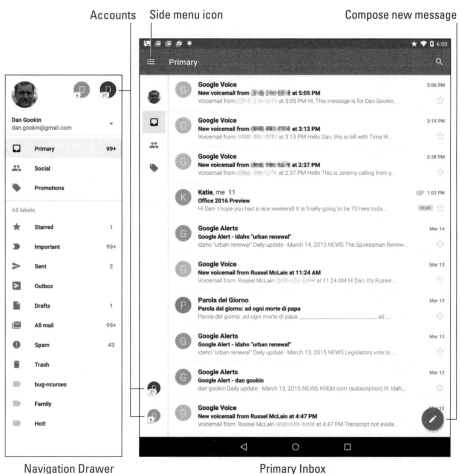

Figure 6-1: The Gmail inbox.

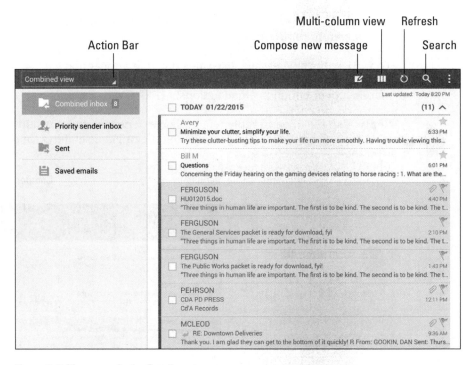

Figure 6-2: Messages in the Email app.

Reply All: Tap this icon to respond to everyone who received the original message, including folks on the Cc line. Use this option only when everyone else must get a copy of your reply.

Forward: Tap this icon to send a copy of the message to someone else.

Delete: Tap this icon to delete a message.

You may not see the Reply All and Forward icons when the tablet is in its vertical orientation. Turn the tablet horizontally to see all three icons, along with the Favorite icon.

Additional email commands can be found by tapping the Action Overflow icon, as shown in the margin. The commands available depend on what you're doing in the Gmail or Email app at the time you touch the icon.

If you've properly configured the Email program, you don't need to delete messages you've read. See the section "Configuring the Delete Email from Server option," later in this chapter.

Write a New Email Message

The Gmail and Email apps not only receive electronic mail but can also be used to spawn new mail. This section describes the various ways to create a message using your tablet.

Starting a message from scratch

Creating a new email epistle works similarly in both the Gmail and Email apps. The key is to find the Compose icon. Tap that icon and then fill in the blanks, adding a recipient, subject, and message text. Figure 6-3 shows how the email composition screen might look. Its features should be familiar to you if you've ever written email on a computer.

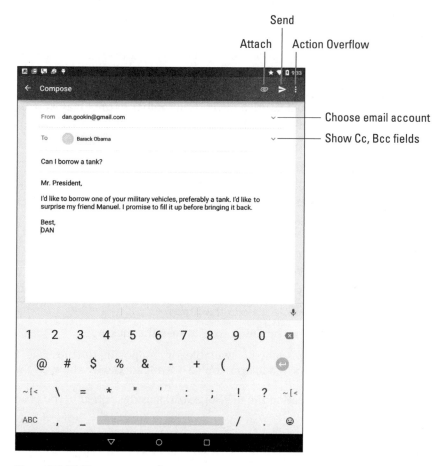

Figure 6-3: Writing a new email message.

To send the message, touch the Send icon, illustrated in Figure 6-3 and shown in the margin.

- To choose an email account for sending, tap the chevron next to your name atop the Compose screen, shown in Figure 6-3. Otherwise, the primary or default email account is used. See the later section "Setting the primary email account."

- You need only type a few letters of the recipient's name. Matching contacts from the tablet's address book appear in a list. Tap a contact to automatically fill in the To field.

- If you can't see the CC and BCC fields, tap the chevron, shown in Figure 6-3, to display those fields. Or you can tap the Action Overflow icon and choose the Add Cc/Bcc command.

- To cancel a message, tap the Action Overflow icon and choose Discard. This action might also be found on the Compose screen. Tap the OK button or Discard button to confirm.

- Save a message by choosing the Save Draft action from the Action Overflow menu. Drafts are saved in the Drafts folder. You can open them there for further editing or sending.

- Some tablets feature a formatting toolbar in the Email app. Use the toolbar to change the way the text looks in your message.

Sending email to a contact

A quick and easy way to compose a new message is to find a contact and then create a message using that contact's information. Heed these steps:

1. **Open the tablet's address book app.**

   The stock Android app is named People, although the name Contacts is also popular.

2. **Locate the contact to whom you want to send an electronic message.**

3. **Touch the contact's email address.**

4. **Choose Gmail or Email to compose the message.**

   Other options may be available for composing the message. For example, a custom email app you've downloaded may show up there as well.

At this point, creating the message works as described in the preceding section.

At Step 4, you may be prompted to use the selected app always or just once. I recommend choosing Just Once until you become more familiar with the email apps. Refer to Chapter 18 for more information on the Always/Just Once choice.

Message Attachments

The key to understanding email attachments on your Android tablet is to look for the paperclip icon. When you find that icon, you can either deal with an attachment for incoming email or add an attachment to outgoing email.

Receiving an attachment

Attachments are presented differently between the Gmail and Email apps, yet your goal is the same: to view the attachment or save it. Sometimes you can do both!

Figure 6-4 shows both the Gmail app and Email app methods of presenting an email attachment. To deal with the attachment, tap it. In most cases, the attachment opens an appropriate app on your tablet. For example, a PDF attachment might be opened by the QuickOffice app.

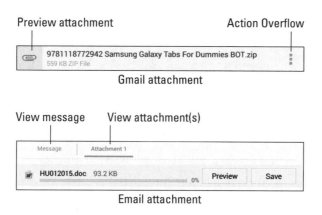

Figure 6-4: Attachment methods and madness.

The Gmail attachment features the Action Overflow icon (refer to Figure 6-4). Tap that icon to control specifically what to do with the app. Actions you might see include

Preview: Open the attachment for viewing.

Save to Drive: Send a copy of the attachment to your Google Drive (cloud) storage.

Save: Save the attachment to the tablet's storage.

Download Again: Fetch the attachment from the mail server.

As with email attachments received on a computer, the only problem you may have is that the tablet lacks the app required to deal with the attachment. When an app can't be found, you have to either suffer through not viewing the attachment or simply reply to the message and direct the person to resend the attachment in a common file format.

- ✓ Sometimes, pictures included in an email message aren't displayed. Tap the message's Show Pictures button to see the images.

- ✓ Common image file formats include PNG and JPEG. Documents are shared by using the HTML (web page), DOCX (Microsoft Word), and PDF (Adobe Acrobat) file formats.

- ✓ You may see a prompt displayed when several apps can deal with the attachment. Choose one and tap the Just This Once button to view the attachment. Also see Chapter 18 for information on the default app prompt.

- ✓ Attachments are saved in the Downloads or Download folder on either the tablet's internal storage or its removable storage (the MicroSD card). See Chapter 17 for details on Android tablet storage, including how to view downloaded files.

Sharing an attachment

When sending an email attachment on an Android tablet, don't think about the method. Instead, think about the attachment: Which app on the tablet created that attachment? When you know that, you're ready to follow these steps:

1. Open the app that created the item you want to attach.

Popular apps for sharing include Photos, Gallery, the web browser app, Maps, Play Store, Drive or any other cloud storage app, and so on.

2. View the item you want to share.

For example, an image, a document, an app in the Play Store, a web page, or a location on a map.

3. Tap the Share icon.

The icon is shown in the margin.

4. Choose the Gmail or Email app.

5. Complete the message as described earlier in this chapter.

The item you're sharing is automatically attached to the message or included as a link.

Sharing an item is the Android tablet method of attaching something to an email message. You're probably more familiar with the computer method, which is to compose the message first and then attach. You can still do that:

Tap the Attachment (paperclip) icon, similar to what's shown in the margin, when creating a new message. Choose an app or category, and then select the item to share.

You've got to admit, however, that finding the item first, and then sharing it, works better on a mobile device.

✔ The variety of items you can attach depends on which apps are installed on the tablet.

✔ The Gmail and Email apps sometimes accept different types of attachments. So if you cannot attach something by using the Gmail app, try using the Email app instead.

Email Configuration

You can have oodles of fun and waste oceans of time confirming and customizing the email experience on your Android tablet. The most interesting things you can do are to modify or create an email signature, specify how mail you retrieve on the tablet is deleted from the server, and assign a default email account.

Creating a signature

Don't be one of the uninformed tablet users whose email signature is the same as everyone else's. Be unique! Set your own signature, just as I did:

```
DAN

This was sent from my Android tablet.
Typos, no matter how hilarious, are unintentional.
```

To create a custom signature for your email accounts, obey these directions:

1. **Open the Settings app.**

2. **Choose the Accounts item.**

   For Samsung tablets, look for the Accounts item on the General tab.

3. **Choose an email account from the list.**

   For example, choose the Personal (IMAP) or Personal (POP3) items, or tap the Email item if you see only it.

4. **Choose Account Settings.**

   This item might be titled Settings.

5. **Choose a specific email account from the left side of the screen.**

6. **Choose Signature.**

   Any existing signature appears on the card, ready for you to edit or replace it.

7. **Type or dictate your signature.**

   If you want to use this signature on other accounts, select and copy the text. See Chapter 4 for details on text editing.

8. **Repeat Steps 5–7 for any additional email accounts.**

The signature you set is appended automatically to all outgoing email you send.

Configuring the Delete Email from Server option

POP3 email, the kind you get from traditional ISPs like Comcast or CenturyLink, is handled differently between an Android tablet and a computer. Unlike reading your email on a computer, messages you fetch on your tablet aren't deleted from the email server. The advantage is that you can retrieve the same messages later by using a computer. The disadvantage is that you end up retrieving mail you've already read and possibly replied to.

You can control whether messages are removed after they're picked up. This setting applies only to POP3 email, not Gmail or IMAP (webmail) accounts. Follow these steps:

1. **Open the Settings app and choose Accounts.**

   Samsung tablets hide the Accounts item on the General tab.

2. **Tap the Personal (POP3) item.**

   This item might simply be titled Email.

3. **Choose the Account Settings item, which might be titled Settings.**

4. **Choose an email account.**

5. **Choose Incoming Settings.**

   Look for the More Settings button if you don't directly see the Incoming Settings item.

6. **Touch the Delete Email from Server item.**

7. **Choose the When I Delete from Inbox option.**

8. **Tap the Done button.**

After you make or confirm this setting, messages you delete in the Email app are also deleted from the mail server. That means the message won't be picked up again, not by the tablet, another mobile device, or any computer that fetches email from that same account.

Setting the primary email account

When you have more than one email account, the main account — the default — is the one used by the Email app to send messages. To change that primary mail account, follow these steps:

1. **Start the Email app.**

2. **From the action bar, choose Combined View.**

3. **Tap the Action Overflow icon and choose Settings.**

4. **On the left side of the screen, select the email account you want to mark as your favorite.**

5. **On the right side of the screen, select the Default Account item.**

The messages you compose and send using the Email app are sent from the account you specified in Step 4.

In the Gmail app, choose the sending account by tapping the chevron next to the From field, as illustrated in Figure 6-3.

Tablet Web Browsing

In This Chapter

▶ Browsing the web on your tablet

▶ Adding a bookmark

▶ Working with tabs

▶ Searching for text on a web page

▶ Sharing web pages

▶ Downloading images and files

▶ Configuring the web browser app

I'm certain that the World Wide Web was designed to be viewed on a computer. The monitor is big and roomy. Web pages are displayed amply, like Uncle Carl on the sofa watching a ballgame. The smaller the screen, however, the more difficult it is to view web pages designed for those roomy monitors. The web on a cell phone? Tragic. But on an Android tablet?

Your tablet doesn't have the diminutive screen of a cell phone, nor does it have a widescreen computer monitor. Instead, the tablet's screen is a good size in between, like a younger, thinner version of Uncle Carl. That size is enjoyable for viewing the web, especially when you've read the tips and suggestions in this chapter.

NIC-lawsuit-rev-5-2
opencda.com
Complete 208 KB

LCDC-Projects_Sou
opencda.com
Complete 796 KB

648px-Conversion_c
upload.wikimedia.org
~nlete 147 KB

✔ If possible, activate the tablet's Wi-Fi connection before you venture out on the web. Although you can use the mobile data connection, a Wi-Fi connection incurs no data usage charges.

✔ Many places you visit on the web can instead be accessed directly and more effectively by using specific apps. Facebook, Gmail, Twitter, YouTube, and other popular web destinations have apps that you may find already installed on your tablet or are otherwise available for free from the Google Play Store.

The Web Browser App

All Android tablets feature a web browsing app. The stock Android app is Google's own Chrome web browser. Your tablet may have another web browser app, which may be named Web, Browser, or Internet.

The good news is that all web apps work in a similar way and offer comparable features. The secret news is that most of these web browsers are simply gussied-up versions of the Chrome web browser. And the sobering news is that I'm writing about only one web browser app in this chapter, which is the Chrome app.

  ✔ If your tablet doesn't have the Chrome app, you can obtain it for free at the Google Play Store. See Chapter 15.

  ✔ An advantage of using Chrome is that your bookmarks, web history, and other features are shared between all devices you use on which Chrome is installed. So if you use Chrome as your computer's web browser, it's logical to use Chrome on your Android tablet as well.

  ✔ The first time you fire up the web browser app on certain Samsung tablets, you may see a registration page. Register your device to receive sundry Samsung bonus stuff — or not. Registration is optional.

The Web on a Tablet

It's difficult these days to find someone who has no experience with the World Wide Web. More common is someone who has used the web on a computer but has yet to sample the Internet waters on a mobile device. If that's you, consider this section your quick mobile web orientation.

Viewing the web

When you first open the web browser app, you're taken to the home page. That may be the tablet manufacturer's home page, the cellular provider's home page, or a home page you've set. For the Chrome app, you see the last page you viewed on the app, or you may see the main Wikipedia page, illustrated in Figure 7-1.

Here are some handy Android tablet web browsing and viewing tips:

  ✔ Pan the web page by dragging your finger across the touchscreen. You can pan up, down, left, or right when the page is larger than the tablet's screen.

  ✔ Pinch the screen to zoom out or spread two fingers to zoom in.

REMEMBER

✔ The page you see may be the mobile page, or a customized version of the web page designed for small-screen devices. To see the nonmobile version, tap the Action Overflow icon and choose Desktop View.

✔ You can orient the tablet vertically to read a web page in Portrait mode. Doing so may reformat some web pages, which can make long lines of text easier to read.

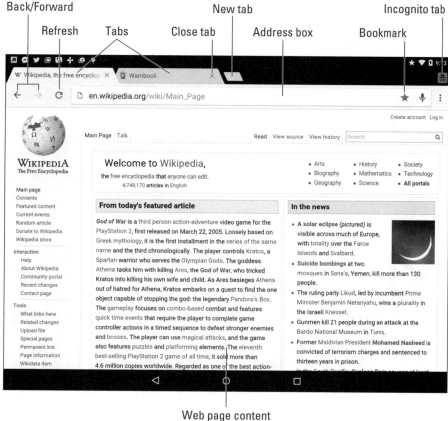

Figure 7-1: The Chrome app beholds Wikipedia's home page.

Visiting a web page

To visit a web page, type its address in the Address box (refer to Figure 7-1). You can also type a search word or phrase if you don't know the exact address of a web page. Tap the Go button on the onscreen keyboard to search the web or visit a specific web page.

You "click" links on a page by touching them with your finger. If you have trouble stabbing the right link, zoom in on the page and try again. You can also long-press the screen to see a magnification window to make accessing links easier.

- Look for special keys when typing a web page address. Some tablets display a .com (dot-com) or .www key. Those keys assist you in rapidly typing web page addresses.

- Long-press the .com key to see other top-level domains, such as `.org`, `.net`, and so on.

- If you don't see the Address box, swipe the web page from the center of the touchscreen downward. If that doesn't work, tap the web page's tab atop the screen.

- To reload a web page, tap the Refresh icon. If you don't see that icon on the screen, tap the Action Overflow icon to find the Refresh or Reload action. Refreshing updates a website that changes often. Using the command can also reload a web page that may not have completely loaded the first time.

- To stop a web page from loading, tap the Stop (X) icon that appears by the Address box.

Browsing back and forth

To return to a previously visited web page, tap the Back icon at the top of the screen (refer to Figure 7-1). If that icon isn't visible, tap the Back navigation icon, shown in the margin.

Tap the Forward icon (refer to Figure 7-1) to go forward or to return to a page you were visiting before you tapped the Back icon.

To review web pages you've visited in the long term, visit the web browser's history page. In Chrome, tap the Action Overflow icon and choose History. If your tablet doesn't use Chrome, try looking on the Bookmarks page for your browsing history: Tap the Action Overflow icon and choose Bookmarks.

- See the later section "Clearing your web history" for information on purging items from the History list.

- If you find yourself frequently clearing the web page history, consider using an incognito tab. See the section "Going incognito."

Saving a favorite web page (bookmarks)

The rest of the web browsing world refers to remembered web pages as being *bookmarked.* That's so 20th century. The term preferred by Google for your Android web browsing adventures is *favorites*. To make a web page one of your favorites, follow these steps:

1. **Navigate to the web page.**

   Favorite web pages are those you plan to visit frequently or want to return to later.

2. **Tap the Star icon.**

   The Star (Favorite) icon is shown in the margin. On some web browser apps, the Bookmark icon is used instead. Good news: That icon often has a tiny star inside. Either way, you see the Add Bookmark card, similar to the one shown in Figure 7-2.

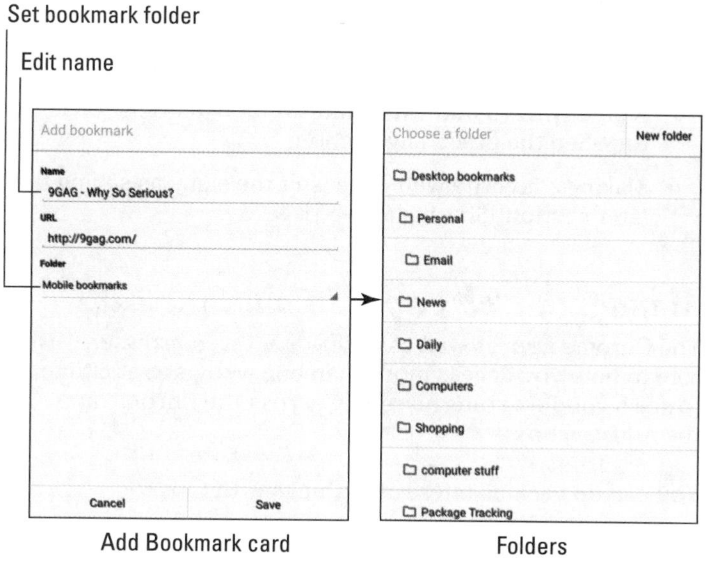

Set bookmark folder

Edit name

Add bookmark		Choose a folder	New folder
Name		☐ Desktop bookmarks	
9GAG - Why So Serious?		☐ Personal	
URL		☐ Email	
http://9gag.com/		☐ News	
Folder		☐ Daily	
Mobile bookmarks		☐ Computers	
		☐ Shopping	
		☐ computer stuff	
Cancel	Save	☐ Package Tracking	

Add Bookmark card   Folders

Figure 7-2: Creating a bookmark.

3. **Edit the bookmark's name, or type in a better name.**

   I prefer short, punchy names as opposed to often long, meandering text.

4. **If you're an organized person, tap the Folder action bar to set a specific folder for the bookmark.**

   The action bar is shown on the left in Figure 7-2. The folders then appear, as shown on the right. Tap a folder to choose a place for the bookmark. If you're an organized person, you'll probably have a complex hierarchy of folders to choose from. If you're not organized, well then, who cares?

5. **Tap the Save button to create the bookmark.**

To view bookmarks in the Chrome app, tap the Action Overflow icon and choose Bookmarks. You see the Bookmarks screen, which appears in Chrome just like a web page. Tap a folder to browse bookmarks; tap a bookmark to visit that page.

To quickly visit a bookmarked website, just start typing the site's name in the Address box. Tap the bookmarked site from the matching list of results displayed below the Address box.

- ✔ The Desktop bookmarks folder lists bookmarks shared with the computer version of Chrome. The Mobile Bookmarks folder lists bookmarks you've created when using a mobile device. My advice is to save all your bookmarks in the Desktop bookmarks folder.

- ✔ Remove a bookmark by long-pressing its entry on the Bookmarks screen. Choose the Delete Bookmark action.

- ✔ I confess that bookmarks are easier to manage when using a computer.

- ✔ A great way to find which sites to bookmark is to view the web page history. See the preceding section.

- ✔ Making a favorite web page isn't the same as saving the page. See the later section "Sharing a web page."

Managing web pages in multiple tabs

The Chrome app, as well as other tablet web browsers, uses a tabbed interface to help you access more than one web page at a time. Refer to Figure 7-1 to see a couple of tabs marching across the Chrome app's screen, just above the Address box.

You can do various interesting things with tabs:

- ✔ **To open a blank tab,** tap the blank tab stub to the right of the last open tab, shown in Figure 7-1. You can also tap the Action Overflow icon and choose New Tab.

- ✔ **To open a link in another tab,** long-press the link and choose Open in New Tab.

- ✔ **To open a bookmark in a new tab,** long-press the bookmark and choose Open in New Tab.

To switch between tabs, tap one. The tab shows the web page title (refer to Figure 7-1).

To close a tab, tap its Close (X) icon. This action applies to both regular tabs and incognito tabs (covered in the next section).

> ✔ Some web browser apps refer to the tabs as *windows*.

> ✔ The tabs keep marching across the screen, left to right. Swipe excess tabs left or right to view the ones that don't appear on the screen.

> ✔ If you close all the tabs, you see a blank screen in the Chrome app. Tap the Add (plus) icon to summon a new tab.

Going incognito

Shhh! For secure browsing, you can open an *incognito* tab: Tap the Action Overflow icon and choose New Incognito Tab. The incognito tab takes over the screen, changing the look of the Chrome app and offering a description page.

When you go incognito, the web browser doesn't track your history, leave cookies, or provide other evidence of which web pages you've visited. It doesn't prevent viruses or sophisticated snooping software.

To switch between incognito tabs and regular tabs, tap the Incognito icon in the upper right corner of the Chrome app's screen, as shown in the margin. Some web browser apps show this icon as a set of overlapping rectangles.

Searching in and on the web

The handiest way to find things on the web is to use the Google Now app, covered in Chapter 14. You can also use the Google Search widget on the Home screen. If it's not there, refer to Chapter 18 for information on adding widgets to the Home screen.

While you're using the web browser app, type search text into the Address bar. Or you can visit any number of search engines, of which Google would most enjoy you choosing Google.

To locate text on a web page, tap the Action Overflow icon and choose Find in Page. As you type the search text, matches appear on the screen. Use the up and down chevrons to page through the document. Tap the Back navigation icon when you've finished searching.

Sharing a web page

There it is! That web page you just *have* to talk about to everyone you know. The gauche way to share the page is to copy and paste it. Because you're reading this book, though, you know the better way to share a web page. Heed these steps:

1. **Go to the web page you desire to share.**

   Actually, you're sharing a *link* to the page, but don't let my obsession with specificity deter you.

2. **Tap the Action Overflow icon and choose Share.**

   The command might be called Share Via or Share Page. Either way, you see an array of apps displayed. The variety and number of apps depends on what's installed on the tablet.

3. **Choose an app.**

   For example, choose Gmail to send the web page's link by email, or Facebook to share the link with your friends.

4. **Do whatever happens next.**

   Whatever happens next depends on how you're sharing the link: Compose the email, write a comment in Facebook, or whatever. Refer to various chapters in this book for specific directions.

You cannot share a page you're viewing on an Incognito tab.

   ✔ Some web browser apps feature a Save action. It lets you save a web page for offline viewing.

   ✔ Also see Chapter 17 for information on printing web pages.

The Art of Downloading

There's nothing to downloading, other than understanding that most people use the term incorrectly. Officially, a *download* is a transfer of information over a network from another source to your gizmo. For your Android tablet, that network is the Internet, and the other source is a web page.

   ✔ The Downloading Complete notification appears after your tablet has downloaded something. You can choose that notification to view the downloaded item.

   ✔ Most people use the term *download* when they really mean *transfer* or *copy*. Those people must be shunned.

   ✔ New apps are installed on your tablet by using the Play Store app, covered in Chapter 15. Installing a new app is a type of downloading, but it's not the same as the downloading described in this section.

   ✔ The opposite of downloading is *uploading*. That's the process of sending information from your gizmo to another location on a network.

Grabbing an image from a web page

The simplest thing to download is an image from a web page: Long-press the image. You see a pop-up menu appear, from which you choose the Save Image action.

To view images you download from the web, you use either the Photos or Gallery app. Downloaded images are saved in the Download album. Refer to Chapter 12 for information on viewing the images on your tablet.

Downloading a file

The web is full of links that don't open in a web browser window. For example, some links automatically download, such as links to PDF files or Microsoft Word documents or other types of files that a web browser is too a-feared to display.

To save other types of links that aren't automatically downloaded, long-press the link and choose the Save Link action. If this action doesn't appear, your tablet is unable to save the link, because either the file is of an unrecognized type or there's a security issue.

Reviewing your downloads

For most Android tablets, you browse the list of items you've obtained from the web by opening the Downloads app. It's found in the Apps drawer. Some variations of this app simply list downloaded items, whereas others may organize the items by date.

To view a download, choose it from the list. The Android tablet uses the appropriate app to view the download. If an app isn't available, an appropriately rude message appears, telling you so.

You can quickly review any single downloaded item by choosing its Download notification.

Web Browser Controls and Settings

More options and settings and controls exist for web browser apps than for just about any other Android app I've used. Rather than bore you with every dang-doodle detail, I thought I'd present just a few of the options worthy of your attention.

Setting a home page

The *home page* is the first page you see when you start a web browser app. Well, every web browser app except for the Chrome app. For the others, heed these directions to set the home page:

1. **Browse to the page you want to set as the home page.**

2. **Tap the Action Overflow icon.**

3. **Choose Set Home Page.**

   You may have to choose the Settings action first and perhaps even dig through other menus, but eventually the Set Home Page command appears. If not, the browser app (like Chrome) doesn't allow you to set a home page.

4. **Tap the action Use Current Page.**

   Because you obeyed Step 1, you don't need to type the web page's address.

If you want your home page to be blank (not set to any particular web page), choose the Blank Page item in Step 4. When this item isn't available, type **about:blank** as the home page address. That's the word *about,* a colon, and then the word *blank,* with no period at the end and no spaces in the middle.

I prefer a blank home page because it's the fastest web page to load. It's also the web page with the most accurate information.

Clearing your web history

When you don't want the entire Internet to know what you're looking at on the web, open an Incognito tab, as described earlier in the section "Going incognito." When you forget to do that, follow these steps to clear one or more web pages from the browser history:

1. **Tap the Action Overflow icon and choose History.**

2. **Tap the X icon next to the web page entry you want to remove.**

   It's gone.

Some web browser apps place the History list on the Bookmarks card: Tap the Bookmarks icon and then tap the History tab to view web page history. Tap the Edit button, then select the items you want to remove. Tap the Delete (Trash) icon to remove those items.

You don't need to clean up your web browsing history when you use an Incognito tab.

Changing the way the web looks

As I ranted at the start of this chapter, the web on a tablet will never look as good as the web on a computer. You do have a few options for making it look better.

First and foremost, remember that you can orient the device horizontally and vertically, which rearranges the way a web page is displayed.

You can spread your fingers to zoom in on any web page, but when you find yourself doing that too often, consider resetting the screen text size:

1. **Tap the Action Overflow icon and choose Settings.**

2. **Choose Accessibility.**

   This item might be titled Screen and Text in some web browser apps.

3. **Use the Text Scaling slider to adjust the text size.**

   The preview text below the slider helps you gauge which size works best.

Setting privacy and security options

Pretty much every web browser app available to Android tablets enables optimum security settings. The only issue you should consider is how information is retained and automatically recalled. You may want to disable some of those features. Obey these steps:

1. **Tap the Action Overflow icon and choose Settings.**

2. **Choose Privacy.**

3. **Tap the Clear Browsing Data button.**

   This step might not be necessary for all web browser apps, which directly show you the list of check mark items.

4. **Place check marks by those items you want removed from the tablet's storage.**

5. **Tap the Clear button.**

Some web browser apps might present options for remembering form data or passwords. If so, remove the check marks by those items. Also, delete any personal data, if that's an option.

With regard to general online security, my advice is always to be smart and think before doing anything questionable on the web. Use common sense. One of the most effective ways that the Bad Guys win is by using *human engineering* to try to trick you into doing something you normally wouldn't do, such as click a link to see a cute animation or a racy picture of a celebrity or politician. As long as you use your noggin, you should be safe.

Also see Chapter 20 for information on applying a secure screen lock, which I highly recommend.

Text, Voice, and Video

The holy grail of communications has always been video chat. Back in the 1960s, the video phone was touted as the harbinger of the future. The film *2001: A Space Odyssey* features a key character making a video phone call to his daughter on the "Bell network." (Cost: $1.70.) Obviously, seeing and speaking on a phone was considered a big deal.

Years after that film was to have taken place, a video phone call is more commonly known as a video chat. It's a feature that your Android tablet is more than capable of offering, along with text messaging, voice chat, and even real phone calls. The future is here — and rather than cost $1.70 for a 2-minute video call, it's *free*.

I'm looking outside at all the falling fall.|

Can We Hangout?

The great Googly way to text message, voice chat, and video chat with your online pals is to use the Hangouts app. It's a communications app, designed by Google to let you connect with one or more of your friends to, well, hang out. It's also a great communications tool.

Using Hangouts

You may find the Hangouts app lurking as an icon on the tablet's Home screen. If not, dig it up in the Apps drawer.

When you first start the Hangouts app, it may ask whether you want to make phone calls. Of course you do! Install the Hangouts Dialer — Call Phones app. If you're not prompted, get the app from the Play Store.

Hangouts hooks into your Google account. Your Google contacts are found by tapping the Contacts tab on the left side of the screen, shown in Figure 8-1. Previous conversations are accessed by tapping the center tab. When the Hangouts Dialer is installed, the third Dialer tab appears on the right side of the screen.

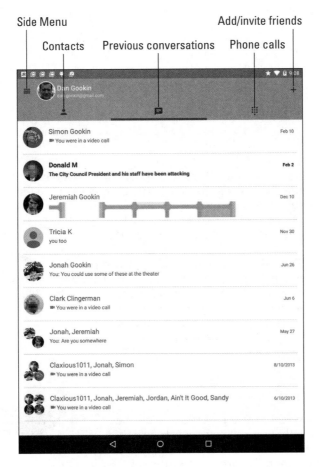

Figure 8-1: Google Hangouts.

 The Hangouts app "listens" for incoming conversation requests, or you can start your own. And you don't have to constantly monitor the Hangouts app: You're alerted to new conversations via a Hangouts notification, as shown in the margin.

To sign out of the app, which means that you won't receive any notifications, tap the Side Menu icon and choose Settings. Choose the Sign Out item on the right side of the screen. Tap OK to confirm.

✔ Conversations are archived in the Hangouts app. To peruse a previous text chat, tap the Conversations tab and choose a conversation from the list. Video calls aren't archived, but you can review when the call took place and with whom.

✔ To remove a previous conversation, long-press it. Tap the Trash icon that appears atop the screen.

✔ Your friend can be on a computer or a mobile device to use Hangouts; it doesn't matter which, but the other person's device must have a camera available to enable video chat.

Typing at your friends

Text chatting is one of the oldest forms of communication on the Internet. It's where people type text back and forth at each other, which can be tedious, but it remains popular. To text-chat in the Hangouts app, obey these steps:

1. **Tap the Contacts tab, or to continue a previous conversation, tap the Previous Conversations tab.**

2. **Choose a contact or previous conversation.**

3. **Use the onscreen keyboard to type a message, as shown in Figure 8-2.**

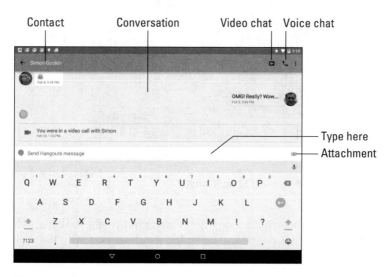

Figure 8-2: Text-chatting.

4. **Tap the Send icon to send your comment.**

The Send icon replaces the Attachment icon when you start to type.

You type, your friend types, and so on until you grow tired or the tablet's battery dies.

Adding more people to the hangout is always possible: Tap the Action Overflow icon and choose New Group Conversation. Choose a friend from those listed to invite them into the hangout.

When you're chatting, or I should say "hanging out," with a group, everyone in the group receives the message.

Talking and video chat

Take the hangout up a notch by tapping the Video Chat icon (refer to Figure 8-2). When you do, your friend receives a pop-up invite, as shown in Figure 8-3. Tap the Answer button to begin talking.

Figure 8-3: Someone wants to video chat!

Figure 8-4 shows what an ongoing video chat might look like. The person you're talking with appears in the big window; you're in the smaller window. Other video-chat participants appear at the bottom of the screen as well, as shown in the figure.

Figure 8-4: Video chat in the Hangouts app.

The onscreen controls (shown in Figure 8-4) may vanish after a second; tap the screen to see the controls again.

To end the conversation, tap the Exit button. Well, say goodbye first, and then tap the button.

✔ When you're nude, or just ugly, decline the video-chat invite. After that, you can choose that contact and reply with a text message or voice chat instead. Explain your embarrassment.

✔ When video chatting with multiple contacts, choose a contact from the bottom of the screen to see that person in a larger format in the center of the screen.

✔ If you want to make eye contact, look directly into the tablet's front-facing camera. It's right above the touchscreen, either centrally located or to the left or right.

Placing a Hangouts phone call

If you've obtained the Hangouts Dialer app, you can use the Hangouts app to place a real live phone call. It's amazingly simple, and it works like this:

1. **Tap the Phone Calls tab in the Hangouts app.**

   Refer to Figure 8-1 for its location. If you don't see the Phone Calls tab, you haven't yet installed the Hangouts Dialer app.

2. **Type a contact name or a phone number.**

3. **Tap the matching contact, or tap the phone number (when it doesn't belong to a contact) to dial.**

   The call is placed.

Tap the red End Call icon when you're done.

✔ To the person you're calling, an incoming Hangouts call looks just like any other call, although the number may be displayed as *Unavailable*.

✔ The good news: Hangouts calls are free!

✔ The bad news: Not every number can be dialed by using the Hangouts app.

Connect to the World with Skype

Skype is one of the most popular Internet communications programs, allowing you to text-, voice-, or video-chat with others on the Internet as well as use the Internet to make real, honest-to-goodness phone calls.

Obtaining Skype for your tablet

The typical Android tablet doesn't come with the Skype app preinstalled. To get Skype, visit the Google Play Store and obtain the Skype app. In case you find multiple apps, get the one that's from the Skype company itself.

To use Skype, you need a Skype account. You can sign up while using the app, or you can visit www.skype.com on a computer to complete the process by using a nice, full-size keyboard and widescreen monitor.

When you start the Skype app for the first time, work through the initial setup screens. You can even take the tour. Be sure to have Skype scour the tablet's address book for contacts you can Skype. This process may take a while, but if you're just starting out, it's a great help.

✔ Skype is free to use. Text chat is free. Voice and video chat with one other Skype user is also free. When you want to call a real phone, or video chat with a group, you need to boost your account with Skype Credit.

✔ It's doesn't cost extra to do a gang video chat in the Hangouts app.

✔ Don't worry about getting a Skype number, unless you plan to receive Skype phone calls on your tablet. Those phone calls include calls from any phone, not just a mobile device using the Skype app. So, unless it's your ultimate desire to transform your Android tablet into a cell phone, don't bother with the Skype number.

Chatting with another Skype user

Text chat with Skype works similarly to texting on a cell phone. The only difference is that the other person must be a Skype user. So in that respect, Skype text chat works a lot like Hangouts chat, covered earlier in this chapter.

To chat, follow these steps:

1. **Start the Skype app and sign in.**

   You don't need to sign in when you've previously run the Skype app. Like most apps, Skype continues to run until you sign out or turn off the tablet.

2. **At the main Skype screen, tap People and choose a contact.**

   Or you can choose one of the contact icons shown on the main screen.

3. **Type your text in the text box.**

   The box is found at the bottom of the screen. It says Type a Message Here.

4. **Tap the blue arrow icon to send the message.**

   As long as your Skype friend is online and eager, you'll be chatting in no time.

At the right end of the text box, you find the Smiley icon. Use this icon to insert a cute graphic into your text.

The Skype Chat notification, shown in the margin, appears whenever someone wants to chat with you. It's handy to see, especially when you may have switched away from the Skype app to do something else on the tablet. Choose that notification to get into the conversation.

Seeing on Skype (video call)

Placing a video call with Skype is easy: Start up a text chat as described in the preceding section. After the conversation starts, tap the Video Call icon, as shown in the margin. The call rings through to the contact, and if that person wants to video chat, they pick up in no time and you're talking and looking at each other.

Placing a Skype phone call

Ah. The big enchilada: Skype can be used to turn your Android tablet into a cell phone. It's an amazing feat. And it works quite well, as long as you have Skype Credit.

To ensure that you have Skype Credit, tap your Account icon on the main Skype screen, shown in Figure 8-5. Tap the Skype Credit item to see a summary of the credit and potentially get more, as illustrated in the figure.

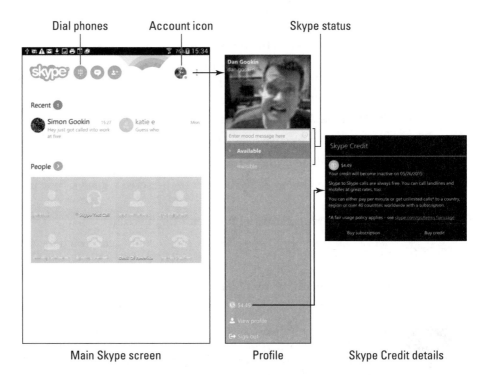

Main Skype screen   Profile   Skype Credit details

Figure 8-5: Finding your Skype Credit.

After you've confirmed your Skype Credit, you can use the tablet to make a "real" phone call, which is a call to any phone number on the planet (Planet Earth). Heed these steps:

1. **Choose a contact to call.**

   Skype contacts are separate from your tablet's address book contacts.

   Your Skype contact must have a phone number listed in his contact information. Otherwise, you have to dial the number directly, which is described near the end of this section.

2. **Tap the Phone icon.**

   If you don't see the Phone icon, the contact's information doesn't include a real, live phone number.

3. **Talk.**

   The Call screen looks similar to the one shown in Figure 8-6.

Figure 8-6: Calling a real phone by using Skype.

4. **To end the call, tap the End Call button.**

   Refer to Figure 8-6 for the button's location.

To dial a number not associated with a contact, tap the Dialpad icon at the top of the main Skype screen (refer to Figure 8-5, left). Punch in the number to dial, starting with 1 (for the United States), then the area code, and then the number. Touch the green Dial icon to place the call.

Lamentably, you can't receive a phone call using Skype on your Android tablet. The only way to make that happen is to pay for a Skype online number. In that case, you can use Skype to both send and receive regular phone calls. This book doesn't cover the Online Number option.

✔ I recommend getting a good headset if you plan on using Skype often to place phone calls.

✔ In addition to the per-minute cost, you may be charged a connection fee for making the call.

✔ You can check the Skype website at www.skype.com for a current list of call rates, for both domestic and international calls.

✔ Unless you've paid Skype to let you use a specific phone number, the phone number shown on the recipient's Caller ID screen is something unexpected — often, merely the text *Unknown.* Because of that, you might want to email the person you're calling and let him or her know that you're placing a Skype call. That way, the call won't be skipped because the Caller ID isn't recognized.

9

Digital Social Life

In This Chapter

▷ Getting Facebook on your tablet

▷ Sharing your life on Facebook

▷ Setting up Twitter

▷ Tweeting

▷ Exploring other social networking opportunities

*L*ong ago, social networking eclipsed email as the number-one reason for using the Internet. It has nearly replaced email, has definitely replaced having a personalized website, and has become an obsession for millions across the globe. Your Android tablet is ready to meet your social networking desires. This chapter covers the options.

Your Life on Facebook

Of all the social networking sites, Facebook is the king. It's *the* online place to go to catch up with friends, send messages, express your thoughts, share pictures and video, play games, and waste more time than you ever thought you had.

  ✓ Although you can access Facebook on the web by using your tablet's web browser app, I highly recommend that you use the Facebook app described in this section.

  ✓ Future software updates to your Android tablet may include a Facebook app or another social networking app. If so, you can read an update on my website at www.wambooli.com/help/android.

Aug 11

Aug 10

: in a video call

Gookin   Aug 10

ere in a video call

okin   Aug 10

ere?

Jun 10

Type a na..

Jeremiah

PEOPLE YOU HANGO

Jeremiah
♂ Famil

Getting the Facebook app

If your Android tablet doesn't come with a Facebook app preinstalled, you can get the Facebook app for free from the Google Play Store. That app is your red carpet to the Facebook social networking kingdom.

The official name of the app is *Facebook for Android*. It's produced by the Facebook organization itself. You can search for this app at the Google Play Store. See Chapter 15.

After obtaining the Facebook app, open it. Sign in by using your Facebook username (typically, an email address) and password. If you don't yet have a Facebook account, tap the item Sign Up for Facebook.

If you're asked to synchronize your contacts, do so. I synchronize all my Facebook contacts with the tablet's address book. That way, my friends' Facebook status and other information appears in the address book app.

Running Facebook on your tablet

The main Facebook screen has several tabs, as shown in Figure 9-1. The tab you'll probably use the most is News Feed. Options for interacting with Facebook appear at the bottom of the screen.

To set Facebook aside, tap the Home icon to return to the Home screen. The Facebook app continues to run until you either sign out of the app or turn off your Android tablet.

To sign out of the Facebook app, tap the Menu icon (refer to Figure 9-1) and choose the Log Out action (from the bottom of the list). Tap the Log Out button to confirm.

- ✒ Refer to Chapter 19 for information on placing a Facebook app launcher or the Facebook widget on the Home screen.
- ✒ The News Feed can be updated by swiping the screen from just below the status bar downward.
- ✒ Use the Like, Comment, or Share buttons below a News Feed item to like, comment, or share something, respectively. You can see any existing comments only when you choose the Comment item.

- ✒ The Facebook app generates notifications for new news items, mentions, chat, and so on. Look for them on the status bar along with the tablet's other notifications.

News Feed Friend requests Messages Notifications More Facebook Contacts

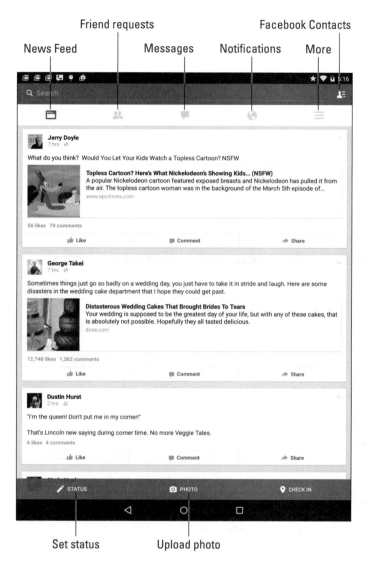

Figure 9-1: Facebook on an Android tablet.

Set status Upload photo

Setting your status

The primary thing you live for on Facebook, besides having more friends than anyone else, is to update your status. It's the best way to share your thoughts with the universe, far cheaper than skywriting and far less offensive than a robocall.

To set your status, follow these steps in the Facebook app:

1. **Switch to the News Feed.**

   Tap the News Feed icon (refer to Figure 9-1).

2. **Tap the Status button at the top of the screen.**

   You see the New Post screen, where you can type your musings, similar to what's shown in Figure 9-2.

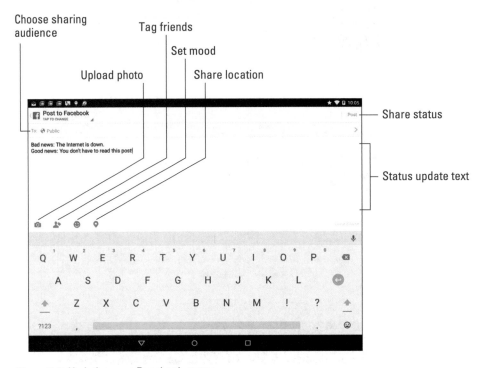

Figure 9-2: Updating your Facebook status.

3. **Tap the action bar to choose where to send the new post.**

   Your choices are the news feed (post to Facebook), a friend's timeline, and a specific group.

4. **Tap the To field.**

   Depending on where you're posting, your choices vary. For posting to Facebook (the news feed), you can choose Public or Friends, where Public makes the post visible to anyone on Facebook and Friends limits viewing to only your friends. Otherwise, choose a user or group for sharing the post.

5. **Tap the What's On Your Mind field to type something pithy, news-worthy, or typical of the stuff you read on Facebook.**

   If you want a lot of attention, type: *Too sad to talk about it now. I need my space.*

6. **Tap the Post button to share your thoughts.**

You can set your status also by using the Facebook widget on the tablet's Home page, if it has been installed: Tap the What's on Your Mind text box, type your important news tidbit, and tap the Share button.

To cancel a post, tap the Back button. Tap the Discard button to confirm.

Uploading a picture to Facebook

One of the many things your Android tablet can do is take pictures. Combine this feature with the Facebook app and you have an all-in-one gizmo designed for sharing the various intimate and private moments of your life with the ogling throngs of the Internet.

The picture posting process starts by tapping the Photo icon in the Facebook app. Refer to Figures 9-1 and 9-2 for popular Photo icon locations on the main screen and the Write Post screen. After tapping the Photo icon, you have two choices:

- ✓ First, you can select an image from pictures shown on the screen. These are images found on your tablet. Tap an image, or tap several images to select a bunch, and then tap the Done button.

- ✓ Second, you can take a picture by using the tablet's camera; tap the Add Photo icon in the upper right corner of the screen, as shown in the margin.

If you elect to use the camera to take a picture, you switch to the Camera app. Snap the photo. You see a review screen, similar to the one shown in Figure 9-3, although not every tablet uses the same Camera app.

Tap the Retry button to take another image, or tap Done or OK and get ready to post the image to Facebook. Tap Cancel to abandon your efforts.

After you select the image, it appears on a new post screen. Continue to create the post as described earlier in this chapter. Tap the Post button. The image can be found as part of your status update or News Feed, and it's also saved to your Mobile Uploads album on Facebook.

Retry   Done/OK   Cancel

Figure 9-3: Adding an image to Facebook.

➤ See Chapter 11 for more information on using the tablet's camera.

➤ I find it easier to take a bunch of images by using the Camera app and then choose an image later to upload it to Facebook.

➤ The Facebook app appears on the Share menus available in other apps on the tablet. Choose that Share command to send to Facebook whatever it is you're looking at or listening to: a video, an image, or some music, for example.

Configuring the Facebook app

Options to control the Facebook app are stored on the Settings screen, which you access by touching the More icon while viewing the main Facebook screen. (Refer to Figure 9-1 for the location of the More icon.) Choose the App Settings action.

Choose Refresh Interval to specify how frequently the app checks for new updates and activities. You might find the 1-hour value to be too long for your frantic Facebook social life, so choose something quicker. Or, to disable Facebook automatic updates, choose Never.

To prevent videos from playing the instant you see one in the News Feed, choose the Video Auto-Play command. Choose Off to disable that feature.

Choose the Notification Ringtone item to the sound that plays when Facebook has a new update. Choose the Silent option to mute update sounds.

Tap the Back icon to return to the main Facebook screen.

The Tweet Life

Twitter is a social networking site, similar to Facebook but far briefer. On Twitter, you write short spurts of text that express your thoughts or observations, or you share links. Or you can just use Twitter to follow the thoughts and twitterings, or *tweets,* of other people.

- A message posted on Twitter is a *tweet.*

- A tweet can be no more than 140 characters long, including spaces and punctuation.

- You can post messages on Twitter and follow others who post messages. It's a good way to get updates and information quickly, from not only individuals but also news outlets, corporations, various organizations, and evil robots.

Setting up Twitter

Your Android tablet most likely didn't come with the Twitter app installed. So your first step into the twitterverse involves getting the app: Visit the Play Store and search for the Twitter app from Twitter, Inc. Install that app; use the directions in Chapter 15 if you need assistance.

After the Twitter app is installed, open it.

You can sign in to Twitter by using your Google (Gmail) account, create a new account, or use an existing account. These options are presented when the Twitter app first runs. For example, tap Create My Account to set up a new account or tap Log In to sign in with an existing account.

You may be asked whether you want the tablet to "use" your Twitter account. If you allow access, your tablet can make Twitter posts for you, which isn't something I want, so I tapped the Cancel button.

Figure 9-4 shows the Twitter app's main screen, which shows the current tweet feed. The Twitter app is updated frequently, so its exact appearance may change after this book has gone to press.

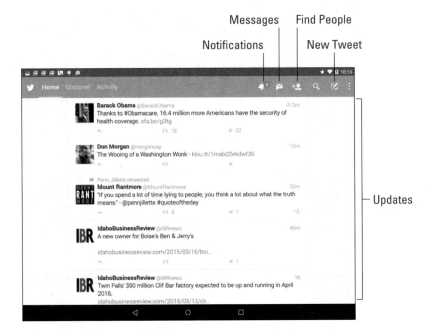

Figure 9-4: The Twitter app.

See the next section for information on *tweeting,* or updating your status using the Twitter app.

The Twitter app comes with companion widgets you can affix to the Home screen. Use the widgets to peruse recent tweets or compose a new tweet. Refer to Chapter 18 for information on affixing widgets to the Home screen.

Tweeting

The Twitter app provides an excellent interface to the many wonderful and interesting things that Twitter does. Of course, the two most basic tasks are reading and writing tweets.

To read tweets, choose the Home category, shown in Figure 9-4. Recent tweets are displayed in a list, with the most recent information at the top. Scroll the list by swiping it with your finger. To update the list, swipe from the middle of the screen downward.

To tweet, touch the New Tweet icon (refer to Figure 9-4). Use the New Tweet screen, shown in Figure 9-5, to compose your tweet.

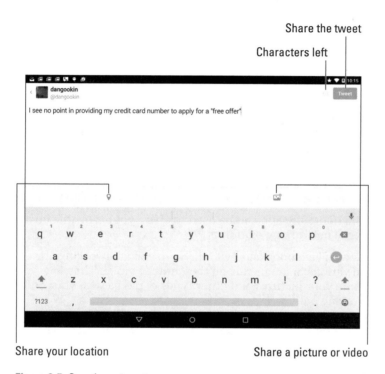

Share the tweet

Characters left

Share your location

Share a picture or video

Figure 9-5: Creating a tweet.

Tap the Location item to add your current whereabouts to the tweet. Tap the Photo icon to add an image or a video from the tablet's gallery.

Touch the Tweet button to share your thoughts with the twitterverse. If you chicken out, touch the Back button and choose Discard.

- ✔ You have only 140 characters, including spaces, for creating your tweet. That includes spaces.

- ✔ The character counter in the Twitter app lets you know how close you're getting to the 140-character limit.

- ✔ The Twitter app appears on various Share menus in other apps. You use those Share menus to send to Twitter whatever you're looking at.

More Social Networking Opportunities

The Internet is brimming with social networking opportunities. Facebook may be the king, but lots of landed gentry are eager for that crown. It almost seems as though a new social networking site pops up every week. Beyond Facebook and Twitter, other social networking sites include, but are not limited to

- ✔ Google+
- ✔ LinkedIn
- ✔ Meebo
- ✔ Myspace

Apps for these services are obtained from the Google Play Store. You can use the app itself to sign up for an account or log in using an existing account.

- ✔ See Chapter 15 for more information on the Google Play Store.
- ✔ Google+ is Google's social networking app, which is related to the Hangouts app. See Chapter 8 for information on using Hangouts.
- ✔ The HootSuite app can be used to share your thoughts on a multitude of social networking platforms.
- ✔ As with Facebook and Twitter, your social networking apps might appear on various Share menus on the Android tablet. That way, you can easily share your pictures and other types of media with your online social networking pals.

Part III
Omni Tablet

Add old-time photo effects to your images. Learn how at www.dummies.com/
extras/androidtablets.

In this part . . .

- Discover your location, find interesting things nearby, and never be lost again.

- Augment your digital photo album by capturing images and recording video.

- Organize images on your tablet and share pictures with others.

- Transfer music from your computer and enjoy it on your Android tablet.

- Schedule your personal and professional life by using the tablet's Calendar app.

- Enjoy an eBook on the road or wherever you take your tablet.

10

There's a Map for That

In This Chapter

▶ Exploring your world with Maps

▶ Adding layers to the map

▶ Finding your location

▶ Sharing your location

▶ Searching for places

▶ Saving a map for later

▶ Using your tablet as a navigator

I'm hoping that teleportation becomes a reality someday. It would be so convenient to travel instantly, to get where you're going without sitting in a cramped cabin. In fact, the only mystery will be whether teleportation has the same knack for losing your luggage as air travel.

One thing our fortunate descendants probably won't complain about is being lost. That's because their Android tablets will tell them exactly where they are, thanks to the Maps app. They'll be able to find all sorts of things, from tacos in pill form to used flying cars to Hello Kitty light sabers. Because it's the future, they might even be able to use the futuristic version of an Android tablet to find their lost luggage.

A Map That Needs No Folding

You can find your location, as well as the location of things near and far, by using the Maps app on your Android tablet. Good news: You run no risk of improperly folding the Maps app. Better news: The Maps app charts the entire country, including freeways, highways, roads, streets, avenues, drives, bike paths, addresses, businesses, and points of interest.

Using the Maps app

You start the Maps app by choosing Maps from the Apps drawer. If you're starting the app for the first time or it has been recently updated, you can read the What's New screen; tap the OK button to continue.

Your tablet communicates with Global Positioning System (GPS) satellites to hone in on your current location. (See the later sidebar "Activate your location!") The position is accurate to within a given range, referenced by a blue circle around your location on the map, as shown in Figure 10-1. If the circle doesn't appear, your location is either pretty darn accurate or you need to zoom in.

Figure 10-1: Your location on a map.

Here are some fun things you can do when viewing the basic street map:

Zoom in: To make the map larger (to move it closer), double-tap the screen. You can also spread your fingers on the touchscreen to zoom in.

Zoom out: To make the map smaller (to see more), pinch your fingers on the touchscreen.

Pan and scroll: To see what's to the left or right or at the top or bottom of the map, drag your finger on the touchscreen; the map scrolls in the direction you drag.

Rotate: Using two fingers, rotate the map clockwise or counterclockwise. Tap the Compass Pointer icon, as shown in the margin, to reorient the map with north at the top of the screen.

Perspective: Touch the screen with two fingers and swipe up or down to view the map in perspective. You can also tap the Location icon to switch to Perspective view, although that trick works only for your current location. To return to flat-map view, tap the Compass Pointer icon.

The closer you zoom in on the map, the more detail you see, such as street names, address block numbers, businesses, and other sites — but no tiny people.

- The blue triangle (shown in the center of Figure 10-1, inside the blue circle) shows in which general direction the tablet is pointing.

- When the tablet's direction is unavailable, you see a blue dot as your location on the map.

- When the location icon is blue, you're viewing your current location on the map. Tap the icon to enter Perspective view. Tap the Perspective icon, shown in the margin, to return to Flat view.

- When all you want is a virtual compass, similar to the one you lost as a kid, get a compass app from the Google Play Store. See Chapter 15 for more information about the Google Play Store.

Adding layers

You add details to the map by applying layers: A *layer* can enhance the map's visual appearance, provide more information, or add other fun features to the basic street map, such as the Satellite layer, shown in Figure 10-2.

The key to accessing layers is to tap the Side Menu icon to view the navigation drawer. It displays optional layers you can add to the map, such as the

Side Menu   Your approximate location and direction

Navigation Drawer   Satellite/Street view

Figure 10-2: The Satellite layer.

Satellite layer, shown in Figure 10-2. Another popular layer is Traffic, which lists updated travel conditions.

To remove a layer, choose it again from the navigation drawer; any active layer appears highlighted. When a layer isn't applied, Street view appears.

Tap the Satellite/Street icon in the lower left corner of the screen to switch between those two layers.

Activate your location!

The Maps app works best when you activate all location technology in the tablet. Open the Settings app and choose the Location item. On Samsung tablets, the Location item is found on the Connections tab. Ensure that the master control by the Location item is set to the On position.

Your Android tablet uses several technologies to hone in on your location, but only when the Location setting is activated. It also uses Wi-Fi, so ensure that the Wi-Fi setting is on as well; see Chapter 16 for details on Wi-Fi. An LTE tablet also uses the mobile data network to help triangulate the tablet's current position.

It Knows Where You Are

It's common to use a map to find out where you're going. New is the concept of using a map to find out where you are. You no longer need to worry about being lost. Using your tablet's Maps app, you can instantly find out where you are and what's nearby. You can even send a message to someone in the tablet's address book to have that person join you — or rescue you.

Finding a location

The Maps app shows your location as a compass arrow or blue dot on the screen. But *where* is that? I mean, if you need to contact a tow truck, you can't just say, "I'm the blue dot on the gray slab by the green thing."

Well, you *can* say that, but it probably won't do any good.

To view your current location, tap the Location icon, as shown in the margin. If you desire more information, or you want more info about any random place, long-press the Maps screen. Up pops a card, similar to the one shown in Figure 10-3. The card gives your approximate address.

Tap the card to see a screen with more details and additional information, shown on the right in Figure 10-3.

✔ This trick works only when the tablet has Internet access. When Internet access isn't available, the Maps app can't communicate with the Google map servers.

✔ The time display under the Travel icon (the car shown on the right side of Figure 10-3) indicates how far away the address is from your current location. You might also see the Route icon, shown in the margin.

Long-press a location
to see the address

Mark the location
as a favorite

Share this location

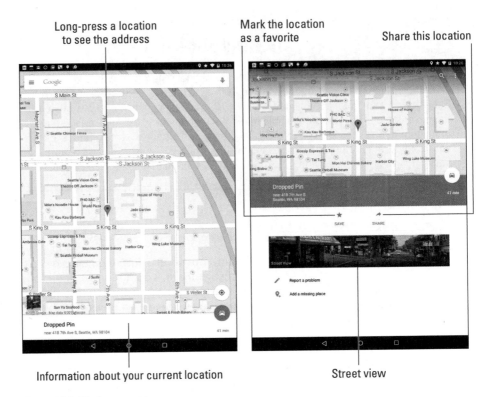

Information about your current location

Street view

Figure 10-3: Finding an address.

 ✔ When you have way too much time on your hands, play with the Street View command. Choosing this option displays the location from a 360-degree perspective. In Street view, you can browse a locale, pan and tilt, or zoom in on details to familiarize yourself with an area, for example — whether you're familiarizing yourself with a location or planning a burglary.

Helping others find your location

 It's possible to use the Maps app to send your current location to a friend. If your pal has a mobile device (phone or tablet) with smarts similar to your Android tablet, he can use the coordinates to get directions to your location. Maybe he'll even bring some tacos in pill form!

To send your current location in an e-mail message, obey these steps:

 1. Long-press your current location on the map.

To see your current location, tap the Location icon in the lower right corner of the Maps app screen.

After long-pressing your location (or any location), you see a card displayed, showing the approximate address.

2. **Tap the card, and then tap the Share icon.**

   The current version of the Maps app doesn't use the standard Android Share icon. Refer to Figure 10-3 for this icon's location and appearance.

3. **Choose the app to share the location.**

   For example, choose Gmail or Email to send the location data in an email message, choose Hangouts to instantly chat with someone, or choose another, appropriate app from among those listed.

4. **Continue using the selected app to complete the process of sending your location to someone else.**

When the recipients receive the message, they can tap the link to open your location in the Maps app — providing that they have an Android device. When the location appears, they can follow my advice in the later section "Android the Navigator" for getting to your location. And don't loan them this book, either; have them purchase their own copy. Thanks.

Find Things

The Maps app can help you find places in the real world, just like the Google Search app helps you find places on the Internet. Both operations work basically the same.

Open the Maps app and type something to find in the Search box, as illustrated in Figure 10-1. The variety of terms you can type in the Search box is explained in this section.

Looking for a specific address

To locate an address, type it in the Search box. For example:

```
1313 N. Harbor Blvd., Anaheim, CA 92803
```

You may not need to type the entire address: As you tap the keys, suggestions appear onscreen. Tap a matching suggestion to view that location. Otherwise, tap the onscreen keyboard's Search key and that location is shown on the map.

After finding a specific address, the next step is getting directions. See the later section "Android the Navigator."

- ✔ You don't need to type the entire address. Oftentimes, all you need is the street number and street name and then either the city name or zip code.

- ✔ If you omit the city name or zip code, the Maps app looks for the closest matching address near your current location.

- ✔ Tap the X button in the Search box to clear the previous search.

Finding a business, restaurant, or point of interest

You may not know an address, but you know when you crave sushi or perhaps the exotic flavors of Manitoba. Maybe you need a hotel or a gas station, or you must find a place that buys old dentures. To find a business entity or a point of interest, type its name in the Search box. For example:

```
Movie theater
```

 This search text locates movie theaters on the current Maps screen. Or, to find locations near you, first tap the Location icon (shown in the margin) and then type the search text.

To look for points of interest at a specific location, add the city name, district, or zip code to the search text. For example:

```
Japanese Market San Diego
```

After typing this command and tapping the onscreen keyboard's Search key, you see the assortment of Japanese (or Asian) markets located in the San Diego metropolitan area, similar to the results shown in Figure 10-4.

To see more information about a result, tap its card, such as the one for Mitsuwa Marketplace in Figure 10-4. View details on the next screen to glean more information.

 To get to the location, tap the Route icon on the location's card. See the later section "Android the Navigator."

- ✔ Every letter or dot on the search results screen represents a matching location. For each dot, a card appears, as shown on the bottom left in Figure 10-4.

- ✔ Spread your fingers on the touchscreen to zoom in on the map.

 - ✔ If you *really* like the location, tap the Save (Star) icon. The location is added to your list of favorite places. A star also appears on the map, indicating that one of your favorite places is nearby. See the next section.

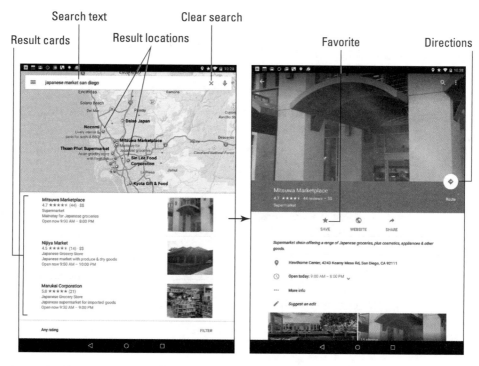

Figure 10-4: Finding a Japanese market near San Diego.

Making a favorite place

Just as you can bookmark favorite websites on the Internet, you can mark favorite places in the real world by using the Maps app. The feature is called Your Places.

 To visit your favorite places or browse your recent map searches, tap the Side Menu icon and choose Your Places from the navigation drawer. Swipe through the list to see recent searches, saved places, and any offline maps you've saved. To revisit a place, tap its entry in the list.

 Mark a location as a favorite by tapping the Save (star) icon on the location's Details card.

Setting your Home and Work locations

Two places you visit most frequently in the real world are where you live and where you work. The Maps app lets you create shortcuts for these locations. They're called, logically enough, Home and Work.

To set the Home and Work locations, follow these steps in the Maps app:

1. **Tap the Side Menu icon to display the navigation drawer.**
2. **Choose Settings.**
3. **Choose the item Edit Home or Work.**
4. **Tap the Edit Home Address item and type in your Home address, or the location you prefer as "home."**

    As you type, choose a matching location from those listed on the screen.

5. **Tap the Back navigation icon.**
6. **Choose Edit Work Address.**
7. **Type the address for your office or wherever you work or pretend to work.**

You can use the Home and Work shortcuts when searching for a location or getting directions. For example, type **Home** into the Search box to instantly see where you live, or whichever place you call home. To get directions from your current location to work, type **Work** as the destination.

Saving a map for offline viewing

The Maps app works only when an Internet connection is active. When you know you'll be away from the Internet, you can save a chunk of the map for offline viewing. Obey these directions:

1. **Locate the map chunk you desire to save.**

    Pan. Square in the area to save on the screen. It can be as large or as small as you need. Obviously, smaller maps occupy less storage.

2. **Tap the Side Menu icon and choose Your Places from the navigation drawer.**

    Offline maps are listed at the bottom of the Your Places screen.

3. **Tap the button View All and Manage.**

    If you don't yet have any offline maps, proceed to Step 4.

4. **Tap the button Save a New Offline Map.**

    Because you already found the location in Step 1, you just need to:

5. **Tap the Save button.**

6. **Type a title for the map and tap the Save button.**

    The map now appears in the list of offline maps on the Your Places screen.

To use an offline map, display the navigation drawer and choose Your Places. Tap the offline map to view, and it shows up on the screen whether an Internet connection is active or not.

- ✏ Offline maps remain valid for 30 days. After that time, you must update the map to keep it current. To update an offline map, tap its Expired entry on the Your Place screen. The offline map is refreshed.

- ✏ Offline maps aren't updated with traffic information.

- ✏ Though you can zoom and pan to peruse an offline map, you cannot use the Maps app to search the map. Searching works only when an Internet connection is active.

Android the Navigator

One command associated with locations found in the Maps app deals with getting directions. The command is called Route, and it shows either the Route icon (see the margin) or a mode of transportation, such as a car, bike, or bus. Here's how it works:

1. **Tap the Route icon on a location's card.**

   After tapping the Route icon, you see a screen similar to the one shown in Figure 10-5. (When the tablet is held vertically, the information is displayed on two screens instead of one.)

2. **Choose a method of transportation.**

   The available options vary, depending on your location. In Figure 10-5, the items are (from left to right) Car, Public Transportation, On Foot, and Bicycle.

3. **Set a starting point.**

   You can type a location or choose from one of the locations shown on the screen, such as your current location, home location, or any location you've previously searched. Tap the Starting Location item to set a different location.

4. **Ensure that the starting location and destination are what you want.**

   If they're backward, tap the Swap icon (refer to Figure 10-5).

5. **Tap a route card.**

   One or more routes are listed on the screen. In Figure 10-5, two cards are shown with different times and distances.

6. **Peruse the results.**

Destination

Starting location

Mode of transportation   Swap   Route

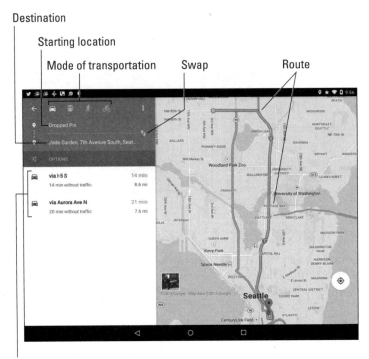

Direction cards

Figure 10-5: Planning a trip.

The map shows your route, highlighted as a blue line on the screen. Detailed directions also appear. Traffic jams show up as red, with slow traffic as yellow.

To see a list of directions, tap a direction card (refer to Figure 10-5). A scrolling list appears on the screen, detailing turn-by-turn directions.

 To begin your journey and enter turn-by-turn navigation mode, tap a direction card and then tap the Navigation icon, shown in the margin. You can mute the voice by tapping the Action Overflow and choosing Mute. Otherwise, toodle on to your destination.

 To exit from Navigation mode, tap the Close icon on the screen.

- If you don't like the route, you can adjust it: Drag the blue line by using your finger. Time and distance measurements shown on the cards change as you adjust the route.

- The Maps app alerts you to any toll roads on the specified route. As you travel, you can choose alternative, non-toll routes, if available. You're prompted to switch routes during navigation; see the next section.

- The blue line appears only on the tablet screen, not on streets in the real world.

- You may not get perfect directions from the Maps app, but it's a useful tool for places you've never visited.

- If you use your tablet in your auto, I strongly recommend that someone else hold it and read the directions. Or use voice navigation and, for goodness sake, don't look at the tablet while you're driving!

- It's possible to navigate by using an offline map. Though the navigation doesn't update, you can user your Wi-Fi tablet to save an offline map and then venture out into the unknown while still using the Maps app. See the earlier section "Saving a map for offline viewing" for details.

- Next to your Android tablet's navigation feature, the other thing you need to get to your destination is a power source. Because navigation consumes a lot of battery power, I strongly recommend getting a car adapter for the tablet. Get an adapter that matches the USB/Power connector on the tablet's edge. Any adapter works; you don't need to ge the pricey one sold by the manufacturer.

Everyone Say "Cheese!"

I have no idea why people say "Cheese" when they get their pictures taken. Supposedly, it's to make them smile. Even in other countries, where the native word for *cheese* can't possibly influence the face's smile muscles, they still say their native word for *cheese* whenever a picture is taken. Apparently, it's a tradition that's present everywhere. Well, except for maybe on the moon, where it's rumored that Buzz Aldrin said "Green cheese."

When you hear folks say "Cheese" around your Android tablet, it will most likely be because you're taking advantage of the tablet's photographic and video capabilities. Or I suppose that you could use the tablet as a festive cheese platter. But when you opt to take pictures or shoot video, turn to this chapter for helpful words of advice.

Android Tablet Camera 101

An Android tablet isn't the world's best camera. And I'm sure that Mr. Spock's tricorder wasn't the best camera in the *Star Trek* universe, either, but it could take pictures. That comparison is kind of the whole point: Your Android tablet is an incredible gizmo that does many things. One of those things is to take pictures, which is the responsibility of the Camera app.

Introducing the Camera app

Google makes a standard Camera app, which is called the Google Camera. Not every tablet uses that app, however. In fact, of all the standard apps on an Android tablet, the Camera app is the one that differs the most.

Generally speaking, the Camera app features at least two shooting modes: still images and video. Additional modes may offer features like a panorama and even special-effects shots. All these shooting modes are handled by the single Camera app.

The Camera app also controls both the tablet's cameras: the main camera, which is on the tablet's backside, and the front-facing camera, which is on the tablet's front above the touchscreen.

Figure 11-1 shows the Google Camera app's main interface in single-shot mode. To switch modes, swipe in from the left side of the screen. The current mode is identified by examining the Shutter/Record icon, as shown in the figure.

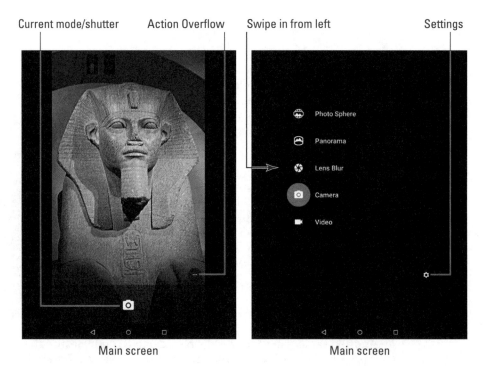

Figure 11-1: The Google Camera app.

Just to show you how different things can be, Figure 11-2 shows the Camera app on a Samsung Galaxy Tab S. This isn't even the same app you'd find on all Samsung Galactic tablets; nope, each one is pretty much unique.

The same items are present in both Figures 11-1 and 11-2, more or less. The Shutter icon still snaps a picture or records video. Beyond that, it's anyone's guess where the options could be. This chapter offers hints and suggestions on how to find key items no matter which Camera app your tablet uses.

  ✔ Camera settings are reflected by icons on the screen. Figure 11-2 shows several examples in the upper right corner, although the icons are not easy to see.

  ✔ You can take as many pictures or record as much video with your tablet as you like, as long as you don't run out of space in the tablet's internal storage or external storage. Speaking of which:

Shortcut area

Switch camera

Shutter

Video Mode

Settings

Flash

Focus Ring

Previous Image

Other shooting modes

MODE

Figure 11-2: The Galaxy Tab S Camera app.

✔ See Chapter 12 for information on previewing and managing pictures and videos.

✔ See Chapter 23 for details on taking a panoramic shot.

Using basic camera controls

Here are some pointers that apply to all variations of the Android tablet's Camera app:

✔ The tablet can be used as a camera in either landscape or portrait orientation. Don't worry either way: The image is always saved with the proper side up.

✔ The tablet's touchscreen serves as the viewfinder; what you see on the screen is exactly what appears in the final photo or video.

✔ Tap the screen to focus on a specific object. You'll see a focus ring or square that confirms how the camera lens is focusing. Not every tablet has a camera that can focus; I've not seen any front-facing camera that can focus.

✔ Zoom in by spreading your fingers on the screen.

✔ Zoom out by pinching your fingers on the screen.

✔ Some tablets let you use the volume key to zoom in or out: Volume Up zooms in, Volume Down zooms out. On other cameras, pressing the volume key works like tapping the Shutter icon to take a picture.

✔ Hold the tablet steady! I recommend using two hands for taking a still shot and for shooting video.

Capturing a still image

Taking a still image requires only two steps. First, ensure that the Camera app is in single-shot mode. Second, tap the Shutter icon to snap the photo.

Set single-shot mode in the Google Camera app by swiping in from the left side of the screen. Tap the Single Shot icon, shown in the margin. Coincidentally, the Shutter icon also looks like the Single Shot icon. Weird.

In other camera apps, choose the icon representing single-shot mode. Sometimes you'll find a toggle that switches between Single-Shot and Video modes. If so, ensure that the setting is on Single-Shot to take a still image.

Set the resolution *before* you shoot. See the later section "Changing still-shot resolution."

Recording video

To record video, switch the Camera app to Video mode. The Shutter icon becomes the Record icon. Tap that icon to start recording. The elapsed time, and maybe even storage consumed, appears on the touchscreen as video is being recorded. Tap the Stop icon to end the recording.

In the stock Android Camera app, swipe your finger from the left edge of the screen toward the center. You see a list of shooting modes, as shown in Figure 11-1, on the right. Tap Video.

When Video mode is active, the Shutter icon changes to the Video icon, shown in the margin. In some Camera apps, the Record icon (a red dot) is used instead. Tap that icon to start recording. Tap the Stop icon to end the video, as shown in Figure 11-3.

- ✔ Some Camera apps feature the Pause icon for recording video. Tap that icon to temporarily suspend recording. Tap the Record icon to resume. The video you record is saved as a single video as opposed to multiple videos.

- ✔ Some versions of the Camera app may allow you to grab a still image while the tablet is recording: Tap the screen. The image is snapped and saved.

Figure 11-3: Shooting video in the Google Camera app.

Reviewing what you just shot

To preview the image or video in the stock Android Camera app, swipe the screen from right to left. This action pulls in the Photos app, where you can view previously shot still images and videos. Tap the left-pointing arrow in the upper left corner of the screen to return to the Camera app.

Most Android tablet Camera apps feature a previous-image thumbnail (refer to Figure 11-2). Tap that thumbnail to examine still images and videos. Tap the Back navigation icon to return to the Camera app.

✔ One reason to review an image you just shot is to delete it. To do so, summon the image or video as described in this section and tap the Delete (Trash) icon. The image is removed immediately, although some tablets may prompt you for confirmation; tap the OK button to delete the image or video.

✔ To manage all images taken by or stored in the tablet, use the Photos app. See Chapter 12.

✔ If your pictures or videos appear blurry, ensure that the camera lens on the back of the tablet isn't dirty. Or you may have neglected to remove the plastic cover from the rear camera when you first set up your tablet.

Camera Settings and Options

Some tablets feature the Camera app, with more features and special effects than you'll find in a Hollywood movie.

Okay, I'm exaggerating. Still, you'll find plenty of options and settings even in the most basic Camera app. This section touches upon the more necessary and vital settings and options.

Switching cameras

You can do more with the tablet's front-facing camera than take those infamous selfie shots. What more *exactly* you can do I can't think of right now, but the key is to be able to switch between front and rear cameras while using the Camera app.

● In the Google Camera app, tap the Action Overflow icon (shown in the margin) and choose the Switch Camera icon, shown in Figure 11-4. When you see yourself, you've done it correctly.

Other camera apps may show the Switch Cameras icon on the main screen. Refer to Figure 11-2, which shows the Switch Cameras icon used by the Samsung Galaxy Tab S Camera app.

Self Timer

Alignment Grid

Flash

Switch Camera

Figure 11-4: Google Camera app actions.

To return to the tablet's rear, or main, camera, repeat the same steps used to switch to the front-facing camera. In the Google Camera app, the icon's appearance changes slightly, but it's still at the same location.

    ✔ When the Switch Camera icon isn't visible, tap the Action Overflow or Settings (Gear) icon, shown in the margin, to look for the Switch Camera action or icon.

    ✔ Other apps that use the camera may have their own techniques for switching from front to rear camera and back again. For example, Hangouts and Skype may automatically use the front-facing camera. See Chapter 8 for details.

Setting the flash

Not all Android tablets feature a flash on the rear camera. If your tablet does, you can set the flash's behavior, as described in Table 11-1.

Table 11-1	Android Tablet Camera Flash Settings	
Setting	**Icon**	**When the Flash Activates**
Auto		During low-light situations but not when it's bright out
On		Always
Off		Never, even in low-light situations

To change or check the flash setting in the Google Camera app, tap the Action Overflow icon on the app's main screen. The current flash setting is represented by an icon on the screen, such as the Auto flash setting shown in Figure 11-4 and referenced in Table 11-1. Tap that icon to change the flash setting.

Some variations of the Camera app show the flash setting on the Camera app's main screen. If so, tap the icon to cycle through the flash settings.

When you can't find the Flash icon on the screen, tap an Action Overflow or Settings icon. I've also seen Camera apps that feature a sliding drawer on which you'll find the Flash icon. Look for a triangle or chevron near the edge of the screen, which could be one of those slide-in drawers.

- A good time to turn on the auto flash is when taking pictures of people or objects in front of something bright, such as Aunt Ellen showing off her prized peach cobbler in front of a burning munitions factory.

- A "flash" setting is also available for shooting video in low-light situations. In that case, the flash LED is on the entire time the video is being shot. This setting is made similarly to setting the flash, although the options are only On and Off. It must be set before you shoot video, and, yes, it devours a lot of battery power.

Changing still-shot resolution

Too many people ignore the image resolution setting, on not only tablets but digital cameras as well. Either that, or they just figure that the highest resolution is the best resolution. That's not always the case.

High-resolution is ideal for printing images and for photo editing. It's not ideal for images you plan on sharing with Facebook or sending as email attachments. Further, higher-resolution pictures occupy more storage space. Don't be disappointed when your tablet fills up with vacation photos because the resolution is too high.

Another problem with resolution is remembering to set it *before* you snap the photo. As you might expect, the techniques for setting resolution vary with the Camera app.

In the Google Camera app, set the image resolution by following these steps:

1. **Display the Camera app's shooting modes.**

   Swipe the screen from left to right.

2. **Tap the Settings icon.**

3. **Choose Resolution & Quality.**

   The Resolution & Quality screen is organized by shooting mode: Camera (still image) and Video. It's further organized by back or front camera.

4. **Choose a mode and a camera.**

   For example, tap Back Camera Photo to set the still-image resolution for the tablet's rear camera.

5. **Choose a resolution or video-quality setting from the list.**

   Options are presented in aspect ratio and in megapixels.

For other Camera apps, the resolution item may be found by tapping the Action Overflow or Settings icon and then choosing a Resolution, Picture Size, or Photo Size action. You may also have to switch cameras (front or rear) before setting the resolution.

~ Set the resolution or video quality *before* you shoot!

~ The *aspect ratio* describes the image's overall dimensions horizontally by vertically. A 4:3 ratio is pretty much standard, just like the tablet's screen. The 16:9 ratio is the widescreen format.

~ A picture's *resolution* describes how many pixels, or dots, are in the image. The more dots, the better the image looks and prints.

~ *Megapixel* is a measurement of the amount of information stored in an image. One megapixel is approximately 1 million pixels, or individual dots that comprise an image. It's often abbreviated *MP*.

Choosing video quality

Video recorded on your Android tablet doesn't use the same type of resolution as taking a still image. Instead, it uses a video quality setting. As with setting the resolution, you set the video quality before you shoot. And setting the highest quality isn't always necessary.

Setting the video quality happens pretty much the same way as setting the still image resolution, as covered in the preceding section. The difference is that you choose the Video or Video Size option instead of the Camera or Photo option.

~ Set the video quality before you shoot!

~ As with setting the still image resolution, the highest video quality isn't always the best. I pick high quality only when I plan to edit the video or show it on a large-screen HDTV or monitor.

✔ The video-quality settings HD and SD refer to High Definition and Standard Definition, respectively. The "p" value represents the vertical resolution, with higher values indicating higher resolution or quality.

✔ Aspect ratio settings might also be available for setting the video quality. The 4:3 ratio is for standard video; 16:9 is for widescreen.

Activating the location tag

Your Android tablet not only takes pictures but also keeps track of where you're located when you take the picture — if you've turned on that option. The feature is called *location tag, geotag, or GPS-tag*.

To confirm the location tag setting, follow these steps in the Google Camera app:

1. **View the Camera modes.**

   Swipe the screen from the left edge toward the center to view the shooting modes.

2. **Tap the Settings icon.**

   The master control by the Save Location item is either on or off, reflecting the location tag setting.

Other Camera apps may require you to tap an Action Overflow or Settings icon to locate the Location Tag item. You may further have to tap a Settings tab to find this specific item.

✔ Deactivating the location tag feature doesn't remove that information from photos you've already taken.

✔ The geotag information is stored in the picture itself. This means that other devices, apps, and computer programs can read the GPS information to determine where the image was taken.

✔ See Chapter 12 for information on reviewing a photograph's location.

Selecting the storage device

When your Android tablet features removable storage, you can set where the Camera app stores images and videos. Generally, the steps work like this:

1. **Tap the Action Overflow or Settings icon.**

2. **Choose Storage Location or a similar option.**

3. Select the location.

The options are Device or Internal for the tablet's internal storage; or MicroSD, Memory Card, or External Storage for the removable media card.

Some Camera apps automatically switch to external storage (the MicroSD card) when that media is inserted. Such apps automatically reset to internal storage when the media card is removed.

Exploring special modes and effects

Camera apps on Android tablets often sport a rich variety of features. Some apps go way beyond the basics and offer custom shooting modes, special effects, filters, animations, and more. These are divided into two categories:

Special modes are shooting modes. For example, the Camera app may offer the Sports shooting mode, ideal for capturing fast action, or Macro mode for getting details on small objects.

Best Shot mode is another type of mode found on some Samsung tablet Camera apps. In that mode, several images are taken rapidly, which you can then review to pick and choose the best parts of the images to create a final composite.

Effects are applied to the image or video beforehand. These include colorization filters — for example, to shoot an image or a video in monochrome or grayscale.

> ✔ Not every Android tablet Camera app offers special shooting modes and effects.

> ✔ Exploring the shooting modes and effects can be fun, but disable them whenever you need to return to normal photography and video recording. The standard modes are Camera or Still Image for taking photos and Video for recording movies. To remove visual effects, choose either the No Effect or Auto option.

Image Management

*W*hat's the point of an Android tablet having a camera unless you can eventually review, peruse, browse, and chortle at those various images and videos? To solve that problem, your tablet features a digital photo album. You use it to view, manage, and manipulate the images stored in the tablet. Further, you can import other images, including photos stored on your computer or found on the Internet. It sounds easy, and I wish I could promise you that, but I've written this chapter anyway.

The Digital Gallery

The traditional Android tablet photo-management/album app is Gallery. It's being replaced by the Photos app. Your tablet may sport one or both apps, which work similarly. The Photos app offers a few more features, plus better integration with online photo sharing, so it's the app covered in this chapter.

Viewing your photos and videos

The Photos app organizes your photos and videos in several ways. The Photos screen, shown in Figure 12-1, lists photos by date. You can choose more specific views by choosing other items from the navigation drawer, also shown in the figure.

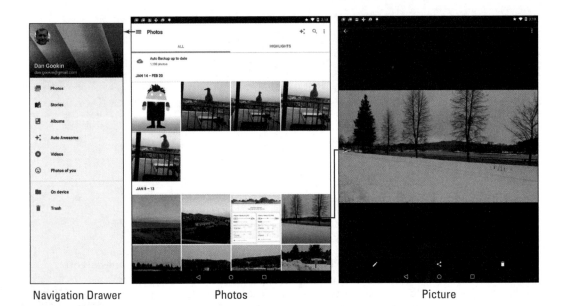

Navigation Drawer   Photos   Picture

Figure 12-1: Image organization in the Photos app.

Tap an image to view it full-screen, as shown on the right in Figure 12-1. You can then swipe the screen left or right to peruse other images.

Videos stored in an album appear with the Play icon. Tap that icon to play the video. As the video is playing, tap the screen again to view onscreen controls.

✔ While viewing an image or a video full-screen, the navigation icons may disappear. Tap the screen to view them.

✔ Tap the Back navigation icon to return to an album after viewing an image or a video.

Starting a slideshow

The Photos app can display a slideshow of your images, but without the darkened room and sheet hanging over the mantle. To view a slideshow, follow these steps:

1. **View an image full-screen.**

2. **Tap the Action Overflow icon.**

3. **Choose Slideshow.**

    Images from that particular album or date appear one after the other on the screen.

Tap the Back navigation icon to exit the slideshow.

 Slideshows don't have to remain in your tablet. If a nearby HDMI TV or monitor features a Chromecast dongle, tap the Chromecast icon on the Slideshow screen, as shown in the margin. Choose a specific Chromecast from the list to view the slideshow on another device.

To end a Chromecast slideshow, tap the Chromecast icon again and tap the Disconnect button.

Finding a picture's location

Your Android tablet can save location information when it takes a picture. The feature is called a *location tag* in the Google Camera app. To use that information in the Photos app, heed these steps:

1. **View the image.**

2. **Tap the Action Overflow icon.**

3. **Choose Details, which might be titled More Info.**

    You see a card displaying image details, similar to what's shown in Figure 12-2. That map information, if available, appears at the top of the card.

See Chapter 11 for more information on the location tag feature, which might also be called a geotag or GPS-tag.

Map preview

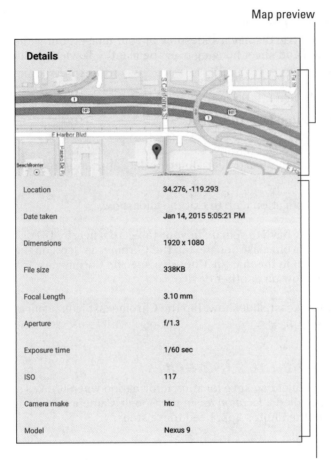

Image trivia and such

Figure 12-2: Image details, including location.

Edit and Manage Images

The best tool for image editing is a computer amply equipped with photo editing software, such as Photoshop or a similar program that's also referred to as "Photoshop" because the term is pretty much generic. Regardless, you can use the Photos app to perform some minor photo surgery. This section covers that topic, as well as general image management.

Editing an image

The Photos app features a special image-editing mode. It offers basic features, such as Crop and Rotate, but also tone manipulation, framing, and other special effects. These powerful editing features are probably why the

Google Camera app is so sparse: True image manipulation should be done after the fact.

To edit an image, follow these steps in the Photos app:

1. **Summon the image you want to edit or otherwise manipulate.**

   Display the image full screen.

2. **Tap the Edit icon.**

   The edit icon is shown in the margin. If you don't see it, tap the screen and it shows up.

The Editing screen is shown in Figure 12-3. A scrolling list of tools appears at the bottom of the screen. Swipe the list left or right to view the lot.

Figure 12-3: Editing an image in the Photos app.

To apply a tool, choose it from the scrolling list. After you select a tool, manipulate the image by using the touchscreen. Some specific examples are found in the next several sections.

For the effects tools, swipe the screen up or down to choose a mode, and then swipe left or right to adjust that mode's intensity. For example, in Figure 12-4, you see the options for Vintage mode.

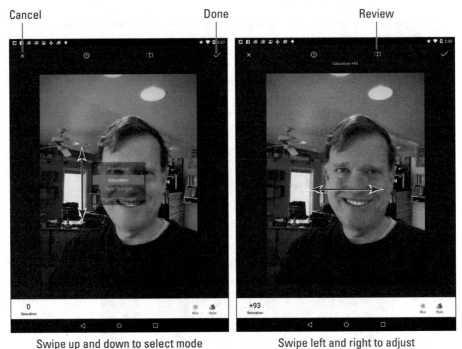

Swipe up and down to select mode   Swipe left and right to adjust

Figure 12-4: Applying image effects.

Tap the Review icon (refer to Figure 12-4) to compare the original and modified images. When you long-press the icon, the original image is shown.

To set your changes, tap the Done icon.

To cancel, tap the Cancel icon.

Choosing Done or Cancel doesn't end Editing mode. To complete the edits and save the image, tap the Done icon on the main editing screen (refer to Figure 12-3).

✔ To view the original version of an image, view that image in the Photos app and tap the Original/Edited icon, shown in the margin. Tapping the icon doesn't restore the image, but it does temporarily show you the original.

✔ To restore an image, removing all edits, edit the image and tap the Action Overflow. Choose Revert. Tap the Revert button to confirm. Tap the Done button to leave Image Editing mode. All edits are removed.

✔ Be careful with those edits! The Photos app attempts to synchronize photos between all your Android devices as well as your Picasa Web image library on the Internet. See the later section "Synchronizing and backing up."

Cropping

An old photography term carried over into the digital world is *crop*. It means "to snip away unwanted portions of an image," like using a pair of scissors on a photo to slice out an old boyfriend (the cheating scum).

To crop an image in the Photos app, follow these steps:

1. **Summon the image for editing.**

   Refer to the preceding section for step-by-step directions.

2. **Choose the Crop tool.**

3. **Adjust the rectangle on the screen to select which portion of the image to keep.**

   Drag the rectangle around. Drag its edges or sides to resize the rectangle.

4. **Save the cropped image.**

5. **Tap the Done icon to exit Editing mode.**

The cropped image is saved in the Photos app.

You can undo the crop by tapping the Restore icon when viewing the image in the Photos app. Refer to the preceding section.

Rotating pictures

When that image isn't really topside up, you can rotate it within the Photos app. Obey these steps:

1. **Summon the cockeyed image for editing.**

   Refer to the earlier section "Editing an image" for specific directions.

2. **Choose the Rotate tool.**

3. **Tap the Rotate Left or Rotate Right button to reorient the image in 90-degree increments.**

   These buttons are found in the lower right corner of the editing screen.

4. **Tap the Done icon to save the rotated image.**

5. **Tap the Done icon to exit image editing mode.**

 It's possible to rotate the image to almost any angle. In Step 3, drag your finger around the touchscreen. The image is automatically resized and cropped to maintain its aspect ratio, but this trick reorients an image up to 45 degrees in any direction.

Deleting images and videos

It's entirely possible, and often desirable, to remove unwanted, embarrassing, or questionably legal images and videos from the Photos app.

 So how do you know what you can delete? Simple: If you see the Delete (Trash) icon on the screen when viewing an image, you can delete that item. Tap the Delete icon. Tap the Delete Everywhere button to confirm. The item is gone.

If you don't see the Trash icon, the item cannot be deleted. It's most likely a copy pulled in from a web photo-sharing service or a social networking site.

  ✔ To undelete an image, tap the Side Menu icon to display the navigation drawer. Choose Trash. Long-press the item to select it, and then tap the Restore icon, shown in the margin.

  ✔ To delete images from Picasa, visit Picasa Web on the Internet at picasaweb.google.com.

  ✔ You can delete a whole swath of images by selecting them as a group. See the next section.

Selecting multiple pictures and videos

Three commands can be applied to groups of images and videos in the Photos app: Share, Copy to Album, and Delete. To select a group, follow these steps:

1. **Long-press an image or a video to select it.**

   Instantly, image-selection mode is activated. The thumbnail you long-pressed grows a check mark.

2. **Continue tapping images and videos to select them.**

3. **Perform an action on the group of images or videos.**

The actions you can perform in Step 3 are

Share: Choose an app to use for sharing the images, such as Gmail to send the lot as an email attachment.

Copy to Album: Select an album to copy the images to, or create a new album. This item is available only when images are selected, not movies or animated GIFs.

Delete: The items are removed. Tap the Delete Everywhere button to confirm.

To deselect items, tap them again. To deselect everything, tap the Back icon.

Set Your Pictures and Videos Free

Keeping your precious moments and memories in your tablet is an elegant solution to the problem of lugging around photo albums. But when you want to show your pictures to the widest possible audience, you need a much larger stage. That stage is the Internet, and you have many ways to send and save your pictures, as covered in this section.

Synchronizing and backing up

The Photos app desires to coordinate your pictures and videos with other Android devices, as well as the Internet. That coordination takes place only when you've activated the Auto Backup feature.

To confirm that Auto Backup is on, look at the Photos screen in the Photos app: Tap the Side Menu icon and choose Photos from the navigation drawer. If the text *Auto Backup Up To Date* appears near the top of the screen, you're good. Images are backed up.

To enable this feature if it's off, look for the text *Turn On,* found on the right side of the Photos screen, near the top. Tap the Turn On button to activate Automatic Backup. Any images not yet backed up are copied to the Internet.

To disable the feature, tap the Action Overflow and choose Settings. Tap Auto Backup, and then slide the master control to the Off position.

> ✔ I strongly recommend disabling this feature if you use your tablet to take images or record video that you don't want anyone to see. Then again, perhaps you should question why you're undertaking such activities in the first place.

> ✔ When Auto Backup is enabled, images on your tablet are copied to your Picasa Web online photo archive. They're stored in the Auto Backup album, which is private by default.

Visiting your Picasa Web account

Part of your Google account includes access to the online photo sharing website Picasa Web. If you haven't yet been to the Picasa Web site on the Internet, use a computer to visit it: `picasaweb.google.com`.

If prompted, log in to your Google account on that website.

Your Picasa account is automatically synchronized with your Android tablet. Any pictures you put on Picasa are echoed to your tablet, accessed through the Photos app. If not, follow these steps to ensure that Picasa is being property synced:

1. **Open the Settings app.**

2. **Choose Accounts.**

   On Samsung tablets, tap the General tab to locate the Accounts item.

3. **Choose Google to access your Google account.**

4. **Tap your Gmail address under the Accounts heading.**

5. **Ensure that a check mark is found by the item Google+ Photos.**

   The item might also be titled Sync Google+ Photos.

If you prefer not to have Picasa synchronize your images, repeat these steps but remove the check mark in Step 5.

To view Picasa Web albums, choose the Albums item from the navigation drawer in the Photos app.

Posting a video to YouTube

The best way to share a video is to upload it to YouTube. As a Google account holder, you also have a YouTube account. Why not populate that account with your latest, bestest videos? Who knows what may go viral next!

To upload a video you've recorded, follow these steps:

1. **Ensure that the Wi-Fi connection is activated.**

   The best way to upload a video is to turn on the Wi-Fi connection, which (unlike the mobile cellular network) doesn't incur data surcharges. In fact, if you opt to use the 4G LTE network for uploading a YouTube video, you see a suitable reminder about the data surcharges.

2. **Open the Photos app.**

3. **View the video you want to upload.**

   You do not need to play the video. Just have it on the screen.

4. **Tap the Share icon.**

   If you don't see the Share icon, tap the screen.

5. **Choose YouTube.**

   The Upload Video screen appears. You may first see a tutorial on trimming the video, which is the next step.

6. **Trim the video, resetting the starting and ending points.**

   This video editing step is optional. If you opt to trim, adjust the starting and ending points for the video by dragging them left or right. As you drag, the video is scrubbed, allowing you to preview the start and end points.

7. **Type the video's title.**

8. **Set other options.**

   Type a description, set the privacy level, add descriptive tags, and so on.

9. **Tap the Upload button.**

   You return to the Photos app, and the video is uploaded. It continues to upload even if the tablet locks.

The Uploading notification appears while the video is being sent to YouTube. Feel free to do other things with your tablet while the video uploads. When the upload has completed, the notification stops animating and becomes the Uploads Finished icon.

To view your video, open the YouTube app. See Chapter 14 for details on using the YouTube app.

   ✔ YouTube often takes a while to process a video after it's uploaded. Allow a few minutes to pass (longer for larger videos) before the video becomes available for viewing.

   ✔ *Upload* is the official term to describe sending a file from your Android tablet to the Internet.

Sharing images with other apps

Just about every app wants to get in on the sharing bit, especially when it comes to pictures and videos. The key is to view an item in the Photos app and then tap the Share icon, as shown in the margin. Choose an app to share the image or video, and that item is instantly sent to that app.

What happens next?

That depends on the app. For Facebook, Twitter, and other social networking apps, the item is attached to a new post. For Gmail, the item becomes an attachment. Other apps treat images and videos in a similar manner, somehow incorporating the item(s) into whatever wonderful thing that app does. The key is to look for that Share icon.

13

Music, Music, Music

In This Chapter

▶ Finding music on an Android tablet
▶ Enjoying a tune
▶ Turning the tablet into a deejay
▶ Buying music online
▶ Organizing your tunes into a playlist
▶ Listening to Internet radio

*Y*our Android tablet's amazing arsenal of features includes its capability to play music. So it effectively replaces any gramophone that you've been lugging around, which is the whole idea behind such an all-in-one gizmo like an Android tablet. And beyond all your Eddie Cantor and Bing Crosby recordings, you can add new tunes to the tablet's music library. It's all covered here.

Listen Here

Your Android tablet is ready to entertain you with music whenever you want to hear it. Simply plug in the headphones, summon the music-playing app, and choose tunes to match your mood.

Browsing your music library

Though your tablet may have come with a Music or My Music app, the great Googly way to audibly entertain yourself on an Android tablet is to use the Play Music app. It accesses music stored on the tablet as well as music stored on the Google cloud.

To view your music library, heed these directions:

1. **Start the Play Music app.**

2. **Tap the Side Menu icon to display the navigation drawer.**

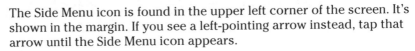

   The Side Menu icon is found in the upper left corner of the screen. It's shown in the margin. If you see a left-pointing arrow instead, tap that arrow until the Side Menu icon appears.

3. **Choose My Library.**

The Play Music app is shown in Figure 13-1 with the My Library screen selected. Your music is organized by category, which appears as tabs atop the screen. Switch categories by tapping a tab, or swipe the screen left or right to browse your music library.

The categories make your music easier to find, as you don't always remember song, artist, or album names. The Genres category is for those times when you're in the mood for a certain type of music but don't know, or don't mind, who recorded it.

✔ Choose the Listen Now category from the navigation drawer to browse songs you frequently listen to or to discover tunes that the tablet guesses you'll like. The more you use the Play Music app, the more you'll appreciate the results shown in the Listen Now category.

✔ Songs and albums feature the Action Overflow icon, similar to the one shown in the margin. Use that icon to view a list of commands associated with the album or artist.

✔ Two types of album artwork are used by the Play Music app. For purchased music, or music recognized by the app, original album artwork appears. Otherwise, the app shows a generic album cover.

✔ When the tablet can't recognize an artist, it uses the title Unknown Artist. This usually happens with music you copy manually to your tablet, but it can also apply to audio recordings you make.

Playing a tune

When you've found the proper tune to enhance your mood, play it! Tap on a song to play that song. Tap on an album to view songs in the album, or tap the album's large Play button, shown in the margin, to listen to the entire album.

While a song plays, controls appear at the bottom of the screen, as shown on the bottom right in Figure 13-1. Tap that strip to view the song full-screen, as shown in Figure 13-2.

Play Music notification   Categories   Action Overflow

Navigation Drawer

Generic album cover art   Current song

Figure 13-1: The Play Music app; Album category.

While the song plays, you're free to do anything else on the tablet. In fact, the song continues to play even when the tablet is locked. Choose the Play Music notification, shown in the margin, to return to the Play Music app, or you can use the controls on the notification drawer even on the Lock screen to pause the song or skip to the next or previous tune.

After the song is over, the next song in the list plays. The order depends on how you start the song. For example, if you start a song from Album view, all songs in that album play in the order listed.

Song queue

Shuffle

Repeat   Previous song   Play/Pause

Next song

Album cover
artwork

Figure 13-2: A song is playing.

The next song doesn't play if you have the Shuffle button activated (refer to Figure 13-2). In that case, the Play Music app randomly chooses another song from the same list. Who knows which one is next?

The next song also might not play when you have the Repeat option on: The three repeat settings, along with the Shuffle settings, are illustrated in Table 13-1. To change settings, tap the Shuffle icon or Repeat icon.

To stop the song from playing, tap the Pause icon, labeled in Figure 13-2.

Table 13-1	Shuffle and Repeat Icons	
Icon	*Setting*	*What Happens When You Touch the Icon*
	Shuffle Is Off	Songs play one after the other.
	Shuffle Is On	Songs are played in random order.
	Repeat Is Off	Songs don't repeat.
	Repeat Current Song	The same song plays over and over.
	Repeat All Songs	All songs in the list play over and over.

> ✒ Use the volume key on the side of the tablet to set the volume.

> ✒ Music on your Android tablet is played by streaming it from the cloud. That means music may not play when an Internet connection is unavailable.

> ✒ You can store music on your tablet by downloading it. Directions are offered in Chapter 15.

> ✒ To change the song order, tap the Song Queue icon, shown in Figure 13-2. Use the tab to the left of each song in the list to change the order; drag the song up or down. Also see the section "Organize Your Music," later in this chapter.

> ✒ You can use the Android tablet's search capabilities to help locate tunes in your music library. You can search by artist name, song title, or album. The key is to touch the Search icon when you're using the Play Music app. Type all or part of the text you're searching for, and then touch the Search icon on the onscreen keyboard. Choose the song you want to hear from the list that's displayed.

> ✒ When a song is playing or paused, its album artwork might appear as the Lock screen wallpaper. Don't let the change alarm you.

"What's this song?"

You might consider getting the handy, music-oriented widget Sound Search for Google Play. You can obtain this widget from the Google Play Store and then add it to the Home screen as described in Chapter 18. From the Home screen, you can use the widget to identify music playing within earshot of your tablet.

To use the widget, tap it on the Home screen. The widget immediately starts listening to your surroundings, as shown in the middle of the sidebar figure. After a few seconds, the song is recognized and displayed. You can choose to either buy the song at the Google Play Store or tap the Cancel button and start over.

The Sound Search widget works best (exclusively, I would argue) with recorded music. Try as you might, you cannot sing into the thing and have it recognize a song. Humming doesn't work, either. I've tried playing the guitar and piano and — nope — that doesn't work either. But it's a great tool for discovering details about what music you're listening to.

Being the life of the party

You need to do four things to make your Android tablet the soul of your next shindig or soirée:

- Connect it to external speakers.
- Use the Shuffle command.
- Set the Repeat command.
- Provide plenty of drinks and snacks.

The external speakers can be provided by anything from a custom media dock or a stereo to the sound system on the Times Square Jumbotron.

You need audio cable with a mini-headphone connector for the tablet's head-phone jack and an audio jack that matches the output device. Look for such a cable at any fine retailer where the employees wear name tags.

After you connect your tablet, start the Play Music app and choose the party playlist you've created. See the later section "Organize Your Music" for information on creating playlists

Enjoy your party, and please drink responsibly.

Add Some Music to Your Life

Consider yourself fortunate if your Android tablet came with music prein-stalled. Otherwise, your music library may be a little light. To pack it full of those songs you adore, you have two options:

- ✓ Buy lots of music from the Google Play Store, which is what Google wants you to do.
- ✓ Borrow music from your computer, which Google also wants you to do, just not as enthusiastically as the first option.

For information on buying music at the Play Store, see Chapter 15. The next section covers borrowing music from your computer.

Getting music into the Google cloud

Realizing that you probably don't want to buy yet another copy of the Beatles' *White Album,* you can take songs from your computer and transfer them to your Google Play Music library on the Internet. Here's how that procedure works:

1. **Locate the music you want to upload to your Play Music library.**

   You can open a music jukebox program, like Windows Media Player, or just have a folder window open that lists the songs you want to copy.

2. **Open the computer's web browser.**

   This would be the computer on which you have lots of music stored.

3. **Visit** https://music.google.com.

   That address represents your music library on the Google cloud. You see a copy of your Play Music library on the screen, including your playlists and any recent songs. You can even listen to your music right there on the computer, but no: You have music to upload.

4. **Click the Upload Music button.**

5. **If you haven't yet done so, download the Music Manager.**

   Click the Download Music Manager button. Complete the installation process. You need to perform this task only once.

6. **Drag music into the web browser window, or click the Select from Your Computer button to add tunes.**

   It takes a while for Google to digest the songs, so be patient.

You can repeat these steps to upload tens of thousands of songs. The limit was once 25,000, but I believe Google increased that number recently.

The songs you upload are available to your Android tablet just like any other songs in the music library.

Synchronizing music directly

Some tablets may let you copy music from the computer directly to the tablet by using the USB cable connection. In that setup, you can use a music jukebox program, such as Windows Media Player, to synchronize music with your Android tablet just as you would any portable music player. Follow these steps:

1. **Connect the Android tablet to your PC.**

   See Chapter 17 if you have difficulty making the connection.

2. **On the PC, choose Windows Media Player from the AutoPlay dialog box.**

   If the AutoPlay dialog box doesn't appear, start the Windows Media Player program.

3. **On the PC, ensure that the Sync list appears, as shown in Figure 13-3.**

   The Android tablet appears in the Sync list on the right side of the Windows Media Player, as shown in Figure 13-3. If it doesn't, click the Next Device link or button until it shows up.

4. **Drag to the Sync area the music you want to transfer to your tablet.**

   In Figure 13-3, you see a list of songs that appear in the Sync list. To add more, drag an album or individual song into the Sync list. Dragging an album sets up all its songs for transfer.

5. **Click the Start Sync button to transfer the music from the PC to your tablet.**

   The Start Sync button may be located atop the list, as shown in Figure 13-3, or it might be found on the bottom.

6. **Close Windows Media Player and disconnect the tablet.**

Your tablet

Click to sync   Sync tab

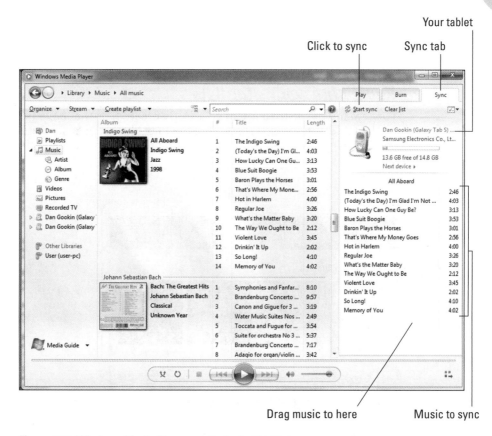

Drag music to here   Music to sync

Figure 13-3: Windows Media Player meets Android tablet.

As I wrote at the start of this section, _some_ tablets let you copy music this way. Even if the transfer appears to be complete, the music may not show up in the Play Music app. If so, great. If not, oh well. You can always try the upload technique described in the preceding section.

✔ You cannot use iTunes to synchronize music with Android devices.

✔ The Android tablet can store only so much music! Don't be overzealous when copying your tunes. In Windows Media Player (refer to Figure 13-3), a capacity-thermometer thing shows you how much storage space is used and how much is available on your tablet. Pay heed to the indicator!

Organize Your Music

The Play Music app categorizes your music by album, artist, song, and so forth, but unless you have only one album and enjoy all the songs on it, that configuration probably won't do. To better organize your music, you can create *playlists.* That way, you can hear the music you want to hear, in the order you want, for whatever mood hits you.

Reviewing your playlists

To view any playlists that you've already created, or that have been preset on the tablet, choose Playlists from the Play Music app's navigation drawer (refer to Figure 13-1). Playlists you've created are displayed on the screen, similar to what's shown in Figure 13-4.

Playlist name

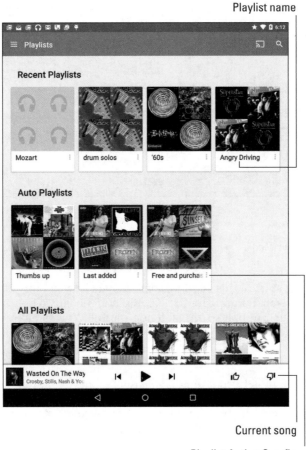

Current song

Playlist Action Overflow

Figure 13-4: Playlists in the Play Music app.

To see which songs are in a playlist, touch the playlist's Album icon. To play the songs in the playlist, touch the first song in the list.

A playlist is a helpful way to organize music when a song's information may not have been completely imported into your Android tablet. For example, if you're like me, you probably have a lot of songs labeled Unknown. A quick way to remedy this situation is to name a playlist after the artist and then add those unknown songs to the playlist. The next section describes how it's done.

Creating your own playlists

The Play Music app features "auto" playlists, three of which are shown in Figure 13-4. Beyond those few, the playlists you see are those you create. Here's how it works:

1. **Locate some music you want to add to a playlist.**

2. **Touch the Action Overflow icon by the album or song.**

3. **Choose Add to Playlist.**

   Ensure that you're viewing a song or an album; otherwise, the Add to Playlist action doesn't show up.

4. **Choose an existing playlist or, to create a new playlist, tap New Playlist.**

   If you choose to create a new playlist, type a name for the playlist and tap the OK button.

The song or album is added to the playlist you selected, or it's placed into a new playlist you created. You can continue to add songs to the playlist by repeating these steps.

- ✔ You can have as many playlists as you like on the tablet and stick as many songs as you like in them. Adding songs to a playlist doesn't noticeably affect the tablet's storage capacity.

- ✔ To remove a song from a playlist, open the playlist and tap the Action Overflow by the song and choose Remove from Playlist.

- ✔ Removing a song from a playlist doesn't delete the song from the music library; see the next section.

- ✔ Songs in a playlist can be rearranged: While viewing the playlist, use the tab on the far left end of a song title to drag that song up or down in the list.

- ✔ To delete a playlist, tap the Action Overflow icon in the Playlist icon's lower right corner (refer to Figure 13-4). Choose Delete and tap OK to confirm.

Removing unwanted music

To remove a song or an album, tap its Action Overflow icon. Choose the Delete action. Tap the OK button to remove the song. Bye-bye, music.

I don't recommend removing music. Most music on your Android tablet is actually stored on the cloud, Google's Play Music service. Therefore, removing the music doesn't affect the tablet's storage, so unless you totally despise the song or artist, removing the music has no effect.

Some music can be stored locally by downloading it to the tablet. That way, the music is always available. See Chapter 15 for details.

Music from the Stream

Although they're not broadcast radio stations, some sources on the Internet — *Internet radio* sites — play music. These Internet radio apps are available from the Google Play Store. Some free services that I can recommend are

- Pandora Radio
- Spotify
- TuneIn Radio

Pandora Radio and Spotify let you select music based on your mood and preferences. The more feedback you give the apps, the better the music selections.

The TuneIn Radio app gives you access to hundreds of Internet radio stations broadcasting around the world. They're organized by category, so you can find just about whatever you want. Many of the radio stations are also broadcast radio stations, so odds are good that you can find a local station or two, which you can listen to on your Android tablet.

These apps, as well as other, similar apps, are available for free. Paid versions might also be found at the Google Play Store. The paid versions generally provide unlimited music with no advertising.

- Google offers an unlimited music listening service. You can sign up by tapping the Get Unlimited Music button, found at the bottom of the Play Music app's navigation drawer. The service is free for 30 days, and then a nominal fee, currently $9.99, is charged monthly.

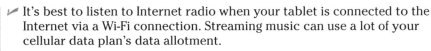

✔ It's best to listen to Internet radio when your tablet is connected to the Internet via a Wi-Fi connection. Streaming music can use a lot of your cellular data plan's data allotment.

✔ Be wary of music subscription services offered through your tablet's manufacturer or cellular provider. I've subscribed to such services only to find them terminated for various reasons. To avoid that disappointment, stick with the services described in this section until you feel comfortable enough to buy into another service.

✔ See Chapter 15 for more information about the Google Play Store.

✔ Internet music of the type delivered by the apps mentioned in this section is referred to by the nerds as *streaming music.* That's because the music arrives on your Android tablet as a continuous download from the source. Unlike music you download and save, streaming music is played as it comes in and isn't stored long-term.

14

Amazing Tablet Feats

In This Chapter

▶ Waking up to your Android tablet
▶ Making tablet calculations
▶ Keeping your appointments
▶ Reading digital books
▶ Playing games
▶ Watching junk on YouTube
▶ Buying or renting films and TV shows

*E*ven given the variety of things your Android tablet can do, you will find some limitations. For example, you cannot use an Android tablet as a yoga block. It makes a poor kitchen cutting board. And despite efforts by European physicists, the Android tablet simply cannot compete with the Large Hadron Collider. Still, for more everyday purposes, I believe you'll find your tablet more than up to the task.

This chapter corrals many (but not all) of the things you can do on your Android tablet. Among the devices it replaces are your alarm clock, calculator, day planner, game machine, eBook reader, and even your TV set. That's not even the full list, but rather everything I could legally cram into this chapter without violating the *For Dummies* chapter length regulations.

Clock

Your Android tablet keeps constant, accurate track of the time, which is displayed at the top of the Home screen as well as on the Lock screen. That's handy, but it just isn't enough, so the tablet ships with an app that tells the time and also may double as an alarm clock.

The app may be called Clock or Alarm. If it's called Alarm, it's probably nothing more than a basic alarm clock. The Clock app, on the other hand, is more of a chronometric app, featuring a timer, stopwatch, alarm, and world clock functions. Of these activities, setting an alarm is pretty useful: In that mode, your tablet becomes your nightstand companion.

Here's how to set a wake-up alarm in the stock Android Clock app:

1. **Tap the Alarm icon or tab atop the Clock app's screen.**

2. **Tap the Add icon.**

   A card appears, which you use to set the alarm time, days, name, and so on.

3. **Fill in details about the alarm.**

   Set the alarm's time, decide whether it repeats daily or only on certain days, choose a ringtone, and complete any other settings as shown on the card. The alarm name appears when the alarm triggers.

4. **Set the alarm.**

   Alarms must be set to activate.

When the alarm triggers, tap the Dismiss icon to tell the tablet, "Okay! I'm up!" Or you can tap the Snooze icon to be annoyed again after a few minutes.

 ✔ Your tablet keeps its clock accurate by accessing an Internet time server. You never have to set the time.

 ✔ Information about a set alarm appears on the Clock app's screen and on the tablet's Lock screen. An Alarm notification, similar to what's shown in the margin, also appears in the status area. These are your clues that an alarm is set and ready to trigger.

 ✔ Unsetting an alarm doesn't delete the alarm. To remove an alarm, tap the alarm and then tap the Delete (Trash) icon. In some incarnations of the Clock/Alarm app, you long-press an alarm and choose the Delete action.

 ✔ The alarm doesn't work when you turn off the Android tablet. However, the alarm does go off when the tablet is locked.

Calculator

The next time you do math, don't bother whipping out your brain. Instead, whip out your Android tablet and summon the Calculator app. The stock Android Calculator app appears in Figure 14-1. Most Android tablet manufacturers mess with this app, so what you see on your tablet might look subtly different, although the basic operation remains the same.

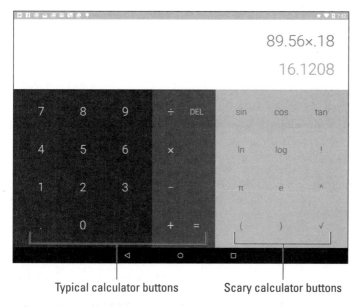

Typical calculator buttons   Scary calculator buttons

Figure 14-1: The Calculator app.

Type your equations by tapping the various buttons on the screen. Parentheses buttons can help you determine which part of a long equation gets calculated first. Use the DEL, CLR, or C key to clear input.

✔ Long-press the calculator's text (or results) to cut or copy the results. This trick may not work in every Calculator app.

✔ I use the Calculator app most often to determine my tip at a restaurant. In Figure 14-1, a calculation is being made for an 18 percent tip on an $89.56 tab. The crab Rangoon was exceptionally fantastic.

Calendar

Your Android tablet is the 21st century version of the old ball-and-chain of the busy person's world: the date book. Thanks to the Calendar app and the Google Calendar service on the Internet, you can toss out your date book.

✔ Google Calendar works with your Google account to keep track of your schedule and appointments. You can visit Google Calendar on the web at www.google.com/calendar

✔ For some weird reason, a few Samsung tablets refer to the Calendar app as the S-Planner. It's the same thing.

✔ Before you throw away your date book, copy into the Calendar app any future appointments and recurring info, such as birthdays and anniversaries.

Browsing your schedule

To see what's happening next, to peruse upcoming important events, or simply to know which day of the month it is, summon the Calendar app. Figure 14-2 shows the Calendar app's Month and Week views. Choose a view by tapping the Action Overflow icon, as illustrated in the figure.

The current day is highlighted in the Calendar app, as shown in Figure 14-2. For some views, the current time is shown as well. To return to the current day, tap the Show Current Day icon, illustrated in the figure.

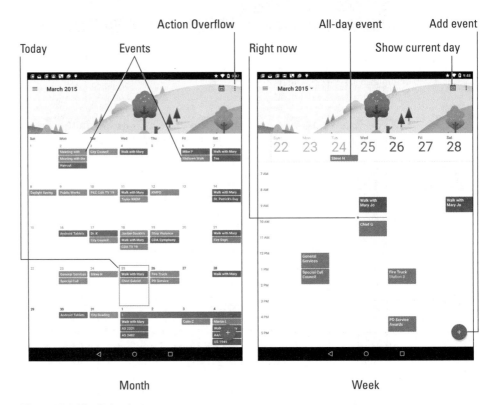

Figure 14-2: The Calendar app.

    ✔ Calendar views not shown in Figure 14-2 include Day and Schedule.

    ✔ Schedule view might be called Agenda or List in some versions of the Calendar app.

    ✔ Some Calendar apps feature 4-day view as well.

    ✔ Use Month view to see an overview of what's going on, and use Week view or Day view to see your appointments.

    ✔ I check Week view at the start of the week to remind me of what's coming up.

    ✔ Swipe the screen left or right to change the view from month to month, week to week, or day to day.

    ✔ Different colors flag your events, as shown in Figure 14-2. The colors represent a calendar category to which events are assigned. See the later section "Creating an event" for information on calendar categories.

Reviewing appointments

To see more detail about an event, tap it. When you're using Month view, tap the date with the event on it to see Week view. Then choose an event to see its details, similar to what's shown in Figure 14-3.

Edit event

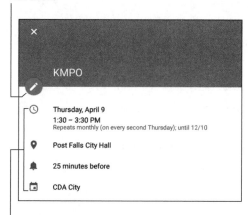

Thursday, April 9
1:30 – 3:30 PM
Repeats monthly (on every second Thursday); until 12/10

Post Falls City Hall

25 minutes before

CDA City

Event details

Figure 14-3: Event details.

The details you see depend on how much information was recorded when the event was created. Some events have only a minimum of information; others may have details, such as a location for the event, the time, and with whom you're meeting.

Tap the Close icon to dismiss the event's details.

✔ Birthdays and a few other events on the calendar may be pulled in from the tablet's address book or from social networking apps. That probably explains why some events can be listed twice — they're pulled in from two sources.

✔ When the event's location is listed, you can tap that location to open the Maps app. See where the event is being held and get directions, as covered in Chapter 10.

✔ The best way to review upcoming appointments is to choose the Schedule view from the Action Overflow.

✔ The Calendar widget also provides a great way to see upcoming events from right on the Home screen. See Chapter 18 for information on applying widgets to the tablet's Home screen.

✔ The Google Now feature lists any immediate appointments or events. See the later section "Google Now."

Creating an event

The key to making the calendar work is to add events: appointments, things to do, meetings, or full-day events such as birthdays or colonoscopies. To create an event, follow these steps in the Calendar app:

1. **Select the day for the event.**

   Or, if you like, you can switch to Day view, where you can tap the starting time for the new event.

2. **Touch the Add Event icon (refer to Figure 14-2).**

   The New Event card or Add Event card appears. Your job now is to fill in the blanks to create the new event.

3. **Add information about the event.**

   The more information you supply, the more detailed the event, and the more you can do with it on your Android tablet and on Google Calendar on the Internet. Here are some of the many items you can set when creating an event:

   • *Title:* The name of the event, person you're going to meet, or place you're headed.

- *Calendar Category:* Choose a specific calendar to help organize and color-code your events.

- *Time/Duration:* If you followed Step 1 in this section, you don't have to set a starting time. Otherwise, specify the time the meeting starts and stops, or choose to set an all-day event such as a birthday or your mother-in-law's visit that was supposed to last for an hour.

- *Location:* Type the location just as though you're searching for a location in the Maps app.

- *Repeat:* Tap the More Options button if you don't see this item. Use the Repeat setting to configure events on a recurring schedule.

- *Notification/Reminder:* Set an email or Calendar notification to signal an upcoming event.

4. Touch the Save or Done button to create the new event.

The new event appears on the calendar, reminding you that you need to do something on such-and-such a day with what's-his-face.

✔ You can change an event at any time: Simply tap the event to bring up more information, and then tap the Edit icon to modify the event, similar to what's shown in Figure 14-3.

✔ For events that repeat twice a week or twice a month, create *two* repeating events. For example, when you have meetings on the first and third Mondays, you need to create two separate events: one for the first Monday and another for the third. Then have each event repeat monthly.

✔ To remove an event, touch the event to bring up more information, and tap the Delete icon. Touch the OK button to confirm. For a repeating event, choose whether to delete only the current event or all future events.

✔ Setting an event's time zone is necessary only when the event takes place in another time zone or spans time zones, such as an airline flight. In that case, the Calendar app automatically adjusts the starting and stopping times for events depending on where you are.

✔ If you forget to set the time zone and you end up hopping around the world, your events are set according to the time zone in which they were created, not the local time.

✔ Reminders are set to direct the tablet to alert you before an event takes place. The alert is either a notification (shown in the margin), or a Gmail message. I prefer notifications, which also display an alert on the tablet's Lock screen.

eBook Reader

Printed books are O so 14th century. These days, reading material is presented electronically in the form of an eBook. The great Googly way to read eBooks is to employ the Play Books app. Still, if you're a Kindle fan, you can also get the Amazon Kindle app from the Play Store (see Chapter 15). Why not use both?

 Begin your reading experience by opening the Play Books app. You'll see any recent books you've read; otherwise, you can view your entire book library: Tap the Side Menu icon (shown in the margin) and choose the My Library command from the navigation drawer.

The library lists any titles you've obtained for your Google Books account, similar to what's shown in Figure 14-4.

Scroll through your library by swiping the screen.

Tap a book's cover to open it. If you've opened the book previously, you're returned to the page you last read. Otherwise, you see the book's first page.

Figure 14-5 illustrates the basic book-reading operation in the Play Books app. You turn pages by swiping the screen right-to-left, assuming that you're reading English or other languages that read in that direction.

The Play Books app also works in both vertical and horizontal orientations. You can lock the screen by choosing the Settings command from the navigation drawer: Choose the Auto-Rotate Screen item and select how you want the screen locked or not.

- If you don't see a book in the library, tap the Action Overflow icon and choose Refresh.

- Books in your Play Books library are stored on the Internet and available to read only when an Internet connection is active. It's possible to keep a book on your tablet by downloading it to the device. Refer to Chapter 15 for details on downloading books.

- To remove a book from the library, tap the Action Overflow icon on the book's cover and then choose the Delete from Library command.

- If the onscreen controls (refer to Figure 14-5) disappear, tap the screen to see them again.

- Tap the A icon to display a menu of options for adjusting the text on the screen and the brightness.

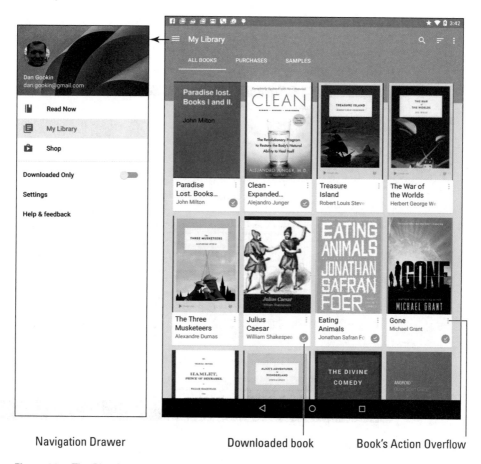

Navigation Drawer   Downloaded book   Book's Action Overflow

Figure 14-4: The Play Books library.

- Unlike dead tree books, eBooks lack an index. That's because text on digital pages can change based on the book's presentation. Therefore, use the Search command (refer to Figure 14-5) to look for items in the text.

- Copies of all your Google Books are available on all your Android devices and on the `http://books.google.com` website.

- Refer to Chapter 15 for information on obtaining books at the Google Play Store, as well as how to download books to your tablet.

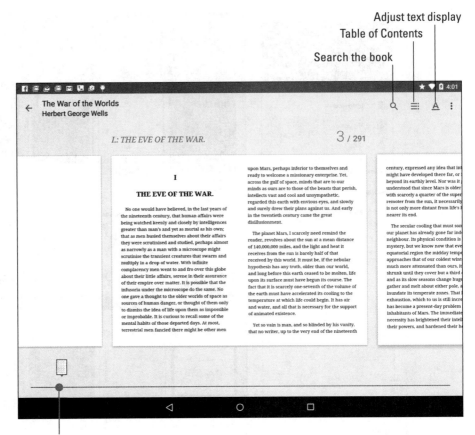

Adjust text display

Table of Contents

Search the book

Drag to scroll through the book

Figure 14-5: Reading an eBook in the Play Books app.

Game Machine

Nothing justifies your expensive, high-tech investment in electronics like playing games. Don't even sweat the thought that you have too much "business" or "work" or other important stuff you can do on an Android tablet. The more advanced the mind, the more the need for play, right? So indulge yourself.

It used to be that your tablet's manufacturer would toss in a few sample games to whet your appetite. That's no longer the case; however, you can obtain an abundance of games, free or not, from the Google Play Store. Look for the "lite" versions of games, which are free. If you like the game, you can fork over the 99 cents or whatever the full version costs.

See Chapter 15 for details on shopping at the Google Play Store.

Google Now

Don't worry about your tablet controlling too much of your life: It harbors no insidious intelligence, and the Robot Uprising is still years away. Until then, you can use the tablet's listening abilities to enjoy the feature called Google Now. It's not quite like having your own personal Jeeves, but it's on its way.

The preferred method to summon Google Now is to swipe your finger upward from the bottom center of the touchscreen. This technique is supposed to work on the Lock screen, the Home screen, or in any app, although your tablet may not support that technique. Otherwise, you can open the Google app in the Apps drawer.

The main Google Now screen looks similar to what's shown in Figure 14-6. Below the Search text box, you'll find cards. The variety and number of cards

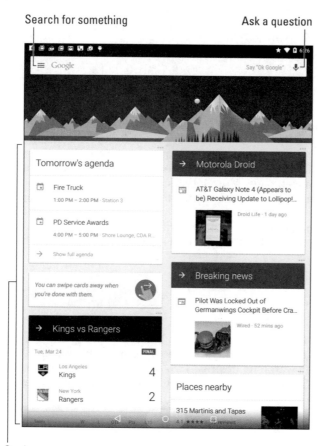

Search for something   Ask a question

Cards

Figure 14-6: Google Now is ready for business. Or play.

Barking orders to Google Now

One way to have a lot of fun is to use Google Now app verbally: Say "Okay, Google." Say it out loud. Any time you see the Google Now app, the tablet is listening to you. Or, when the tablet is being stubborn, touch the Microphone icon.

You can speak simple search terms, such as "Find pictures of Megan Fox." Or you can give more complex orders, among them:

✏ Will it rain tomorrow?

✏ What time is it in Frankfurt, Germany?

✏ How many euros equals $25?

✏ What is 103 divided by 6?

✏ How can I get to Disneyland?

✏ Where is the nearest Canadian restaurant?

✏ What's the score of the Lakers–Celtics game?

✏ What is the answer to life, the universe, and everything?

When asked such questions, Google Now responds with a card and a verbal reply. When a verbal reply isn't available, you see Google search results.

You can also use Google Now to verbally control your tablet. To use the camera, say "Okay, Google, take a picture" or "Okay, Google, record a video." Future versions of Google Now may offer additional spoken commands.

depend on how often you use Google Now. Though you can't manually add cards, the more the app learns about you, the more cards appear.

You can use Google Now to search the Internet, just as you would use Google's main web page. More interestingly than that, you can ask Google Now questions; see the nearby sidebar "Barking orders to Google Now."

Google Now might also be found on the far left Home screen page: Keep swiping the Home screen left-to-right until it shows up — if your tablet supports this feature.

Video Entertainment

Someday, it may be possible to watch "real" TV on an Android tablet, but why bother? You'll find plenty of video apps available on your tablet to sate your television-watching desires. Two of the most common are YouTube and Play Movies. So although you may not be able to pick up and enjoy the local

Action News Team every day at 5 p.m., you're not bereft of video enjoyment on your tablet.

Enjoying YouTube

YouTube is the Internet phenomenon that proves that real life is indeed too boring and random for television. Or is it the other way around? Regardless, you can view the latest YouTube videos by using the YouTube app on your Android tablet.

Search for videos by tapping the Search icon. Type the video's name, a topic, or any search terms to locate videos. Zillions of videos are available.

The YouTube app displays suggestions for any channels you're subscribed to, which allows you to follow favorite topics or YouTube content providers.

To view a video, touch its name or icon in the list.

✔ Because you have a Google account, you also have a YouTube account. I recommend that you log in to your YouTube account when using YouTube on your Android tablet: Tap the Action Overflow icon and choose the Sign In command. Log in if you haven't already. Otherwise, you see your account information, your videos, and any video subscriptions.

✔ Refer to Chapter 12 for information on uploading a video you've recorded on your Android tablet to your account on YouTube.

✔ To view the video in a larger size, tilt the tablet to the horizontal orientation.

TIP

Chromecast your videos

The best way to view your tablet's videos is by casting them to an HDTV or a monitor. Google sells a casting device called the Chromecast. Other casting gizmos are available as well, although Chromecast works natively with Android tablets.

After setting up the Chromecast dongle, switch your TV or monitor to its HDMI input. (On my TV it's Input 4.) On your tablet, tap the Chromecast icon (▣) in the YouTube or Play Movies & TV app. After tapping the icon, choose the Chromecast device, which must be on the same Wi-Fi network as the tablet. The video then plays on the HDMI TV or monitor, while you can use the tablet to control playback.

> ✔ Use the YouTube app to view YouTube videos, rather than use the tablet's web browser app to visit the YouTube website.
>
> ✔ Not all YouTube videos are available for viewing on mobile devices.

Buying and renting movies

You can use the Play Movies & TV app to watch videos you've rented or purchased at the Google Play Store. Open the app and choose the video from the main screen. Items you've purchased show up in the app's library.

The actual renting or purchasing is done at the Google Play Store. Check the Store often for freebies and discounts. More details for renting and purchasing movies and shows is found in Chapter 15.

> ✔ Movies and shows rented at the Play Store are available for viewing for up to 30 days after you pay the rental fee. After you start the movie, you can pause and watch it again and again during a 24-hour period.
>
> ✔ Not every film or TV show is available for purchase. Some are rentals only.

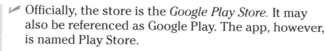

15

Play Store Shopping

In This Chapter

▶ Shopping at the Google Play Store

▶ Downloading an app

▶ Shopping for music, books, and movies

▶ Building a wish list

▶ Sending an app suggestion to a friend

▶ Keeping media on the tablet

*T*he place to find more digital stuff for your Android tablet is a digital marketplace known as the Google Play Store. You can obtain music, books, movies, TV shows, and most importantly, apps. A lot of the stuff available is free. Some of it costs money, but only pennies. Bottom line: The Google Play Store is the place to go when you need to expand upon your tablet's capabilities.

Hello, Google Play Store

Although it seems like a kid's clothing place you'd find in a mall, the Google Play Store is where you obtain new apps, books, movies, music, and other goodies for your Android tablet. The Play store lets you expand upon the paltry sampling of these items included with your tablet.

✔ Officially, the store is the *Google Play Store*. It may also be referenced as Google Play. The app, however, is named Play Store.

✔ The Google Play Store was once known as the Android Market, and you may still see it referred to as the Market.

> ✔ You obtain more goodies from Play Store over an Internet connection. Therefore:

> ✔ I highly recommend that you connect your tablet to a Wi-Fi network if you plan to obtain apps, books, or other digital goodies at the Play Store. Wi-Fi not only gives you speed but also helps avoid data surcharges. See Chapter 16 for details on connecting your tablet to a Wi-Fi network.

> ✔ The Play Store app is frequently updated, so its look may change from what you see in this chapter. Refer to my website for updated info and tips: www.wambooli.com/help/android.

Browsing the Google Play Store

You access the Google Play Store by opening the Play Store app, found on the Apps screen and, possibly, also on the Home screen.

After opening the Play Store app, you see the main screen, similar to what's shown in Figure 15-1. If not, tap the Side Menu icon (shown in the margin) to display the navigation drawer. Choose Store Home to see the app's main screen.

To browse, tap a category atop the screen. Available categories include apps, games, movies, TV shows, music, books, and magazines. Suggestions are offered below the main categories, as shown in Figure 15-1. Swipe the suggestions up and down to peruse the lot.

As an example, suppose that you want to browse for an app: Choose the Apps category. The next screen lists popular and featured items plus additional categories you can browse by swiping the screen from right to left. The category titles appear toward the top of the screen.

When you have an idea of what you want, such as an app's name or even what it does, searching works fastest: Tap the Search icon at the top of the Play Store screen, shown in Figure 15-2. At the main Play Store screen, tap the Google Play bar to search (refer to Figure 15-1). Type all or part of the item's title, such as an app name, album name, book author, or perhaps a description.

To see more information about an item, tap it. You see a more detailed description, screen shots, or perhaps a video preview, as shown in Figure 15-2.

> ✔ The first time you enter the Google Play Store, or after the Play Store app is updated, you have to accept the terms of service. To do so, tap the Accept button.

> ✔ You can be assured that all apps that appear in the Google Play Store can be used with your Android tablet. There's no way to download or buy one that's incompatible.

Side Menu icon   Tap to search   Categories

Navigation drawer

Figure 15-1: The Google Play Store.

- ✔ Pay attention to an app's ratings. Ratings are added by people who use the apps — people like you and me. Having more stars is better. You can see additional information, including individual user reviews, by choosing the app.

- ✔ Another good indicator of an app's success is how many times it's been downloaded. Some apps have been downloaded more than 10 million times. That's a good sign.

- ✔ In Figure 15-2, the app's description (on the right) shows the Install button. Other buttons that may appear on an app's description screen include Open, Update, and Uninstall. The Open button opens an app that's already installed on your tablet; the Update button updates an already installed app; and the Uninstall button removes an installed app. See Chapter 18 for more information on app management.

Side Menu icon   Swipe categories   Go Back   Search

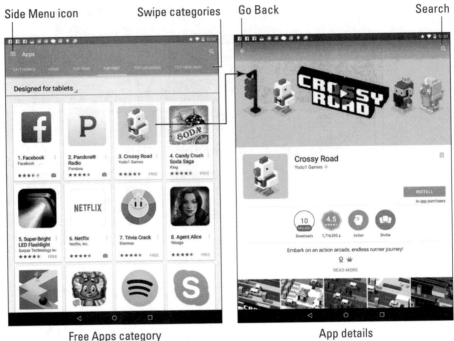

Free Apps category   App details

Figure 15-2: App details.

Obtaining an app

After you locate the app you've always dreamed of, the next step is to down-load it, by copying it from the Google Play Store on the Internet into your Android tablet. The app is then installed automatically, building up your collection of apps and expanding what your Android tablet can do.

Good news: Most apps are available for free. Better news: Even the apps you pay for don't cost dearly. In fact, it seems odd to sit and stew over whether paying 99 cents for a game is worth it.

I recommend that you download a free app first, to familiarize yourself with the process. Then try your hand at a paid app.

Free or not, the process of obtaining an app works pretty much the same. Follow these steps:

1. **If possible, activate the Wi-Fi connection to avoid incurring data overages.**

    See Chapter 16 for information on connecting your Android tablet to a Wi-Fi network.

2. **Open the Play Store app.**

3. **Find the app you want, and open its description.**

   The app's description screen looks similar to the one shown on the right side in Figure 15-2.

   The difference between a free app and a paid app is found on the button used to obtain the app. For a free app, the button says Install. For a paid app, the button shows the price.

4. **Tap the Install button to get a free app; for a paid app, tap the button with the price on it.**

   Don't fret! You're not buying anything yet.

   You see a screen describing the app's permissions. The list isn't a warning, and it doesn't mean anything bad. The Play Store is just informing you which of your tablet's features the app could access.

5. **Tap the Accept button.**

   If you're purchasing an app, you must tap the Buy button to complete the purchase. See the next section for details.

6. **Wait while the app downloads.**

   The Downloading notification appears atop the screen as the app is downloaded. You're free to do other things on your tablet while the app is downloaded and installed.

7. **Tap the Open button to run the app.**

   Or if you were doing something else while the app was downloading and installing, choose the Successfully Installed notification, as shown in the margin. The notification features the app's name with the text *Successfully Installed* below it.

At this point, what happens next depends on the app you've downloaded. For example, you may have to agree to a license agreement. If so, tap the I Agree button. Additional setup may involve setting your location, signing in to an account, or creating a profile.

After you complete the initial app setup, or if no setup is necessary, you can start using the app.

- Apps you download are added to the Apps drawer, made available like any other app on your tablet.

- Some apps may install launcher icons on the Home screen after they're installed. See Chapter 18 for information on removing the icon from the Home screen, if that is your desire.

- Also see Chapter 18 for information on uninstalling apps.

Avoiding Android viruses

How can you tell which apps are legitimate and which might be viruses or evil apps that do odd things to your Android tablet? Well, you can't. In fact, most people can't, because most evil apps don't advertise themselves as such.

The key to knowing whether an app is evil is to look at what it does, as described in this chapter. If a simple grocery-list app uses the tablet's microphone and the app doesn't need to use the microphone, it's suspect.

In the history of the Android operating system, only a handful of malicious apps have been distributed, and most of them were found on devices used in Asia. Google routinely removes malicious apps from the Play Store, and a feature of the Android operating system even lets Google remotely wipe such apps from all Android devices. So you're pretty safe.

Generally speaking, avoid "hacker" apps, porn apps, and apps that use social engineering to make you do things on your tablet that you wouldn't otherwise do, such as visit an unknown website to see racy pictures of politicians or celebrities.

Purchasing something at the Play Store

To purchase an app, music, eBook, or anything else at the Play Store, you tap the Buy button. A card appears listing available payment methods. These include any credit cards you've used previously, plus any redeemed Google credit.

Figure 15-3 shows the Buy card for purchasing an app. The app costs $6.99. The chosen payment method is a Master Card ending in 5501. That payment method is used automatically after the Buy button is tapped.

To select another payment method, follow these steps when the Buy card is presented:

1. **Tap the chevron by the price.**

   The chevron is shown next to the $6.99 price at the top of Figure 15-3.

2. **Choose Payment Methods.**

   Of, if you're fortunate enough to have a Google Play gift card, tap Redeem to cash in.

Current payment method

Cash in a gift card

Choose another form of payment

Figure 15-3: The Play Store's Buy card.

3. **Choose a credit or debit card, PayPal, or a gift card.**

   The credit or debit cards listed are those you've used before. Don't worry: Your information is safe.

   If you don't yet have a credit or debit card registered, choose the option Add Credit or Debit Card, and complete the onscreen steps to set up your payment.

4. **Type your Google password.**

   This step provides for security. I strongly recommend that you never choose the option Never Ask Me Again.

5. **If prompted, tap the Every Time option.**

   By choosing this option, you ensure that your password is required for every purchase you make at the Play Store.

At this, point, the item you purchased is made available. Apps are instantly downloaded and installed; music, eBooks, movies, and videos are available but not necessarily downloaded. See the later section "Keeping stuff on the device."

- ✔ Eventually, you receive a Gmail message from the Google Play Store, confirming your purchase. The message contains a link you can select to review the refund policy in case you change your mind about the purchase.

- ✔ Be quick on that refund: For a purchased app, you have only two hours to get your money back. You know when the time limit is up, because the Refund button on the app's description screen changes to Uninstall.

Getting more music

The Play Store is also the go-to app for purchasing more music; specifically, for the Play Music app (covered in Chapter 13). To find some tunes, follow these steps:

1. **Tap the Music category on the main Play Store screen.**

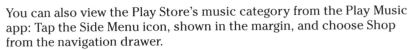

   You can also view the Play Store's music category from the Play Music app: Tap the Side Menu icon, shown in the margin, and choose Shop from the navigation drawer.

2. **Use the Search icon to help you locate music, or just browse the categories.**

   Eventually, you see a page showing details about the song or album, similar to what's shown in Figure 15-4.

   Choose a song from the list to hear a preview. The button next to the song or album indicates the purchase price, or it says Free for free music.

Never buy anything twice

Any apps, music, books, or other items you buy from the Play Store are yours as long as you keep your Google account or until the Robot Uprising, whichever comes first. That means you don't have to buy anything a second time.

For example, if you have an Android phone and you already paid for a slew of apps, you can obtain those same apps for your Android tablet: Just visit the Play Store and install the apps. The same rule goes for music, books, or anything you've previously paid for.

To review already purchased apps in the Play Store, choose the My Apps item in the navigation drawer (refer to Figure 15-1, on the left). Tap the All tab at the top of the screen. You'll see all the apps you've ever obtained at the Google Play Store, including apps you've previously paid for. Those apps are flagged with the text *Purchased*. Select the item to reinstall the paid app.

Buy the whole album

Add to wish list

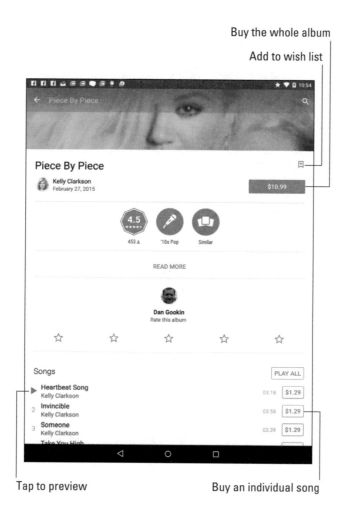

Tap to preview   Buy an individual song

Figure 15-4: Music in the Play Store.

3. **Tap the Free button to get a free song, or tap the Price button to purchase a song or an album.**

   Don't worry; you're not buying anything yet.

4. **To buy music, choose your credit card or payment source.**

   Refer to the earlier section "Purchasing something at the Play Store" for purchase details.

5. **Tap the Buy or Confirm button.**

   The song or album is added to your tablet's music library.

Refer to Chapter 13 for more information on using the Play Music app to listen to songs obtained from the Google Play Store.

- ✔ All music sales are final. Don't blame me; I'm just writing down Google's current policy for music purchases.

- ✔ Keep an eye out for special offers at the Play Store. They're a great way to pick up some free songs and albums.

- ✔ Music you purchase from the Google Play Store is available on any Android device with the Play Music app installed, providing you use the same Google account on that device. You can also listen to your tunes by visiting the play.google.com/music/listen.com site on any computer connected to the Internet.

Buying eBooks

The process for buying eBooks on your Android tablet works the same as that for buying an app or music: Search for a title or browse the Books section of the Play Store app. Some books, particularly classics, are available for free. Others must be purchased. The steps used in the earlier section "Purchasing something at the Play Store" apply to eBooks as well as apps and music.

See Chapter 14 for information on the Play Books app, your Android tablet's eBook reader.

Renting or purchasing videos and TV shows

When it comes to movies and TV shows available at the Google Play Store, you have two options: rent or purchase.

When you choose to rent a video, the rental is available to view for the next 30 days. Once you start watching, however, you have only 24 hours to finish — you can also watch the video over and over again during that time span.

Purchasing a video is more expensive than renting it, but you can view the movie or TV show at any time, on any Android device. You can also download the movie so that you can watch it even when an Internet connection isn't available.

One choice you must make when buying a movie is whether to purchase the SD or HD version. The SD version is cheaper, and the HD version plays at high definition only on certain output devices.

- ✔ See the earlier section "Purchasing something at the Play Store" for details on the purchase process.

- ✔ See Chapter 14 for information on the Play Movies app.

Play Store Tricks

I don't want you to be a Play Store expert. If you're like me, you just want to get the app you want and get on with your life. When you're ready to get more from the Play Store, peruse some of the items in this section.

Using the wish list

While you dither over getting a paid app, music, book, or any other purchase at the Play Store, consider adding it to your wish list: Tap the Wish List icon when viewing the app. The Wish List icon is shown in the margin, although its color changes depending on which category you're viewing in the Play Store app.

To review your wish list, tap the Side Menu icon in the Play Store app (refer to Figure 15-1). Choose the My Wishlist item from navigation drawer. You see all the items you've flagged. When you're ready to buy, choose one and buy it!

Sharing an item from the Play Store

Sometimes you love your Play Store purchase so much that you just can't contain your glee. When that happens, consider sharing the item. Obey these steps:

1. **Open the Play Store app.**

2. **Browse or search for the app, music, book, or other item you want to share.**

3. **When you find the item, tap it to view its description screen.**

4. **Tap the Share icon.**

    You may have to swipe down the screen to locate the Share icon, shown in the margin. After tapping the Share icon, you see a menu listing various apps.

5. **Choose an app.**

    For example, choose Gmail to send a Play Store link in an email message.

6. **Use the chosen app to share the link.**

    What happens next depends on which sharing method you've chosen.

The end result of these steps is that your friend receives a link. That person can tap the link on his mobile Android device and be whisked instantly to the Google Play Store, where the item can be obtained.

Methods for using the various items on the Share menu are found throughout this book.

Keeping stuff on the device

Books, music, movies, and TV shows you obtain from the Play Store are not copied to your Android tablet. Instead, they're stored on the Internet. When you access the media, it's streamed into your device as needed. This setup works well, and it keeps your tablet from running out of storage space, but it works only when an Internet connection is available.

When you plan on being away from an Internet connection, such as when you are flying across country and are too cheap to pay for inflight Wi-Fi, you can download Play Store music, eBook, and movie purchases and save them on your tablet.

To see which media is on your tablet and which isn't, open the Play Books, Play Music, or Play Movies & TV app. Follow these steps, which work identically in each app:

1. **Tap the Side Menu icon.**

2. **In the navigation drawer, locate the Downloaded Only item.**

3. **Slide the master control to the On position.**

   Just tap the gizmo and it toggles between On and Off settings.

4. **Choose the My Library item from the navigation drawer.**

   You see only those items on your tablet. The rest of your library, you can assume, is held on the Internet.

To see your entire library again, repeat these steps but in Step 3 slide the master control to the Off position.

 Items downloaded to your tablet feature the On Device icon, similar to the one shown in the margin. The icon's color differs between music, eBooks, and movies.

 To keep an item on your tablet, look for the Download icon, shown in the margin. Tap that icon, and the item is fetched from the Internet and stored on your device.

Keeping movies and lots of music on your Android tablet consumes a lot of storage space. That's okay for short trips and such, but for the long term, consider purging some of your downloaded media.

To remove an item you've downloaded, tap the On Device icon. Tap the Remove button to confirm.

Don't worry about removing downloaded media. You can always access items you've purchased (or obtained free) when an Internet connection is active. And you can download items over and over without having to pay again.

Part IV
Nuts and Bolts

Activate the Dropbox app's automatic photo-backup feature, at
www.dummies.com/extras/androidtablets.

In this part . . .

- ✏ Learn how to seek out and find Wi-Fi networks, connect, and use the Internet.

- ✏ Discover how to exchange files between your Android tablet and a PC by using a USB cable.

- ✏ Customize the tablet's Home screen with apps and widgets.

- ✏ Add security to an Android tablet by applying a password or providing lock screen information.

- ✏ Explore the world with your Android tablet at the ready.

- ✏ Learn how to save battery life and discover which items on the tablet are using the most battery juice.

16

It's a Wireless Life

In This Chapter

▶ Using the mobile data network
▶ Enabling Wi-Fi
▶ Accessing a Wi-Fi network
▶ Connecting to a WPS router
▶ Pairing with a Bluetooth peripheral
▶ Transferring information with Android Beam

*A*t one time, being burdened with a nest of wires was considered an aspect of truly advanced technology. Today, the opposite is true. Your Android tablet lives a carefree and wireless existence. In addition to its beefy battery, the device communicates in a carefree and wireless manner, with both the Internet and other gizmos. Welcome to the wireless life.

The Wonderful World of Wireless

Your Android tablet demands an Internet connection. To sate that desire, the tablet communicates with the information superhighway in a wireless way. Given how wireless networking has proliferated around the globe, finding an available wireless network is no longer a big deal. No, the issue is how to coax the tablet into making the connection happen.

Using the mobile data network

LTE Android tablets are designed to connect to the Internet by using the mobile data network. That's the same digital cellular network used by smartphones. Several types of this network are available, based on the network's speed:

- ✔ **4G LTE:** The fourth generation of wide-area data network and the fastest.

- ✔ **3G:** The third-generation network, which is the fastest network used when a 4G signal isn't available.

- ✔ **1X:** Several types of the original, slower cellular data signals are still available. They all fall under the 1X banner. It's slow.

Your tablet always uses the best network available. So, when the 4G LTE network is within reach, it's used for Internet communications. Otherwise, the 3G network is chosen, and then 1X networking in an act of last-ditch desperation.

- ✔ A status icon representing the network connection type appears atop the touchscreen, right next to the Signal Strength icon.

- ✔ Accessing the digital cellular network isn't free. You likely signed up for some form of subscription plan for a certain quantity of data. When you exceed that quantity, the costs can become prohibitive.

- ✔ See Chapter 21 for information on how to avoid cellular data overcharges when taking your Android tablet out and about.

- ✔ Also see Chapter 23 for information on monitoring your mobile data usage as well as tips on sharing the tablet's mobile data connection.

Understanding Wi-Fi

The mobile data connection is nice, and it's available pretty much all over, but it costs you money every month. A better option is *Wi-Fi,* or the same wireless networking standard used by computers for communicating with each other and the Internet.

To make Wi-Fi work on an Android tablet requires two steps. First, you must activate the tablet's Wi-Fi radio. The second step is connecting to a specific wireless network. The next two sections cover these steps in detail.

- ✔ When your tablet is connected to a Wi-Fi network, it uses that network rather than the mobile data network.

- ✔ Wi-Fi stands for *wi*reless *fi*delity. It's brought to you by the numbers 802.11 and various letter suffixes too many to mention.

Activating Wi-Fi

Follow these steps to activate your Android tablet's Wi-Fi radio:

1. **Open the Settings app.**

2. **Choose the Wi-Fi item.**

   On Samsung tablets, tap the Connections tab to locate the Wi-Fi item.

3. **Ensure that the Wi-Fi Master Control is set to the On position.**

To deactivate the Wi-Fi radio, which also disconnects the Wi-Fi network connection, repeat the steps in this section but set the master control to the Off position.

  ✔ Use the Wi-Fi Quick Setting to instantly activate or deactivate the Wi-Fi connection. See Chapter 3 for information on accessing the Quick Settings.

  ✔ Once Wi-Fi is activated, the tablet connects automatically to any memorized Wi-Fi networks. See the next section for info on memorized networks.

  ✔ It's perfectly okay to keep the tablet's Wi-Fi radio on all the time. It does drain the battery, but you really need that Internet access to get the most from your Android tablet.

  ✔ Using Wi-Fi to connect to the Internet doesn't incur data usage charges.

Connecting to a Wi-Fi network

After you've activated the Android tablet's Wi-Fi radio, you can connect to an available wireless network. Obey these steps:

1. **Open the Settings app.**

2. **Choose Wi-Fi.**

   On some Samsung tablets, you find the Wi-Fi item on the Connections tab.

3. **Choose a wireless network from the list.**

   Available Wi-Fi networks appear on the screen, similar to what's shown in Figure 16-1. When no wireless networks are listed, you're sort of out of luck regarding wireless access from your current location.

4. **If prompted, type the network password.**

   Tap the Show Password check box so that you can see what you're typing; some of those network passwords can be *long.*

Signal strength

Password-protected network   Wi-Fi Master Control

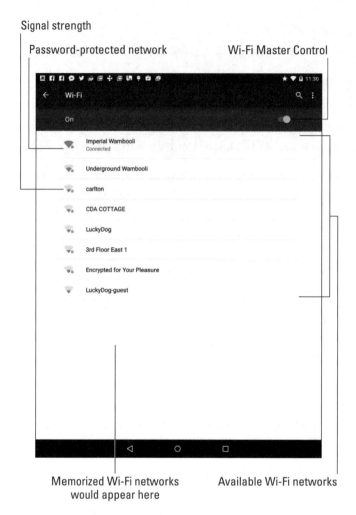

Memorized Wi-Fi networks   Available Wi-Fi networks
would appear here

Figure 16-1: Hunting down a wireless network.

5. Tap the Connect button.

The network is connected immediately. If not, try the password again.

When the tablet is connected to a wireless network, you see the Wi-Fi Connected status icon, similar to the one shown in the margin. This icon indicates that the tablet's Wi-Fi is on, connected, and communicating with a Wi-Fi network.

✔ Some public networks are open to anyone, but you have to use the tablet's web browser app to find a login web page. Heed that page's directions to get network access. To find the page, simply browse to any page on the Internet, and the login web page shows up.

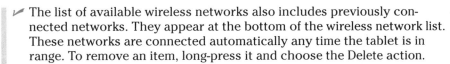

   ✔ The list of available wireless networks also includes previously con-
      nected networks. They appear at the bottom of the wireless network list.
      These networks are connected automatically any time the tablet is in
      range. To remove an item, long-press it and choose the Delete action.

   ✔ Not every wireless network has a password. Even though that absence
      makes connection work easier, be careful when connecting to such a
      network. It's possible that the Bad Guys can monitor your connection,
      stealing passwords and other information.

   ✔ To disconnect from a Wi-Fi network, simply turn off Wi-Fi. See the
      preceding section.

   ✔ Use Wi-Fi whenever you plan to remain in one location for a while. Unlike
      a mobile data network, a Wi-Fi network's broadcast signal has a limited
      range. If you wander too far away, your tablet loses the signal and is
      disconnected.

Connecting to a hidden Wi-Fi network

Some wireless networks don't broadcast their names, which adds security
but also makes connecting more difficult. In these cases, follow these steps to
make the Wi-Fi network connection:

1. **Open the Settings app and choose Wi-Fi.**

   For Samsung tablets, locate the Wi-Fi item on the Connections tab in the
   Settings app.

2. **Tap the Action Overflow and choose Add Network.**

   The item might be titled Add Wi-Fi Network, or it may appear as the Add
   (Plus) icon on the screen.

3. **Type the network name into the Enter the SSID box.**

4. **Choose the security setting.**

5. **Type a password.**

   The password may be optional, although heed my advice from the
   preceding section regarding password-less networks.

6. **Tap the Save button or Connect button.**

Details such as the security setting and password are obtained from the same
person who provided you with the network name or SSID.

SSID stands for Service Set Identifier. Any further information on this
acronym would needlessly lower your blood pressure, so I'll leave it at
that.

Connecting to a WPS router

Many Wi-Fi routers feature WPS, which stands for Wi-Fi Protected Setup. It's a network authorization system that's really simple and quite secure. If the wireless router features WPS, you can use it to quickly connect your Android tablet to the network.

To make the WPS connection, follow these steps:

1. **Touch the WPS connection button on the router.**

   The button either is labeled WPS or uses the WPS icon, shown in the margin.

2. **On your tablet, open the Settings app and choose Wi-Fi.**

   On your Samsung tablet, look on the Settings app's Connection tab to locate the Wi-Fi item.

3. **If you don't see any WPS options on the screen, tap the Action Overflow icon and choose Advanced.**

4. **Choose WPS Push Button or WPS Pin Entry, depending on how the router does the WPS thing.**

5. **If the router is a WPS push-button router, push the WPS button on the router. If the router is a WPS PIN router, type the number shown on the tablet's screen on the router.**

Connection with the router may take a few minutes, so be patient. The good news is that, as on all Wi-Fi networks, once the initial connection is established, the tablet automatically connects in the future.

The Bluetooth World

Bluetooth has nothing to do with the color blue or dental hygiene. No, it's a wireless protocol for communication between two or more Bluetooth-equipped devices. Your Android tablet just happens to have a Bluetooth wireless radio in its bosom, so it can chat it up with Bluetooth devices, such as keyboards, headphones, printers, and robotic mice armed with deadly lasers.

Understanding Bluetooth

To make Bluetooth work, you need a Bluetooth peripheral, such as a wireless keyboard. The goal is to pair that peripheral with your tablet. The operation works like this:

1. **Turn on the Bluetooth wireless radio on both your tablet and the peripheral.**

2. **Make the peripheral you're trying to connect to discoverable.**

   The peripheral must announce that it's available and willing to go steady with other electronics in the vicinity.

3. **On your tablet, choose the peripheral from the list of Bluetooth devices.**

4. **If required, confirm the connection.**

   For example, you may be asked to input a code or press a button.

5. **Use the Bluetooth peripheral.**

You can use the Bluetooth peripheral as much as you like. Turn off the tablet. Turn off the peripheral. When you turn both on again, they're automatically reconnected.

 Bluetooth devices are labeled with the Bluetooth logo, shown in the margin. It's your assurance that the gizmo can work with other Bluetooth devices.

Activating Bluetooth on your tablet

You must turn on the tablet's Bluetooth radio before you can enjoy using any Bluetoothy peripherals. Here's how to activate Bluetooth on an Android tablet:

1. **Open the Settings app.**

2. **Choose Bluetooth.**

   On some Samsung tablets, tap the Connections tab to locate the Bluetooth item.

3. **Ensure that the Bluetooth master control is set to the On position.**

   Slide the icon to the right to activate.

 When Bluetooth is on, the Bluetooth status icon appears. It uses the Bluetooth logo, shown in the margin.

To turn off Bluetooth, repeat the steps in this section, but slide the master control to the Off position.

 You'll also find a Bluetooth switch in the tablet's Quick Settings, as foretold in Chapter 3.

Pairing with a Bluetooth peripheral

To make the Bluetooth connection between your tablet and some other gizmo, such as a Bluetooth keyboard, follow these steps:

1. **Ensure that the tablet's Bluetooth radio is on.**

   Refer to the preceding section.

2. **Make the Bluetooth peripheral discoverable.**

   Turn on the gizmo and ensure that its Bluetooth radio is on. Keep in mind that some Bluetooth peripherals have separate power and Bluetooth switches. If so, press the Bluetooth button or take whatever action is necessary to make the peripheral discoverable.

3. **On the Android tablet, open the Settings app.**

4. **Choose Bluetooth.**

   On Samsung tablets, tap the Connections tab in the Settings app to locate the Bluetooth item.

   The Bluetooth screen shows already paired and available peripherals, similar to what's shown in Figure 16-2. If not, tap the icon or choose the command to scan for devices. You may have to tap the Action Overflow to see the command, which can be titled Refresh, Scan, or Search for Devices.

5. **Choose the Bluetooth peripheral from the list.**

6. **If necessary, type the device's passcode or otherwise acknowledge the connection.**

   For example, with a Bluetooth keyboard, you may see a prompt on the tablet showing a series of numbers. Type those numbers on the keyboard and then press the Enter or Return key. That action completes the pairing.

After the device is paired, you can begin using it.

Connected devices appear in the Bluetooth Settings window, under the heading Paired Devices, such as the Logitech Ultrathin KB Cover shown in Figure 16-2.

   ✔ To break the connection, you can either turn off the gizmo or turn off the Bluetooth radio on your Android tablet. Because the devices are paired, when you turn on Bluetooth and reactivate the device, the connection is instantly reestablished.

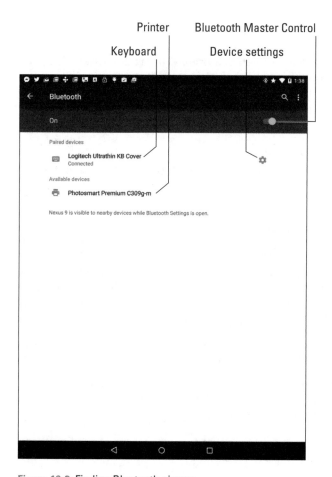

Figure 16-2: Finding Bluetooth gizmos.

✔ It's rare to unpair a device. Should you need to, visit the Bluetooth screen (refer to Figure 16-2) and tap the Settings icon by the device's entry. Choose the Unpair command or just tap the OK button to terminate the pairing.

✔ Unpair only the devices that you plan never to use again. Otherwise, simply turn off the Bluetooth device when you're done using it.

✔ The Bluetooth radio consumes a lot of power. Don't forget to turn off the device, especially a battery-powered one, when you're no longer using it with your tablet.

Android, Beam It to Me

A handful of Android tablets feature an NFC radio, where *NFC* stands for Near Field Communications and *radio* is a type of vegetable. NFC allows your tablet to communicate wirelessly with other NFC devices. That connection is used for the quick transfer of information. The technology is called Android Beam.

Turning on NFC

You can't play with the Android Beam feature unless the tablet's NFC radio has been activated. To confirm that it has, or to activate it, follow these steps:

1. **Open the Settings app.**

2. **Locate the NFC item.**

   On a stock Android device, you find the NFC item by choosing the More item beneath the Wireless & Networks heading. On Samsung tablets with this feature, tap the Connections heading to find the NFC item.

3. **Ensure that the NFC item is activated.**

   Either place a check mark next to the NFC item or ensure that its Master Control icon is in the On position.

With NFC activated, you can use your tablet to communicate with other NFC devices. These include other Android tablets, Android phones, and payment systems for various merchants.

NFC is not the same as the Nearby Devices feature found on some Samsung tablets. The Nearby Devices feature is used for sharing media over a network.

Using Android Beam

The Android Beam feature works when you touch your tablet to another NFC device. As long as the two devices have an NFC radio and the Android Beam feature is active, they can share information. You can beam items such as a contact, map location, web page, YouTube video, or just about anything you're viewing on the tablet's touchscreen.

When two Android Beam devices touch — usually back-to-back — you see a prompt appear on the screen: Touch to Beam. Tap the screen, and the item you're viewing is immediately sent to the other device. That's pretty much it.

- Generally speaking, if an app features the Share icon, you can use Android Beam to share an item between two NFC gizmos.

- Both devices present the Touch to Beam prompt when they get close. If the other person touches his screen at the same time you do, information is swapped between both devices.

- The NFC field is most frequently found on the tablet's rump. The pitiful documentation that came with your Android tablet may illustrate the exact spot.

Using Jim Beam

Follow these steps to enjoy a bottle of Kentucky straight bourbon whiskey:

1. **Unscrew cap.**

2. **Pour.**

3. **Enjoy.**

It isn't truly necessary to pour the whiskey into another container for consumption, though many users find a glass, mug, or red Solo cup useful.

Alcohol and social networking do not mix.

Connect, Share, and Store

*A*s much as it tries, your Android tablet just can't be completely wireless. Unless you have a wireless charging pad for the tablet, you're going to need the USB cable to resupply the battery with juice. But the USB cable is more than a power cord: It's also a method of communications — specifically, file transfer between your tablet and a computer. This chapter carefully describes how that transfer works. Also discussed is the anxiety-laden issue of storage and sharing, which is presented in a deceptively cheerful manner.

The USB Connection

The most direct way to connect an Android tablet to a computer is by using a wire — specifically, the wire nestled at the core of a USB cable. You can do lots of things after making the USB connection, but everything starts with connecting the cable.

Connecting the tablet to a computer

The USB cable that comes with your Android tablet can be used to physically connect both the tablet and a computer. It's cinchy, thanks to

Sound

Display

Storage

Power saving..

Battery

lication ma..

Total space
16.00 GB

System memor
4.91 GB

Applications
1.83 GB

Pictures, videos
20.63 MB

Audio (music, ri
156 KB

Downloads
1.29 MP

three-dimensional physics, 21st century electronics, and the following two important pieces of advice:

✔ One end of the USB cable plugs into the computer.

✔ The other end plugs into the Android tablet.

The connectors on either end of the USB cable are shaped differently and cannot be plugged in incorrectly. If one end of the cable doesn't fit, try the other end. If it still doesn't fit, try plugging it in upside down.

✔ After the USB connection has been made successfully, the USB notification appears atop the screen, similar to the one shown in the margin. Not every tablet displays this icon.

✔ The tablet-computer connection works best with a powered USB port. If possible, plug the USB cable into the computer itself or into a powered USB hub.

✔ Tablets with a USB 3.0 jack come with a USB 3.0 cable. You can still use the old-style, USB 2.0 micro-USB cables on such devices: Simply plug the micro-USB connector into the larger side of the USB 3.0 jack on the tablet's edge.

✔ For data transfer to take place at top speeds over the USB 3.0 cable, you must connect the tablet's USB 3.0 cable into the USB 3.0 port on a computer. These ports are color-coded blue.

✔ Android tablets lack the capability of using the USB connection to communicate with common USB peripherals, such as a mouse, thumb drive, and so on. Some tablets may come with a multimedia dock that offers this connectivity, but it can't happen with a direct USB connection.

Configuring the USB connection

The USB connection is configured automatically whenever you plug your Android tablet into a computer. Everything should work peachy. When it doesn't, you can try manually configuring the USB connection: Swipe down the notifications drawer and choose the USB notification.

The USB Computer Connection screen lists two options for configuring the USB connection:

Media Device (MTP): This setting persuades the computer to believe that the tablet is a portable media player or thumb drive. This option is the most useful.

Camera (PTP): This setting misleads the computer into thinking that the tablet is a digital camera.

If the computer fails to recognize the tablet, switch USB connection settings. Or, if you're using a Macintosh, see the later section "Connecting your tablet to a Mac." Also, if the tablet is locked, you must unlock it (work the screen lock) before its storage can be accessed.

✔ Some tablets may use their own file transfer software, which is annoying but you must deal with it. For example, older Samsung tablets required you to use the Samsung Kies utility to transfer files. Samsung's newer tablets don't come with this limitation.

✔ No matter which USB connection option you've chosen, the tablet's battery charges whenever it's connected to a computer's USB port — as long as the computer is turned on, of course.

✔ If your Android tablet has a MicroSD card, its storage is also mounted to the computer, as well as to the tablet's internal storage. You do not need to configure that storage separately to make the USB connection.

✔ PTP stands for Picture Transfer Protocol. MTP stands for Media Transfer Protocol.

Connecting your tablet to a PC

Upon making the USB connection between an Android tablet and a PC, a number of things happen. Don't let these things frighten you.

First, you may see some activity on the PC: drivers being installed and such. That's normal behavior any time you first connect a new USB gizmo to a Windows computer.

Second, you may see one of two different AutoPlay dialog boxes, as shown in Figure 17-1. Whether you see one or the other depends on how the tablet's USB connection is configured. Both dialog boxes show similar options.

Finally, choose an option from the AutoPlay dialog box or just close the dialog box. From that point on, you can use your computer to work with the files on your tablet. Later sections in this chapter provide the details.

✔ In Windows 8, things work differently: Look for a prompt on the screen that says Tap to Choose What Happens with This Device. Click or touch the prompt to view suggestions similar to those found in the AutoPlay dialog boxes (refer to Figure 17-1).

✔ Even if the AutoPlay dialog box doesn't appear, you can still access media and files stored on the tablet from your computer. The later section "Files Back and Forth" has details.

The tablet as media player   The tablet as digital camera

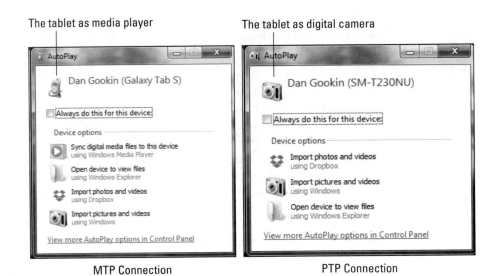

MTP Connection   PTP Connection

Figure 17-1: Windows AutoPlay dialog boxes.

Connecting your tablet to a Mac

You need special software to deal with the Android-to-Macintosh connection. That's because the Mac doesn't natively recognize Android devices. Weird, huh? It's like Apple wants you to buy some other type of tablet. I just don't get it.

To help deal with the USB connection on a Mac, obtain the Android File Transfer program. On your Mac, download that program from this website:

```
www.android.com/filetransfer
```

Install the software. Run it. From that point on, whenever you connect your Android tablet to the Mac, you see a special window appear, similar to the one shown in Figure 17-2. It lists the tablet's folders and files. Use that window for file management, as covered later in this chapter.

If the tablet has a MicroSD card inserted, you see two buttons on the Android File Transfer program window: Tablet and Card. Click one or the other to see files and folders on that storage location. (The buttons aren't shown in Figure 17-2, because that tablet doesn't feature removable storage.)

Disconnecting the tablet from a computer

The process is cinchy: When you're done transferring files, music, or other media between your PC and the tablet, close all programs and folders you

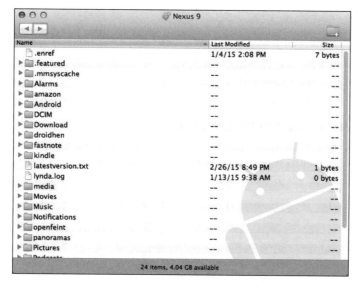

Figure 17-2: The Android File Transfer program.

have opened on your computer — specifically, those you've used to work with the tablet's storage. Then you can disconnect the USB cable. That's it.

   ✔ It's a Bad Idea to unplug the tablet while you're transferring information or while a folder window is open on your computer. Doing so can damage the tablet's internal storage, rendering unreadable some of the information that's kept there. To be safe, close those programs and folder windows you've opened before disconnecting.

   ✔ Unlike other external storage on the Macintosh, there's no need to eject the tablet's storage when you're done accessing it. Quit the Android File Transfer program on the Mac, and then unplug the tablet — or vice versa. The Mac doesn't get angry, either way.

Files Back and Forth

The USB connection can be used to transfer files, but that's not the only way to get files between your tablet and another device. Files can also flee to or from your tablet by using cloud storage. And when the need arises, the tablet can connect with a printer and dispense with a file by creating a hard copy.

   ✔ Transferring a file from the tablet to the computer or vice versa is no guarantee that you can do productive things with it. Specifically, don't copy an eBook from your computer to the tablet and expect to be able to read it. See Chapter 14 for information on eBooks.

✔ You can access your Google Play Music, Play Books, and Play Movies & TV content by using a web browser on a computer. See Chapters 13 and 14 for details.

✔ Pictures can be synchronized between devices by using Picasa Web albums. See Chapter 12.

Sharing files with the cloud

Perhaps the best and easiest way to swap files between your Android tablet and just about any other device is to use *cloud storage*. That's just fancy talk for storing files on the Internet.

All Android tablets come with Google cloud storage called the Google Drive. Use the Drive app to access that storage. On a computer, visit `drive.google.com` to view the storage. From that site, you can also obtain the Google Drive program for your computer, which I recommend.

All files saved to your Google Drive are synchronized instantly with all devices that access that storage. Change a file in a Google Drive folder and that file is instantly updated on your tablet.

To move an item from your Android tablet to your computer, start by viewing the item. Follow these steps:

1. **Locate the item you want to send to the computer.**

   It can be a picture, movie, web page, YouTube video, or just about anything.

2. **Tap the Share icon.**

   If you don't see the Share icon, the item you're viewing cannot be copied to the Google Drive.

3. **Choose Drive.**

   If you prefer to use other cloud storage, choose that app icon instead.

4. **Tap the Save icon.**

   Before you tap the icon, you can optionally edit the item's filename and choose a specific folder for saving the file.

Likewise, to make a file available to the tablet, copy that file to the Google Drive folder on your computer. When you next access the Drive app on the tablet, open the proper folder and find the file.

✔ Other cloud storage apps include the popular Dropbox, Microsoft's OneDrive, the Amazon Cloud, and more. Each of these works similarly to Google Drive, allowing you to share and swap files between the tablet and a computer or any other device that accesses that cloud storage.

✔ Cloud storage apps are free and you can use a token amount of storage at no cost. Beyond that amount, you must pay a monthly fee.

Transferring files by using the USB connection

The direct way to transport files between a computer and Android tablet is to connect both devices by using a USB cable. Once established, you use the connection to move files one way, the other, or both ways. Here's how it works:

1. **Connect the Android tablet to the computer by using the USB cable.**

   Specific directions are offered earlier in this chapter.

2. **On a PC, choose the option Open Folder/Device to View Files from the AutoPlay dialog box; on a Mac, wait for the Android File Transfer program to appear on the screen.**

   If the AutoPlay dialog box doesn't appear, you can view files manually: Open the Computer window, and then locate and open the tablet's icon to begin browsing files.

   The tablet's folder window shows files and folders just like any folder window. The difference is that the files and folders are on your Android tablet, not on the computer.

3. **On the computer, open the folder to which or from which you want to copy or move files.**

   The key is to have two folders open, as shown in Figure 17-3. One folder shows the files on the tablet; the other, files on the computer.

4. **Drag the file icons to copy them between the two folders.**

   The same file dragging technique is used to transfer files between an Android tablet and a Macintosh. The difference is that files on the tablet appear in the Android File Transfer window.

5. **Close the folder windows and disconnect the USB cable when you're done.**

When your Android tablet has a MicroSD card installed, Windows displays two AutoPlay dialog boxes and two entries for the storage (refer to Figure 17-3). Each AutoPlay dialog box represents a different storage source — internal storage as well as the MicroSD card.

Tablet's Download folder

One entry for each storage location

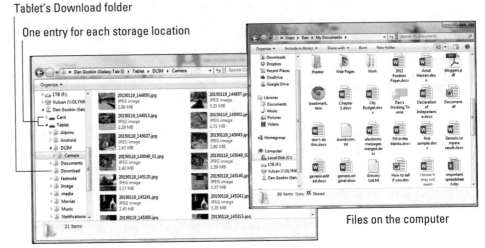

Files on the computer

Files on the tablet

Figure 17-3: Copying files to the Android tablet.

- ✔ The most common things to transfer include music, photos, videos, and even vCards, which are used to build the tablet's address book.

- ✔ The best way to synchronize music with your Android tablet is to use a music jukebox program in Windows. See Chapter 13.

- ✔ If you don't know where to copy files to your Android tablet, place the files into the Download folder, shown in Figure 17-3.

- ✔ If your Android tablet features removable storage, you can use it to transfer files: Remove the MicroSD from the tablet and insert it into a computer. From that point on, the files on the media card can be read by the computer just as they can be read from any media card. Also see the later section "Unmounting the MicroSD card."

Printing

You may not think of it as part of moving files back and forth, but using a printer with your Android Tablet is a type of file transfer. It just so happens that the other device is a printer, not a computer.

Android tablet printing works like this:

1. **View the material you want to print.**

   You can print a web page, photo, map, or any number of items.

2. **Tap the Action Overflow and choose the Print action.**

   If you don't see the Print action, your tablet lacks this feature.

3. Choose a printer.

The current printer is shown on the action bar, as shown in Figure 17-4. If it's okay, you're good. To view additional printers, tap the action bar, illustrated in the figure. You see a list of all printers available on the tablet's currently connected Wi-Fi network.

4. To change any print settings, tap the Show More Details chevron.

The items presented let you set which pages you want to print, change the number of copies, and make other common printer settings.

5. Tap the Print button.

The item prints.

Select printer Action Bar   Show more details   Print

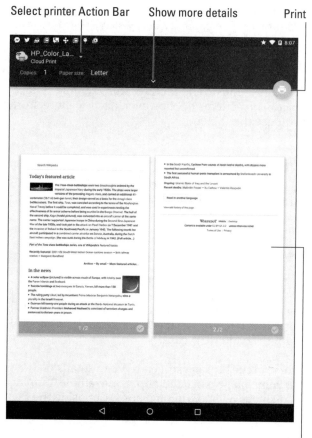

Print preview

Figure 17-4: Android tablet printing.

Not every app supports printing. The only way to know is to work through Steps 1 and 2 in this section. If you don't see the Print action, you can't print.

Android Tablet Storage

Somewhere, deep in your Android tablet's bosom, lies a storage device. That storage works like the hard drive in a computer, and for the same purpose: to keep apps, music, videos, pictures, and a host of other information for the long term. This section describes what you can do to manage that storage.

- Android tablets come with 8GB, 16GB, or 32GB of internal storage. In the future, models with larger storage capacities might become available.

- Removable storage in the form of a MicroSD card is available on some Android tablets. The capacity of a MicroSD card can vary between 8GB and 64GB or greater.

- A GB is a *gigabyte,* or 1 billion bytes (characters) of storage. A typical 2-hour movie occupies about 4GB of storage, but most things you store on the tablet — music and pictures, for example — take up only a sliver of storage. Those items do, however, occupy more storage space the more you use the tablet.

Reviewing storage stats

You can see how much storage space is available on your Android tablet's internal storage by following these steps:

1. **Open the Settings app.**

2. **Choose the Storage item.**

   On Samsung tablets, you'll find the Storage item on the General tab in the Settings app.

   You see a screen similar to the one shown in Figure 17-5. It details information about storage space on the tablet's internal storage and, if available, the MicroSD card.

Tap a category on the Storage screen to view details on how the storage is used or to launch an associated app. For example, tapping App (refer to Figure 17-5) displays a list of running apps. Choosing the Pictures, Videos item lets you view pictures and videos.

- Things that consume the most storage space are videos, music, and pictures, in that order.

- To see how much storage space is unoccupied, refer to the Available item.

Used space   Free space

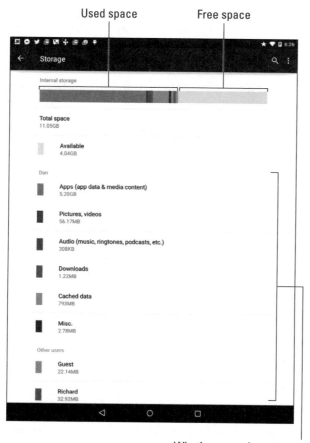

What's consuming storage

Figure 17-5: Android tablet storage information.

> Don't feel gypped if the Total Space value is far less than the stated capacity of your Android tablet. For example, your tablet may have 16GB of storage but the Storage screen reports on 11.05GB of total space. The missing space is considered overhead, as are several gigabytes taken by the government for tax purposes.

Managing files

You probably didn't get an Android tablet because you enjoy managing files on a computer and you wanted another gizmo to hone your skills. Even so, you can practice the same type of file manipulation on the Android tablet as you would on a computer. Is there a need to do so? Of course not! But if you want to get dirty with files, you can.

Some Android tablets come with a file management app. It's called File or My Files, and it's a traditional type of file manager, which means that if you detest managing files on your computer, you'll experience the same pain and frustration on your tablet.

When your tablet lacks a file management app, you can swiftly obtain one. You'll find an abundance of file management apps available at the Google Play Store. One that I admire and use is the ASTRO file manager/browser from Metago. See Chapter 15 for more information on the Google Play Store.

- If you simply want to peruse files you've downloaded from the Internet, open the Downloads app, found in the Apps drawer. Refer to Chapter 7.
- Pictures and videos on the tablet are stored in the DCIM/Camera folder, which is found on both internal storage and the MicroSD card.
- Music on the tablet is stored in the Music folder, organized by artist.

Unmounting the MicroSD card

The MicroSD card provides removable storage on some Android tablets. When the tablet is turned off, you can insert or remove the MicroSD card at will; directions are provided in Chapter 1. The MicroSD card can also be removed when the tablet is turned on, but you must first unmount the card. Obey these steps:

1. **Open the Settings app.**

2. **Choose Storage.**

   On Samsung tablets, tap the General tab to locate the Storage item.

3. **Choose Unmount SD Card.**

   This item is found near the bottom of the screen.

4. **Ignore the warning and tap the OK button.**

5. **When you see the action Mount SD Card, it's safe to remove the MicroSD card from the tablet.**

It's important that you follow these steps to safely remove the MicroSD card. If you don't, and you just pop out the card, it could damage the card and lose information.

You can insert a MicroSD card at any time. See Chapter 1 for details.

Formatting MicroSD storage

Your Android tablet should instantly recognize a MicroSD card after it's inserted. If not, you can try formatting the card to see if that fixes the problem.

All data on the MicroSD card is erased by the formatting process.

To format a MicroSD card, first insert it into the tablet. Directions are found in Chapter 1. Follow these steps to determine whether a format is in order:

1. **Open the Settings app.**

2. **Choose the Storage item.**

   On Samsung tablets, you find the Storage item on the General tab.

3. **Choose the action Format SD Card.**

4. **Tap the Format SD Card button.**

5. **Tap the Delete All button to confirm.**

   The MicroSD card is unmounted, formatted, and then mounted again and made ready for use.

After the card is formatted, you can use it to store information, music, apps, photos, and stuff like that.

✐ Some tablets may not let you format the MicroSD card when the device is connected to a computer. Disconnect the tablet (unplug the USB cable) and try again.

✐ The Camera app for most tablets automatically stores images on the MicroSD card. This setting can be changed; see Chapter 11.

18

Apps and Widgets

In This Chapter

▶ Organizing apps on the Home screen
▶ Working with widgets
▶ Rearranging the Home screen
▶ Creating folders
▶ Performing app updates
▶ Removing apps
▶ Selecting default apps
▶ Organizing the Apps drawer

*O*ut of the over 1.3 million apps available for your Android tablet, you probably want to keep a handful of your favorites ready and available. The best way to keep them accessible, neat, and tidy is to place their launcher icons on the Home screen. Indeed, the whole point of having a Home screen is to keep handy apps and widgets.

Apps and Widgets on the Home Screen

You can be an idle observer, frustrated that the apps you need don't occupy their own postage-stamp of real estate on the Home screen, or you can customize the Home screen to show those apps you use all the time.

The app icons on the Home screen are called *launchers,* or *launcher icons.*

Adding apps to the Home screen

As you find yourself using an app frequently, consider slapping a launcher icon for the app on the Home screen. Here's how that works:

1. **Visit the Home screen page on which you want to stick the launcher icon.**

   The page must have room for the launcher icon. If it doesn't, swipe the screen left or right to hunt down a page. Or, if you're organizing pages by app type, visit the proper page. For example, on my tablet, the second page is just for games.

2. **Tap the Apps icon to display the Apps drawer.**

   On some tablets, ensure that the Apps tab (not the Widgets tab) is chosen.

3. **Long-press the app icon you want to add to the Home screen.**

   After a moment, the Home screen page you chose in Step 1 appears, similar to the one shown in 18-1.

4. **Drag the app to a position on the Home screen page.**

   Launcher icons on the Home screen are aligned to a grid. Other launchers may wiggle and jiggle as you find a spot. That's okay.

5. **Lift your finger to place the app.**

   Don't worry if the launcher isn't in the exact spot you want. The later section "Moving launchers and widgets" describes how to rearrange items on the Home screen.

The app hasn't moved: What you see is a launcher, which is like a copy or shortcut. You can still find the app in the Apps drawer, but now the app is available — more conveniently — on the Home screen.

✔ Don't worry about placing new app launchers on the Home screen. When you obtain a new app (as described in Chapter 15), its launcher icon is automatically affixed to the Home screen.

✔ Some tablets feature a Home screen menu, which you can also use to add apps to the Home screen. By using this menu, you can skip over Steps 1 and 2 in this section; you still have to long-press the icon and drag it to a Home screen page.

✔ You can't cram more launchers on the Home screen than will fit in the grid. As an alternative, consider rearranging launchers by moving some to another Home screen page, as covered in the later section "Moving launchers and widgets." Also see the section "Working with folders" for another solution. Finally, if your tablet allows you to add more Home screen pages, you can solve the problem that way; see Chapter 19.

Drag the icon to a   Favorites tray
position on the
Home screen

Figure 18-1: Placing an app icon on the Home screen.

Placing an app on the Favorites tray

Some tablets feature a row of launcher icons that remains the same no matter which Home screen page you're viewing. It's called the *Favorites tray*, and it's an ideal spot for apps you use most frequently.

Launchers are added to the Favorites tray in one of two ways:

✔ Drag a launcher off the Favorites tray, either to the Home screen page or to the Remove or Delete icon. That action makes room for a new icon to be placed on the Favorites tray.

✔ Drag a launcher from the Home screen to the Favorites tray, in which case any existing icon swaps places with the icon that's already there.

Of these two methods, the second one may not work on all tablets. In fact, the second method may create an app folder on the Favorites tray, which is probably not what you want.

See the later section "Working with folders" for information on creating and using Home screen folders, which can also dwell on the Favorites tray.

 The best apps to place on the Home screen are those that show notifications for new messages, similar to the icon shown in the margin. These launchers are ideal to place on the Favorites tray.

Slapping down widgets

Just as you can add apps to the Home screen, you can also add widgets. A *widget* works like a tiny, interactive or informative window, often providing a gateway into another app on the tablet.

Two common ways exist to add widgets to the Home screen. The current stock Android method is to view the Widgets drawer. The older method involved accessing widgets from the Apps drawer. Both methods are covered in these steps:

1. **Switch to a Home screen page that has enough room for the new widget.**

   Widgets come in a variety of sizes. The size is measured by launcher dimensions: A 1x1 widget occupies the same space as a launcher icon. A 2x2 widget is twice as tall and twice as wide as a launcher icon.

2. **Access the widgets.**

   If your tablet has a Widgets drawer, long-press a blank part of the Home screen and tap the Widgets icon. If you don't see the icon, try locating widgets on the Apps drawer: Tap the Apps icon and then tap the Widgets tab atop the screen.

3. **Long-press the widget you want to add.**

   Swipe through the pages to find widgets, which are listed alphabetically and show preview images just like apps. Also shown are the widget's dimensions.

4. **Drag the widget to the Home screen.**

   Move the widget around to position it. As you drag the widget, existing launcher icons and widgets jiggle to make room.

5. **Lift your finger.**

   If the widget grows a border, it can be resized. See the next section.

After adding some widgets, you may be prompted for additional information — for example, a location for a weather widget, a contact name for a contact widget, and so on.

✔ The variety of available widgets depends on the apps installed. Some apps come with widgets; some don't. Some widgets are independent of any app.

✔ Fret not if you change your mind about the widget's location. See the later section "Moving launchers and widgets" for obtaining the proper *feng shui*.

✔ To remove a widget, see the section "Removing an item from the Home screen."

Resizing a widget

Some widgets are resizable. You can change a widget's size right after plopping it down on the Home screen — or at any time, really: The secret is to long-press the widget. If it grows a box, as shown in Figure 18-2, you can change the widget's dimensions.

Drag up or down   Drag left or right

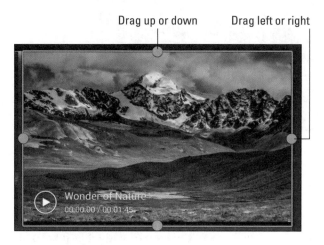

Figure 18-2: Resizing a widget.

To resize, drag one of the orange dots in or out. Tap elsewhere on the touchscreen when you're done resizing.

Moving launchers and widgets

Launcher icons and widgets aren't fastened to the Home screen with anything stronger than masking tape. That's obvious because it's quite easy to pick up and move an icon, relocating it to a new position or removing it completely. It all starts by long-pressing the item, as shown in Figure 18-3.

Delete item   Long-press to "lift"

Drag to another page

Figure 18-3: Moving a launcher icon.

Drag the item to another position on the Home screen. If you drag to the far left or far right of the screen, the icon or widget is sent to another Home screen page.

Removing an item from the Home screen

To banish a launcher or widget from the Home screen, move the launcher or widget to the Remove icon that appears on the Home screen. The Remove icon may be an X, the word *Remove* (refer to Figure 18-3), or a Delete icon, similar to what's shown in the margin.

✔ Removing an app or widget from the Home screen doesn't uninstall the app or widget. See the later section, "Uninstalling an app."

✔ Your clue that an item is ready to be deleted is that it's highlighted in red when it hovers over the Remove or Trash icon.

Working with folders

For further organization of the Home screen, consider gathering similar apps into folders. For example, I have a Listen folder that contains all my streaming music apps. Your tablet may have come with a Google folder, which contains all the various apps provided by Google. These folders can not only help organize your apps, they can also solve the problem of an overly crowded Home screen.

Folders are created in different ways, depending on the tablet. The stock Android method to create a folder is to drag one launcher icon on top of another. The folder is created.

Another technique is to look for a Folder creation icon: Drag the launcher icon up to that icon, which creates a new folder. Or, perhaps, you long-press the Home screen and tap the Create Folder action. Drag icons into the new folder.

Folder icons are composed of the launcher icons inside, along with a circle. Examples of various folder icons are shown in Figure 18-4.

Figure 18-4: Folder icon varieties.

Add more apps to the folder by dragging them over the folder's icon.

Open a folder by tapping it. Tap a launcher in the folder to start an app. Or, if you don't find what you want, tap the Back icon to close the folder.

✔ Folders are managed just like other icons on the Home screen. You can long-press them to drag them around or delete them. When you delete a folder, you remove the launcher icons from the folder; deleting the folder doesn't uninstall the apps.

- ✔ Change a folder's name by opening the folder and then tapping the folder's name. Type the new name by using the onscreen keyboard.

- ✔ To remove a launcher icon from a folder, open the folder and drag out the icon. When the second-to-last last icon is dragged out of a folder, the folder is removed. If not, drag the last icon out, and then remove the folder as you would any other item on the Home screen, as described in the preceding section.

App Management

When I think of managing apps on my Android tablet, I say, "Oh, pish!" That's because, first of all, I enjoy saying the word _pish_. But more importantly, you don't really need to manage apps. The Android operating system deftly handles that task for you. When the topic of app management does become a necessity, consider the advice offered in this section.

Reviewing your apps

To peruse the apps you've downloaded from the Google Play Store, follow these steps:

1. **Open the Play Store app.**

2. **Choose My Apps from the navigation drawer.**

   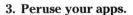

   Tap the Side Menu icon, as shown in the margin.

3. **Peruse your apps.**

Your apps are presented in two categories: Installed and All, as shown in Figure 18-5. Apps listed on the Installed tab are found on your tablet. Apps listed in the All tab include all apps on your tablet, as well as any apps you've downloaded but that may not currently be installed.

See the next section for information on using the Update All button, shown in Figure 18-5.

- ✔ Tap an app in the list to view its details. Some of the options and settings on the app's Details screen are discussed elsewhere in this chapter.

- ✔ Uninstalled apps remain on the All list because you did, at one time, download the app. To reinstall them (and without paying a second time for paid apps), choose the app from the All list and touch the Install button.

Apps on the tablet   Apps in need of an update

Side Menu icon   All your Android apps   Update apps

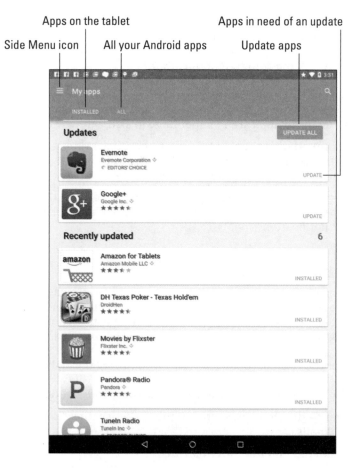

Figure 18-5: Locating all your tablet's apps.

Updating apps

New versions, or updates, of apps happen all the time. They're automatic. Occasionally, you're called upon to perform a manual update. How can you tell? The Updates Available notification appears, looking similar to what's shown in the margin.

To deal with a manual update, open the Play Store app to view all your installed apps; details for viewing your apps are presented in the preceding section. What you're looking for is the Update or Update All button, as shown in Figure 18-5. Tap that button to apply necessary app updates. If prompted to accept the app's permission, tap the Accept button.

You can view the app update process in the Play Store app, or go off and do something else with your tablet.

Here's how to deal with that notification:

✔ Yes, you do need an Internet connection to update apps. If possible, try to use Wi-Fi so that you don't incur any data surcharges on your cellular bill. Android apps aren't super huge in size, but why take the risk?

✔ Unlike updating a major computer operating system, if the Internet connection is broken during an update, the apps update automatically continues once the connection is reestablished.

✔ Most apps automatically update; you need not do a thing. The updates do generate a notification icon, shown in the margin. Feel free to dismiss that notification.

Uninstalling an app

I can think of a few reasons to remove an app. It's with eager relish that I remove apps that don't work or that somehow annoy me. It's also perfectly okay to remove redundant apps, such as when you're trying to find a decent music-listening app and you end up with a dozen or so that you never use.

Whatever the reason, remove an app by following these directions:

1. **Display the list of installed apps on your Android tablet.**

   Refer to the steps presented in the earlier section "Reviewing your apps" for details.

2. **Locate the app that offends you.**

3. **Tap the Uninstall button.**

4. **Tap the OK button to confirm.**

   The app is removed.

The app continues to appear on the All list even after it's been removed. That's because you downloaded it once. That doesn't mean, however, that the app is still installed.

✔ You can always reinstall paid apps that you've uninstalled. You aren't charged twice for doing so.

✔ You can't remove apps that are preinstalled on the tablet by either the manufacturer or cellular provider. I'm sure there's a technical way to uninstall such apps, but seriously: Just don't use the apps if you want to remove them and discover that you can't.

Choosing a default app

Every so often, you may see the Complete Action Using prompt, which may look similar to the one shown in Figure 18-6. Regardless of its appearance, you're prompted to choose from one or more apps to complete an action, and given the choice of Just Once or Always.

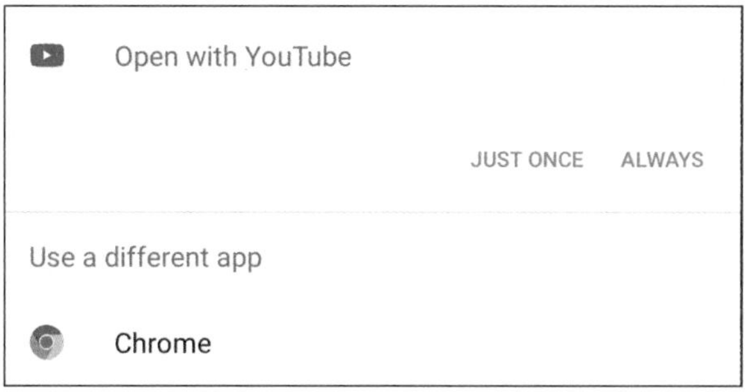

> ▶ Open with YouTube
>
> JUST ONCE   ALWAYS
>
> Use a different app
>
> ◉ Chrome

Figure 18-6: The Complete Action Using question is posed.

When you choose Always, the same app is always used for whatever action took place: composing email, listening to music, cropping a photo, navigation, and so on.

When you choose Just Once, you see the prompt again and again.

My advice is to choose Just Once until you get sick of seeing the Complete Action Using prompt. At that point, choose Always.

The fear, of course, is that you'll make a mistake. Keep reading in the next section.

Clearing default apps

Fret not, gentle reader. The settings you chose for the Complete Action Using prompt can be undone. For example, if you select the Chrome app from Figure 18-6, you can undo that choice by following these steps:

1. **Open the Settings app.**

2. **Tap Apps.**

3. **Choose the app that always opens.**

    This is the tough step, because you must remember which app you chose to "Always" open.

4. **Tap the Clear Defaults button.**

If you have a Samsung tablet, you might have a shortcut to clear default apps: Open the Settings app and tap the Applications tab. (On some Galaxy Tabs, tap the General tab instead.) Choose Default Applications from the left side of the screen.

When you clear the defaults for an app, you see the Complete Action Using prompt again. The next time you see it, however, make a better choice.

Shutting down an app run amok

Sometimes, an app goofs up or crashes. You may see a warning message on the touchscreen, informing you that the app has been shut down. That's good. What's better is that you too can shut down apps that misbehave or those you cannot otherwise stop. Follow these steps:

1. **Open the Settings app.**

2. **Tap the Apps item.**

   On Samsung tablets, tap the Applications tab; or on some Galaxy Tabs, tap the General tab. Choose Application Manager from the left side of the screen.

3. **Tap the Running tab.**

4. **Choose the errant app from the list.**

   Touch the app. For example, if the Annoying Sound app is bothering you, choose it from the list.

5. **Touch the Stop or Force Stop button.**

   The app quits.

 Using the Stop or Force Stop button is a drastic act. Don't kill off any app or service unless the app is annoying or you are otherwise unable to stop it. Avoid killing off Google Services, which can change the tablet's behavior or make the Android operating system unstable.

Moving an app to the MicroSD card

On Android tablets with removable storage, you may see an option on an app's Info screen to move the app from internal storage to the MicroSD card. My advice: Don't.

First, apps don't occupy a lot of storage, so moving them to external storage isn't saving you anything. Second, you run the risk of losing the

app should the storage vanish. Indeed, launcher icons for those apps disappear from the Home screen. Finally, the current trend is for Android tablets *not* to feature removable storage. So even if moving apps to the MicroSD card works for you, it's not a long-term solution.

Keep reading in the next section for more ways you can manipulate apps on
your Android tablet.

The problem with randomly quitting an app is that data may get lost or damaged. At the worst, the tablet may become unstable. The only way to fix that
situation is to restart the device.

Apps Drawer Organization

Some tablets offer tools for arranging apps in the Apps drawer. These tools
allow you to present the apps in an order other than alphabetical, rearrange
the apps, or even collect apps and place them into folders.

The key to organizing the Apps drawer is to look for the Action Overflow or
Menu icon. If it's available, tap that icon and look for the View command or
View Type command. Choosing this command presents options for changing
the Apps drawer presentation. For example, on some tablets, you can choose
Customizable Grid view, which allows you to drag icons around to redecorate
the Apps drawer.

Your tablet might also allow you to create app folders on the Apps drawer.
These folders are used to collect and organize apps in one location, similar to
how folders work on the Home screen folder.

As with organizing the Apps drawer, tap the Action Overflow or Menu icon
to look for the Create Folder command. Generally speaking, folders on the
Apps drawer work like folders on the Home screen: Open the folder to view
icons, drag an icon into or out of the folder, and so on. Refer to the section
"Working with folders," earlier in this chapter, for more details.

19

Customize Your Android Tablet

In This Chapter

▶ Changing the background image

▶ Working with Home screen pages

▶ Changing the screen brightness

▶ Putting shortcuts on the Lock screen

▶ Controlling Lock screen notifications

▶ Activating keyboard features

▶ Setting sound options

*I*t's entirely possible to own an Android tablet for decades and never once customize it. It's not that customization is impossible; it's that most people just don't bother. Maybe they don't know how to customize it; maybe they don't try; or maybe they're deathly afraid that the tablet will seek revenge.

Poppycock!

It's *your* tablet! Great potential exists to make the device truly your own. You can change the way it looks to the way it sounds. Revenge is not part of the equation.

Home Screen and Display Settings

The Home screen is where the action happens on your Android tablet. To help hone the Home screen to meet your demands, several customization options are available. You can change the background image, control the automatic lock timeout, and even add or remove Home screen pages. This section uncovers the secrets.

Decorating the Home screen

The key to Home screen decorating can be subtly different from tablet to tablet. Perhaps the most predictable method is to long-press a blank part of the Home screen; do not long-press a launcher icon or widget. Upon success, you may see Home screen management options, similar to those shown in Figure 19-1.

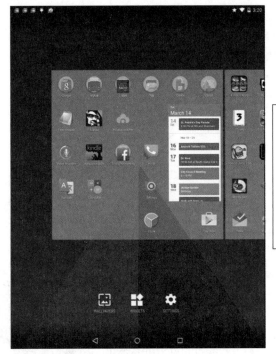

Home screen management icons   Home screen management menu

Figure 19-1: The Home screen menu.

The most popular method of showing the options is to present them as icons, shown on the left in Figure 19-1. Your tablet may instead present the options on a menu, shown on the right. These options include the following items:

Wallpaper: Change the background image on the Home screen.

Widgets: Add widgets to the Home screen. An Apps option might also be available, or combined as Apps and Widgets.

Folder: Create folders for storing launcher icons on the Home screen.

Page: Add, remove, or manage Home screen pages.

Later sections in this chapter describe how to use each command.

- ✔ You cannot long-press the Home screen when it's full of launcher icons and widgets. Swipe to a screen that's all or partially empty.

- ✔ Use folders to help organize apps on the Home screen, especially when the Home screen starts to overflow with launcher icons. See Chapter 18.

- ✔ Some older Android tablets featured a menu button below the touch-screen. Press that button to view the Home screen menu, which looks similar to the option on the right in Figure 19-1.

Hanging new wallpaper

The Home screen background can be draped with two types of wallpaper: traditional and live. Traditional wallpaper can be any image, such as a picture you've taken or an image provided by the tablet's manufacturer. Live wallpaper is animated or interactive.

To set a new wallpaper for the Home screen, obey these steps:

1. **Long-press the Home screen and tap either the Wallpapers or Set Wallpaper command or icon.**

2. **Choose the Home screen option if prompted to set the Home screen or Lock screen wallpaper.**

   See the later section "Setting the Lock screen background" for information on changing the Lock screen's wallpaper.

3. **Tap a wallpaper to see a preview.**

   Swipe the list left or right to peruse your options. You see the previous wallpaper images plus those provided by the tablet manufacturer. On the far right, you'll find the live wallpapers.

4. **Tap the Set Wallpaper button to confirm your choice.**

   The new wallpaper takes over the Home screen.

If you prefer to use an image from the tablet's photo library, tap the Pick Image or More Images button in Step 3. Choose an image. Crop the image by manipulating the cropping rectangle on the screen. Tap the Done button to set the wallpaper.

With some tablets, you must first choose the wallpaper type. You see three options:

Wallpapers: Choose a preset wallpaper.

Live Wallpapers: Select an animated Home screen background.

Image app: Use the named app (Gallery, Photos, or whatever) to choose an image stored on the tablet.

When choosing your own image, you'll be asked to crop. Tap the Set Wallpaper button to assign the image as the tablet's Home screen background.

- ✏ Be careful how you crop the wallpaper image when you choose one of your own photos. Zoom out (pinch your fingers on the touchscreen) to ensure that the entire image is cropped properly for both the tablet's horizontal and vertical orientations.

- ✏ Live wallpapers can be obtained from the Google Play Store. See Chapter 15.

- ✏ The Zedge app is an über-repository of wallpaper images, collected from Android users all over the world. Zedge is free at the Google Play Store.

- ✏ See Chapter 12 for more information on how to crop an image.

Managing Home screen pages

The number of pages on the Home screen isn't fixed. You can add pages. You can remove pages. You can even rearrange pages. This feature might not be available to all Android tablets and, sadly, it's not implemented in exactly the same way.

The stock Android method of adding a Home screen page is to drag an icon left or right, just as though you were positioning that icon on another Home screen page. When a page to the left or right doesn't exist, the tablet automatically adds a new, blank page.

Other tablets may be more specific in how pages are added. For example, you can choose a Page command from the Home screen menu, shown earlier, in Figure 19-1.

Samsung tablets feature a Home screen page overview, shown in Figure 19-2. To edit Home screen pages, pinch the Home screen: Touch the screen with two fingers and drag them together. You can then manage Home screen pages as illustrated in the figure.

Generally speaking, to rearrange the pages, long-press and drag it to a new spot. When you're done, tap the Back or Home icon.

- ✏ The maximum number of Home screen pages may be three, five, seven, or nine, depending on your tablet. The minimum is one.

- ✏ On some tablets, the far left Home screen page is the Google Now app.

- ✏ Some tablets allow you to set the primary Home screen page, which doesn't necessarily have to be the center Home screen page. I've seen different ways to accomplish this task. The most common one is to tap the Home icon in a thumbnail's preview, which is what's illustrated in Figure 19-2.

Primary page

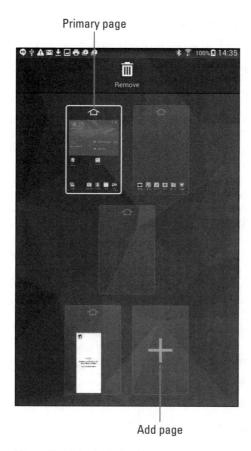

Add page

Figure 19-2: Manipulating Home screen pages.

Setting the screen lock timeout

You can manually lock your tablet at any time by pressing the Power/Lock key. That's probably why it's called the Power/*Lock* key, although I have my doubts. When you don't manually lock the tablet, it automatically locks after a given period of inactivity.

You have control over the automatic lock-timeout value, which can be set from just a few seconds to several minutes. Obey these steps:

1. **Open the Settings app.**

2. **Choose Display.**

   On some Samsung tablets, you need to first tap the Device tab before you can locate the Display item.

3. **Choose the Screen Timeout item.**

   This option is titled Sleep on some tablets.

4. **Select a timeout value from the list.**

   I prefer a value of 10 minutes.

The lock timer measures inactivity; when you don't touch the screen, the timer starts ticking. About 5 seconds before the timeout kicks in, the touchscreen dims. Then the touchscreen turns off and the tablet locks. If you touch the screen before then, the timer is reset.

The Lock screen has its own timeout. If you unlock the tablet but don't work the screen lock, the tablet locks itself automatically after about tem seconds. This timeout value cannot be adjusted.

Adjusting display brightness

You can set the screen brightness to very dim or very bright, or you can let the tablet determine the setting by using the ambient light in the room.

To set brightness, follow these steps:

1. **Open the Settings app and tap the Display item.**

   On Samsung tablets, look for the Display item on the Device tab.

2. **Tap the Brightness item.**

3. **Use the slider to adjust the touchscreen's intensity.**

If you'd rather have the tablet adjust the brightness for you, locate the Adaptive Brightness item and slide its master control to the On position. Not every tablet may feature this option.

✔ The Adaptive Brightness setting might be called Automatic Brightness.

✔ You might also find a Brightness setting in the tablet's Quick Settings area. See Chapter 3 for information on accessing the Quick Settings.

Lock Screen Settings

The Lock screen is different from the Home screen, although the two locations share similar traits. As with the Home screen, you can customize the Lock screen. You can change the background, add app launcher shortcuts, and perform all sorts of tricks.

✔ Lock screen features might not be available for all Android tablets.

✔ For information on setting screen locks, refer to Chapter 20.

Setting the Lock screen background

For most Android tablets, the Lock screen wallpaper is the same as the Home screen wallpaper. A few tablets, however, let you set separate Lock screen wallpaper.

To determine whether your tablet provides for separate Lock screen wallpaper, follow the same steps as outlined in the earlier section "Hanging new wallpaper." If you see a prompt to set the Lock screen wallpaper, choose it. Then select a wallpaper for the Lock screen that's different from the Home screen.

Adding Lock screen shortcuts

Some Android tablets feature the Camera icon in the lower right corner of the screen. Swipe that icon to unlock the tablet and run the Camera app. It's a quick way to take a picture.

Samsung tablets allow for up to five launcher icons to appear on the Lock screen, but only when the Swipe screen lock is selected. You can use these Lock screen launchers to both unlock the tablet and immediately start the app: Simply swipe the app launcher icon on the Lock screen.

To configure Lock screen shortcuts on some Samsung tablets, heed these steps:

1. **Open the Settings app.**
2. **Tap the Device tab, and then choose Lock Screen from the left side of the screen.**
3. **On the right side of the screen, locate the Shortcuts item and slide its master control to the On position.**

   If you don't see this item, your tablet lacks this feature.

4. **Tap the Shortcuts item.**

   You see the icons that will appear on the Lock screen.

You can add or remove Lock screen launchers: Tap the Add icon to choose another app. A maximum of five Lock screen shortcuts can be selected. Long-press an app icon and drag it to the Delete icon to remove it from the Lock screen launcher list.

Displaying Lock screen notifications

The Lock screen can list the tablet's notifications, just as they appear on the notifications drawer. You can determine whether all notifications appear or just highlights (for added security), or you can deactivate the feature.

To control Lock screen notifications, follow these steps:

1. **Open the Settings app.**

2. **Tap the Sound & Notification item.**

3. **Choose When Device Is Locked.**

4. **Select a Lock screen notification level.**

   Three options are shown:

   • Show All Notification content.

   • Hide Sensitive Notification Content.

   • Don't Show Notifications at All.

5. **Choose a notification level.**

The Hide Sensitive Notification Content item simply displays notices, not message previews. And, of course, the Don't Show Notifications at All setting suppresses Lock screen notifications.

The Samsung Galaxy Tab S can also display Lock screen notifications in the form of information cards. To activate the Lock screen cards, follow these directions:

1. **Open the Settings app.**

2. **Tap the Device tab, and choose Lock Screen from the left side of the window.**

3. **Choose Lock Screen Card.**

4. **Place a green check mark by the cards you want to appear on the Lock screen.**

   To disable this feature, uncheck all the items.

You can simply admire the Lock screen notifications, or to use them, double-tap. The app that generated the notification (or card) is started, and you can see more details.

Keyboard Settings

Quite a few options are available for the Google Keyboard, some of which enable special features and others which supposedly make the onscreen typing experience more enjoyable. I'll leave it up to you to determine whether that's true.

Getting keyboard feedback

The onscreen keyboard can help with your typing by generating haptic feedback. This is either in the form of a pleasing click sound or by vibrating the tablet. To check these settings, follow these steps:

1. **Open the Settings app.**

2. **Choose Language & Input.**

   Samsung tablets keep the Language and Input item on either the General or Controls tab in the Settings app.

3. **Choose Google Keyboard.**

4. **Choose Preferences.**

   The two items that control haptic feedback are Vibrate on Keypress and Sound on Keypress.

5. **Use the master control to set vibration and sound options.**

On Samsung tablets, tap the Settings icon by Samsung keyboard. You'll then find check boxes for Sound and Vibration.

Not every tablet features vibration.

Ensuring that predictive text is active

Predictive text is on all the time when you use the Google Keyboard. Not every Android tablet uses that keyboard, so to ensure that the feature is active, follow these steps:

1. **Open the Settings app.**

2. **Choose Language & Input.**

   On Samsung tablets, you may have to first tap the General or Controls tab to locate the Language and Input item.

3. **Tap the item Google Keyboard.**

   On Samsung tablets, tap the Settings icon by the Samsung Keyboard item.

4. **Ensure that the item Predictive Text is active.**

   On some tablets, place a check mark by that item; on others, slide the master control to the On position.

If your tablet doesn't show the Predictive Text item, it's most likely on all the time and can't be turned off. Do ensure that the Next-Word Suggestions item is active: On the Google Keyboard Settings screen, tap Text Correction and then confirm that the master control by the item Next-Word Suggestions is in the On position.

See Chapter 4 for more information on using the predictive text feature.

Activating keyboard gestures

Gesture typing allows you to create words by swiping your finger over the onscreen keyboard. Chapter 4 explains the details, although this feature may not be active on your tablet. To ensure that it is, follow these steps:

1. **Open the Settings app.**

2. **Choose Language & Input.**

3. **Choose Google Keyboard.**

4. **Choose Gesture Typing.**

5. **Ensure that all the Master Control icons are set to the On position.**

   Only the Enable Gesture Typing item needs to be enabled, although activating the other items does enhance the experience.

For some Samsung tablets, the setting is called Keyboard Swipe. Activate it from the Samsung Keyboard Settings screen by following these steps:

1. **Open the Settings app.**

2. **Tap the General Tab.**

   On some Galaxy Tabs, tap the Controls tab if you can't find Language and Input on the General tab.

3. **Choose Language and Input.**

4. **Tap the Settings icon by Samsung Keyboard.**

5. **Choose Keyboard Swipe.**

   This item might be called SwiftKey Flow on older Samsung tablets. Also be aware that not every Galaxy Tab offers this feature.

6. **Tap the item Continuous Input.**

Refer to Chapter 4 to learn more about gesture typing.

Turning on dictation

Voice input should be active on all Android tablets, but that's no guarantee. The secret is to find the Dictation (Microphone) icon on the keyboard. The icon looks similar to the one shown in the margin.

On some Samsung keyboards, long-press the Multifunction key to locate the Dictation icon.

When you can find the Dictation key, and before you defenestrate the tablet in frustration, follow these steps to ensure that this feature is active:

1. **Open the Settings app.**

2. **Choose Language & Input.**

   Samsung tablets title this item Language and Input, and it's found on the Controls tab or on the General tab.

3. **Ensure that Google Voice Typing is listed; if a check box is available, ensure that a check mark is in the box.**

   If not, tap the box to place a check mark there.

The Microphone key now appears on the onscreen keyboard. Using that key is covered in Chapter 4.

Audio Adjustments

The Sound & Notification screen in the Settings app is where you control the various ways your Android tablet can make noise. It's capable of more than beeping, and the volume can be set as well as the vibration options.

To witness the Sound screen for yourself, open the Settings app and tap the Sound & Notification item. On some tablets, the item is called Sound. On Samsung tablets, the Sound item is found on the Device tab in the Settings app.

Worthy options on the Sound screen include the following, although the specific names used on your tablet may be slightly different from what's shown here:

Default Notification Ringtone: Choose which sound you want to hear for a notification alert. Choose a sound or choose None or Silent (at the top of the list) for no sound.

Vibration: Choose the Vibration item to set whether the tablet vibrates during a notification and, potentially, how vigorously it vibrates. If you don't see this option, your Android tablet either doesn't let you control vibration or it lacks the vibration feature.

Volumes: Though you can set the Android tablet volume using the Volume buttons on the side of the gizmo, the Volumes command on the Sound screen lets you set the volume for different types of sound events, such as music, games, and notifications.

Other items might also be available, controlling features specific to the tablet.

Android Tablet Security

In This Chapter

▶ Adding or changing a screen lock

▶ Setting a secure screen lock

▶ Locating a lost tablet

▶ Erasing your tablet's data

▶ Creating accounts for others

▶ Setting up a child's account

*I*n the last century, you didn't need to log in to your computer. Banking and shopping were done in person. And passwords were used only to keep girls out of the boys' fort. Things today are different. Security is vital. Passwords are necessary to secure your personal information for all your online personas.

Lock Your Tablet

If you keep anything important on your Android tablet or you have multiple users on the same tablet or you access a corporate email account, you need Lock screen security. I'm referring to more security than the simple swipe screen lock.

Finding the screen locks

The keys to your Android tablet's screen locks are found within the Settings app. Here's how to get there:

1. **Open the Settings app.**

2. **Choose Security.**

   On Samsung tablets, tap the Device tab and look for the Lock Screen item on the left side of the screen.

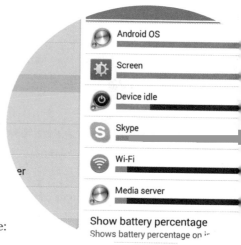

3. **Choose Screen Lock.**

   If you don't see the Screen Lock item, look for the item titled Set Up Screen Lock or Change Screen Lock.

4. **Work any existing screen lock to continue.**

   Eventually you see the Choose Screen Lock screen, which might instead be called Select Screen Lock.

Several locks are shown on the Select Screen Lock screen. The stock Android screen locks are

- **Swipe:** Unlock the tablet by swiping your finger across the screen.
- **Pattern:** Trace a pattern on the touchscreen to unlock the tablet.
- **PIN:** Unlock the tablet by typing a personal identification number (PIN).
- **Password:** Type a password to unlock the tablet.

Other locks may be available, including Face Unlock, Fingerprint, Signature, and even the None lock, which isn't a lock at all.

- The most secure locks are the PIN and password. Using one or the other is required if the tablet has multiple users or a kid's account or it accesses a secure email server.

- If your tablet is encrypted, you may be prompted to require the screen lock (pattern, PIN, or password) to start the device. My recommendation is to require the screen lock; choose the option Require *Lock* to Start Device, where *lock* is the type of screen lock being applied.

- I know of no recovery method available if you forget your tablet's PIN or password screen locks. If you use them, write them down somewhere inconspicuous, just in case.

Removing the screen lock

You don't remove the screen lock on your Android tablet as much as you replace it. Specifically, to remove the pattern, PIN, or password screen lock, set the swipe lock. Follow the directions in the preceding section to get to the Select Screen Lock screen and change the existing screen lock to something else.

Setting a PIN

The PIN lock is second only to the password lock as the most secure for your Android tablet. To access the tablet, you must type a PIN, or personal identification number. This type of screen lock is also employed as a backup for less secure screen-unlocking methods, such as the pattern lock.

The *PIN lock* is a code between 4 and 16 numbers long. It contains only numbers, 0 through 9. To set the PIN lock for your Android tablet, follow the directions in the earlier section "Finding the screen locks" to reach the Select Screen Lock screen. Choose PIN from the list of locks.

Use the onscreen keypad to type your PIN once and tap the Continue button. Type the same PIN again to confirm that you know it. Tap OK. The next time you unlock the tablet, you need to type the PIN to gain access.

Assigning a password

The most secure way to lock an Android tablet is to apply a full-on password. Unlike a PIN, a *password* can contain numbers, symbols, and both upper- and lowercase letters.

Set a password by choosing Password from the Select Screen Lock screen; refer to the earlier section "Finding the screen locks" for information on getting to that screen. The password you select must be at least four characters long. Longer passwords are more secure.

You're prompted to type the password whenever you unlock your Android tablet or whenever you try to change the screen lock. Tap the OK button to accept the password you've typed.

Creating an unlock pattern

One of the most common ways to lock an Android tablet is to apply an *unlock pattern*. The pattern must be traced exactly as it was created in order to unlock the device and get access to your apps and the tablet's other features. To create an unlock pattern, follow along:

1. **Summon the Select Screen Lock screen.**

   Refer to the earlier section "Finding the screen locks."

2. **Choose Pattern.**

   If you've not yet set a pattern lock, you may see a tutorial describing the process; tap the Next button to skip over the dreary directions.

3. **Trace an unlock pattern.**

   Use Figure 20-1 as your inspiration. You can trace over the dots in any order, but you can trace over a dot only once. The pattern must cover at least four dots.

4. **Tap the Continue button.**

I began the pattern here   Keep tracing

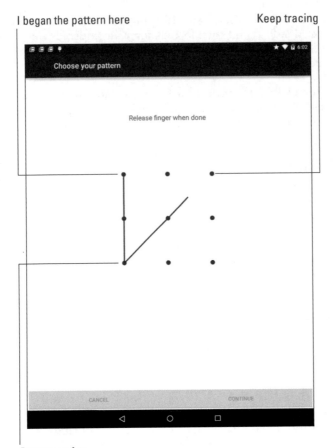

Pattern so far

Figure 20-1: Set the unlock pattern.

5. **Redraw the pattern.**

   You need to prove to the doubtful tablet that you know the pattern.

6. **Tap the Confirm button.**

   Your tablet may require you to type a PIN or password as a backup to the pattern lock. If so, follow the onscreen directions to set that lock as well.

To ensure that the pattern appears on the Lock screen, place a check mark by the option Make Pattern Visible. For even more security, you can disable this option, but you must remember how — and where — the pattern goes.

Also: Clean the touchscreen! Smudge marks can betray your pattern.

Setting unusual screen locks

Several tablets offer other screen locks, which can be silly or fancy and perhaps not that secure. Among them are the face unlock, signature lock, and fingerprint lock. Choose these screen locks from the Select Screen Lock window. Work through the setup process. You may also need to set a PIN or password as a backup to the locks, which generally aren't considered that secure.

- ✔ The face unlock works by using the tablet's front camera. To unlock the device, you stare at the screen. As long as you haven't had any recent, major plastic surgery, the tablet unlocks.

- ✔ The signature lock is unique to the Samsung Galaxy Note. Use the S-Pen to scribble your John Hancock on the touchscreen. The tablet unlocks.

- ✔ Tablets equipped with a fingerprint scanner allow you to swipe your favorite digit across a scanner to unlock the device. On the Samsung Galaxy Tab S, the Home button doubles as the fingerprint scanner.

Other Tablet Security

The screen lock only keeps the Bad Guys at bay. Further tablet security is necessary if you really want to protect your personal information. For example, if your precious digital servant gets lost or stolen, you probably want it back. Or perhaps you need to ensure that your data is encrypted or even erased. This section covers some security options and features.

Adding owner info text

If your Android tablet someday gets lost, it would be nice if a good Samaritan found it. What would be even more helpful is if you had some information on the Lock screen to help that kind person find you and return your gizmo.

To set the owner info for your Android tablet, follow these steps:

1. **Visit the Settings app.**

2. **Choose the Security or Lock Screen category.**

   On some Samsung tablets, the Lock Screen category is found on the Device tab.

3. **Choose Owner Info or Owner Information.**

4. **Ensure that a check mark appears next to the Show Owner Info on Lock Screen option.**

5. **Type text in the box.**

   You can type more than one line of text, though the information is displayed on the Lock screen as a single line.

Whatever text you type in the box appears on the Lock screen. Therefore, I recommend typing your name, address, phone number, email, and so on. That way, should you lose your tablet and an honest person finds it, he or she can get it back to you.

The Owner Info may not show up when None is selected as a screen lock.

Finding a lost tablet

Someday, you may lose your beloved Android tablet. It might be for a few panic-filled seconds, or it might be for forever. The hardware solution is to weld a heavy object to the tablet, such as a vending machine, yet that strategy kind of defeats the entire mobile/wireless paradigm. The software solution is to use a cell phone locator service, which also works for tablets.

Cell phone locator services employ apps that use a tablet's mobile data signal as well as its GPS to help locate the missing gizmo. Even if you have a Wi-Fi–only tablet, the service still works, which is why I recommend it. These types of apps are available at the Google Play Store. One that I've tried and recommend is Lookout Mobile Security.

Lookout features two different apps. One is free, which you can try to see whether you like it. The paid app offers more features and better locating services. As with similar apps, you must register at a website to help you locate your tablet, should it go wandering.

- ✔ Visit Chapter 15 for information about the Google Play Store, where you can obtain copies of the Lookout security app and search for other tablet-finding apps.

- ✔ Some tablet manufacturers may offer their own service, such as Samsung's Find My Mobile. You need a Samsung account to use the service, but it does work well with many (not all) of its tablets.

Encrypting your tablet

When the information on your galactic tablet must be really, really secure, you can take the drastic step of encrypting the internal and external storage. For most Android tablet users, this step is a bit much. However, if you're using your tablet to store the Colonel's secret recipe, you might want to consider it.

First, apply a secure screen lock, such as the PIN or password.

Second, ensure that the tablet is either plugged in or fully charged. Encryption takes a while, and you don't want your gizmo pooping out before the process is complete.

Third, follow these steps to encrypt your tablet's internal storage:

1. **Open the Settings app and choose the Security item.**

   On Samsung tablets, tap the General tab to find the Security item.

2. **Choose Encrypt Tablet or Encrypt Device.**

   If you haven't followed my advice in this section, you'll need to charge the tablet or set a password or both.

3. **Tap the Encrypt Tablet button.**

4. **Wait.**

You can choose the item Encrypt External SD Card to perform the same operation on its storage as well.

Once encrypted, only by unlocking the tablet will anyone be able to access its storage.

My advice is not to encrypt your tablet but instead to use a strong password. Adding remote security, as described in the preceding section, is also a good thing to do.

Performing a factory data reset

The most secure thing you can do with information on your Android tablet is to erase it all. The procedure is known as a *factory data reset*. It effectively restores the device to its original state, just like when you got it new.

A factory data reset is a drastic thing. It not only removes all information from storage but also erases all your accounts. Don't take this step lightly! In fact, if you're using this procedure to cure an ill, I recommend first getting support.

When you're ready to erase all the tablet's data, follow these steps:

1. **Start the Settings app and choose Backup & Reset.**

   On Samsung tablets, tap the General tab to locate the Backup and Reset item.

2. **Choose Factory Data Reset.**

3. **Tap the Reset Tablet button.**

   It might be called Reset Device on your tablet.

4. **If prompted, work the screen lock.**

   This level of security prevents others from idly messing with your Tab.

5. **Tap the Erase Everything or Delete All button to confirm.**

   All the information you've set or stored on the tablet is purged, including all your accounts, any apps you've downloaded, music — everything.

Practical instances when this action is necessary include selling your tablet or giving it to someone else to use. That's the perfect time to perform a factory data reset.

It's Everyone's Tablet!

Computers have long had the capability to allow multiple users on the same device. Each person has their own account and customized items within their account. It's a good idea for a computer, but for a tablet?

Android tablets can sport multiple users. Though I would suggest that each person get their own tablet (accompanied by a copy of this book), that's not always practical. A better solution is to give each human a user account on the device. That includes accounts for the kiddies.

Adding another user

Your tablet already has one account — yours! It appears as a tiny circle on the Lock screen, usually in the upper right corner, similar to the one shown on the left in Figure 20-2.

You add accounts by following these steps:

1. **Apply a secure screen lock to your account.**

   See the earlier section "Lock Your Tablet." I strongly recommend a PIN or password screen lock.

2. **Grab the other person.**

   Though you, as the Lord High User of your tablet, can create the new account, you need the other person to complete the job.

3. **Open the Settings app and choose Users.**

   On Samsung tablets, look on the Device tab or General tab for the Users item.

   If you're unable to find the Users category, your tablet doesn't have this feature.

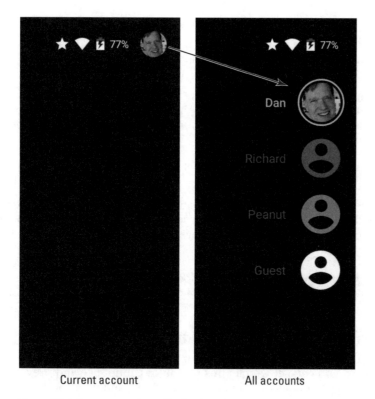

Current account   All accounts

Figure 20-2: User accounts on the Lock screen.

4. **Tap the Add icon or Add User or Profile button.**

5. **Choose User.**

   See the later section "Configuring a kid's account" for information on the Restricted Profile account type.

6. **Tap the OK button after ignoring the Add User info.**

7. **Tap the Set Up Now button, and hand the tablet over to the other person so that they can continue configuring the device.**

At this point, the other person configures your Android tablet exactly as you did when you first set up the device. This process includes adding a Google/ Gmail account, setting various options, and so on. Eventually the account is created and the other user can start using the tablet.

  ✓ Settings, apps, email, and other options for each user are unique and separate. You cannot access another account unless you know how to work that user's screen lock.

- ✔ I recommend each user have his account protected with a medium- to high-security screen lock.

- ✔ The tablet's first user (most likely you) is the main user, the one who has primary administrative control.

- ✔ Remove an account by following Steps 3 through 5 in this section. Tap the Delete (Trash) icon next to the account you want to remove. If you don't see the icon, tap the account and look for the icon on the next screen.

Switching users

To access another account, tap the account circle on the Lock screen, as shown in Figure 20-2. If additional accounts are available, they appear similar to the one shown on the right in the figure. Tap an account bubble to switch to that account.

When you're done using the tablet, lock the screen. Other users can then access their own accounts from the Lock screen, as described in this section.

Configuring a kid's account

Don't just hand over your Galaxy Tab to Peanut! Craft him a kid's account. That way, you can set which apps he can or cannot use and prevent him from downloading millions of dollars of apps, music, and video.

To add a kid's account, follow the steps in the earlier section "Adding another user." Choose the Restricted Profile account type.

After creating the account, you see the Application/Content Restrictions screen. Here's what to do next:

- ✔ Tap the account name, New Restricted Account, to replace it with your child's name — or whatever name they choose.

- ✔ Place a check mark by the Location Access item if you want their location tracked as they use the tablet. Most parents prefer to keep this item unchecked.

- ✔ Swipe through the list of programs and place check marks by the ones you would allow your tiny tot to use. These would include various games or whatever other apps you deem appropriate.

- ✔ Some apps feature the Settings icon, such as Google, Netflix, and Play Movies & TV. Tap that icon to make further adjustments, such as determining what level of entertainment would be appropriate for your child.

See the preceding section for information on switching to the kid's account.

On the Road

In This Chapter

▶ Traveling with your Android tablet

▶ Using the tablet on an airplane

▶ Activating Airplane mode

▶ Taking an Android tablet overseas

▶ Avoiding data roaming charges

As a mobile device, your Android tablet is designed to go wherever you go. And if you throw the tablet, it can go beyond where you go, but that's not my point. Because it is wireless and has a generous battery, the tablet is built to go on the road. Where can you take it? How can it survive? What if it runs off by itself? These are the issues regarding taking your tablet elsewhere, all of which are covered in this chapter.

You Can Take It with You

How far can you go with an Android tablet? As far as you desire to go. As long as you can carry the tablet with you, it goes where you do. How it functions may change depending on your environment, and you can do a few things to prepare before you go, which are all covered in this section.

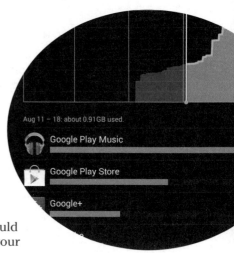

Aug 11 – 18: about 0.91GB used.

🎧 Google Play Music

▶ Google Play Store

Google+

Preparing to leave

Unless you're being unexpectedly abducted, you should prepare several things before leaving on a trip with your Android tablet.

First and most important, of course, is to charge the thing. I plug in my Android tablet overnight before I leave the next day. The tablet's battery is nice and robust, so power should last until well after you reach your destination.

Second, consider loading up on some reading material, music, and a few new apps before you go.

For example, consider getting some eBooks for the road. I prefer to sit and stew over the Play Store's online library before I leave, as opposed to wandering aimlessly in some airport sundry store, trying hard to focus on the good books rather than on the salty snacks. Chapter 14 covers reading eBooks on your Android tablet.

Picking up some music might be a good idea as well. Visit Chapter 13.

I usually reward myself with a new game before I go on a trip with my tablet. Visit the Play Store and see what's hot or recommended. A good puzzle game can make a nice, long international flight go by a lot quicker.

See Chapter 15 for information on obtaining games from the Google Play Store. Also refer to that chapter for information on keeping eBooks, music, and videos on your tablet when an Internet connection isn't available. You'll want to download that material before you leave.

Finally, don't forget your tickets! Many airlines offer apps. The apps may make traveling easy because they generate notifications for your schedule and provide timely gate changes or flight delays — plus, you can use the Tab as your e-ticket. Search the Play Store to see whether your preferred airline offers an app.

Going to the airport

I'm not a frequent flier, but I am a nerd. The most amount of junk I've carried with me on a flight is two laptop computers and three cell phones. I know that's not a record, but it's enough to warrant the following list of travel tips, all of which apply to taking an Android tablet with you on an extended journey:

- ✔ Take the Android tablet's AC adapter and USB cable with you. Put them in your carry-on luggage.

- ✔ Most airports feature USB chargers, so you can charge the tablet in an airport, if you need to. Even though you need only the cable to charge, bring along the AC adapter, anyway.

- ✔ At the security checkpoint, place your Android tablet in a bin by itself or with other electronics. The exceptions are when you've been approved for pre-check or you're using a preapproved tablet carrying pouch.

- ✔ Use the Calendar app to keep track of your flights. The event title serves as the airline and flight number. For the event time, use the take-off and landing schedules. For the location, list the origin and destination airport codes. And, in the Description field, put the flight reservation number. If you're using separate calendars (categories), specify the Travel calendar for your flight. See Chapter 14 for more information on the Calendar app.

✔ Scan for the airport's Wi-Fi service. Most airports don't charge for the service, although you may have to agree to terms by using the tablet's web browser app to visit the airport's website.

Flying with an Android tablet

It truly is the trendiest of things to be aloft with the latest mobile gizmo. Like taking a cell phone on a plane, however, you have to follow some rules.

The good news is that because your Android tablet isn't a smartphone, you can leave it on for the duration of the flight. All you need to do is place the tablet into Airplane mode. Follow these steps just before take-off:

1. **Open the Settings app.**

2. **Tap the More item in the Wireless & Networks area.**

   On a Samsung tablet, tap the Connections tab.

3. **Slide the master control by the Airplane Mode item to the On position.**

   The tablet turns off its Wi-Fi and Bluetooth radios.

When the Android tablet is in Airplane mode, a special icon appears in the status area, similar to the one shown in the margin.

To exit Airplane mode, repeat the steps mentioned in this section.

✔ An Airplane Mode Quick Settings button is also available: Summon the Quick Settings and tap the Airplane Mode icon. See Chapter 3 for more information on the Quick Settings.

✔ Some tablets feature an Airplane Mode action on the Device Options menu: Press and hold down the Power button and choose Airplane Mode.

✔ Airplane mode might be called Flight mode on some tablets.

✔ If the airline features onboard wireless networking, and you're not skittish about overpaying for dreadfully slow Internet access, you can reactivate the tablet's Wi-Fi radio after you place the device into Airplane mode. After doing so, use the web browser app to display any web page. What you see instead is the inflight Wi-Fi access screen. Heed the directions and you're online.

Getting to your destination

After you arrive at your destination, the tablet may update the date and time according to your new location. One additional step you may want to take is to set the tablet's time zone. By doing so, you ensure that your schedule adapts properly to your new location.

To change the tablet's time zone, follow these steps:

1. **Open the Settings app.**

2. **Choose Date and Time.**

   On some Samsung tablets, tap the General tab to locate the Date and Time item.

3. **If you find an Automatic Time Zone setting, ensure that a check mark appears by that option.**

   If so, you're done; the tablet automatically updates its time references. Otherwise, continue with Step 4.

4. **Choose Select Time Zone.**

5. **Pluck the current time zone from the list.**

If you've set appointments for your new location, visit the Calendar app to ensure that their start and end times have been properly adjusted. If you're prompted to update appointment times based on the new zone, do so.

When you're done traveling or you change your time zone again, make sure that the tablet is updated as well. When the Automatic Time Zone setting isn't available, follow the steps in this section to reset the tablet's time zone.

The Android Tablet Goes Abroad

Yes, your Android tablet works overseas. The two resources you need to consider are a way to recharge the battery and a way to access Wi-Fi. As long as you have both, you're pretty much set. You also must be careful about mobile data (cellular) roaming surcharges when using an LTE tablet.

Using overseas power

You can easily attach a foreign AC power adapter to your tablet's AC power plug. You don't need a voltage converter — just an adapter. After it's attached, you can plug your tablet into those weirdo overseas power sockets without the risk of blowing up anything. I charged my Android tablet nightly while I spent time in France, and it worked like a charm.

Accessing Wi-Fi in foreign lands

Wi-Fi is pretty universal. The same protocols and standards are used everywhere, so if the tablet can access Wi-Fi at your local Starbucks, it can access Wi-Fi at the Malted Yak Blood Café in Wamboolistan. As long as Wi-Fi is available, your Android tablet can use it.

- See Chapter 16 for details on using Wi-Fi with your Android tablet.

- Internet cafés are more popular overseas than in the United States. They are the best locations for connecting your tablet and catching up on life back home.

- Many overseas hotels offer free Wi-Fi service, although the signal may not reach into every room. Don't be surprised if you can use the Wi-Fi network only while you're in the lobby.

- Use your Android tablet to make phone calls overseas by getting some Skype Credit. Skype's international rates are quite reasonable. The calls are made over the Internet, so when the tablet has Wi-Fi access, you're good to go. See Chapter 8 for more information on making Skype calls.

Disabling data roaming

The word *roam* takes on an entirely new meaning when it's applied to an LTE tablet (which features a cellular modem). Whenever you venture outside of your carrier's service area, the tablet may end up latching onto another mobile data network. When that happens, the tablet is *roaming*.

Roaming sounds handy, but there's a catch: It almost always involves a surcharge for using another mobile data network — an *unpleasant* surcharge.

Relax: Your cellular tablet alerts you whenever you're roaming. The Roaming icon appears in the status area, similar to the one shown in the margin. You may even see the word *Roaming* on the Lock screen and witness the name of the foreign cellular provider where the local provider's name normally appears.

If you'd like to eschew using the alien mobile network and, potentially, avoid any unpleasant charges, disable the tablet's Data Roaming option. Follow these steps:

1. **Open the Settings app.**

2. **In the Wireless & Networks section, tap the More item.**

   On Samsung tablets, tap the Connections tab in the Settings app. The More item may be titled More Networks.

3. **Choose Mobile Networks or Cellular Networks.**

4. **Ensure that the Data Roaming option isn't selected.**

   On some tablets, the option is titled Global Data Roaming Access. Choose it and then choose the option Deny Data Roaming Access.

Your tablet can still access the Internet over the Wi-Fi connection while it's roaming. Connecting to a Wi-Fi network doesn't make you incur extra charges on your cellular bill.

✔ Before you travel abroad, contact your cellular provider and ask about overseas data roaming. A subscription service or other options may be available, especially when you plan to stay overseas for an extended length of time.

✔ If roaming concerns you, simply place the tablet into Airplane mode, as covered earlier in this chapter. In Airplane mode, your tablet can access Wi-Fi networks, but its cellular modem is definitely disabled.

Maintenance, Troubleshooting, and Help

In This Chapter

▷ Cleaning an Android tablet
▷ Checking on the battery
▷ Saving battery power
▷ Solving annoying problems
▷ Searching for support
▷ Troubleshooting issues
▷ Getting answers

M aintenance for your Android tablet is a lot easier than it was in the old days. Back in the 1970s, tablet computer owners were required to completely disassemble their devices and hand-clean every nut and sprocket with solvent and a wire brush. Special cloth was necessary to sop up all the electrical oil. It was a nightmare, which is why most people never did tablet maintenance back then.

Today, things are different. Android tablet mainte- nance is rather carefree, involving little more than cleaning the thing every so often. No disassembly is required. Beyond covering maintenance, this chapter offers suggestions for using the battery, gives you some helpful tips, and provides a Q&A section.

The Maintenance Chore

Relax. Maintenance of an Android tablet is simple and quick. Basically, I can summarize it in three words: Keep it clean. Beyond that, another maintenance task worthy of attention is backing up the information stored on your tablet.

Keeping it clean

You probably already keep your Android tablet clean. Perhaps you're one of those people who uses their sleeves to wipe the touchscreen. Of course, better than your sleeve is something called a *microfiber cloth*. This item can be found at any computer- or office-supply store.

✔ Never use any liquid to clean the touchscreen — especially ammonia or alcohol. Those harsh chemicals damage the touchscreen, rendering it unable to detect your input. Further, they can smudge the display, making it more difficult to see.

✔ Touchscreen-safe screen cleaners are available for those times when your sleeve or even a microfiber cloth won't cut it. Ensure that you get a screen cleaner designed for a touchscreen.

✔ If the screen keeps getting dirty, consider adding a *screen protector.* This specially designed cover prevents the screen from getting scratched or dirty but still allows you to use your finger on the touchscreen. Be sure that the screen protector is designed for use with the specific brand and model of your Android tablet.

Backing up your stuff

For a majority of the information on your Android tablet, backup is automatic. Your Google account takes care of Gmail, the calendar, your contacts, and even your apps. If you don't download music, eBooks, or movies, nothing ever needs to be backed up — at least not manually.

To ensure that your account information is being backed up, heed these steps:

1. **Open the Settings app.**

2. **Choose Accounts.**

   On Samsung tablets, tap the General tab to locate Accounts.

3. **Choose Google.**

4. **Tap your Gmail address.**

5. **Ensure that check marks appear by every item in the list.**

   These are the items that synchronize between the tablet and your Google account on the Internet.

   You're not done yet!

6. **Tap the Back navigation until you're returned to the main Settings app screen.**

7. **Choose Backup & Reset.**

The command may also read as Back Up and Reset, or a similar variation.

8. **Ensure that the item Back Up My Data is enabled.**

Beyond your Google account, which is automatically backed up, the rest of the information can be manually backed up. You can copy files from the tablet's internal storage to the cloud or your computer as a form of backup. See Chapter 17 for information on coordinating files between the Android tablet and a computer.

Yes, I agree: Manual backup isn't an example of technology making your life easier.

Updating the system

Every so often, a new version of the Android tablet's operating system becomes available. It's an *Android* update because Android is the name of the operating system, not because the Android tablet thinks that it's some type of robot.

When an automatic update occurs, you see an alert or a message, indicating that a system upgrade is available. The message may be as subtle as a notification icon, or it might be a card onscreen informing you that an update is necessary. My advice: Install the update and get it over with. Don't dally.

✔ If possible, connect the tablet to a power source during a software update. You don't want the battery to die in the middle of the operation.

✔ You can manually check for updates: In the Settings app, choose About Tablet or About Device. (On Samsung tablets, look on the General tab.) Choose System Updates or Software Update. When the system is up-to-date, the screen tells you so. Otherwise, you find directions for updating the Android operating system.

✔ Touching the Check Now button isn't magic. When an update is available, the tablet lets you know.

✔ Non-Android system updates might also be issued. For example, the tablet's manufacturer may send out an update to the Android tablet's guts. This type of update is often called a *firmware* update. As with Android updates, my advice is to accept all firmware updates.

Battery Care and Feeding

Perhaps the most important item you can monitor and maintain on your Android tablet is its battery. The battery supplies the necessary electrical juice by which the device operates. Without battery power, your tablet is basically an expensive trivet. Keep an eye on the battery.

Monitoring the battery

Android tablets display the current battery status at the top of the screen, in the status area, next to the time. The icons used to display the battery status are similar to the icons shown in Figure 22-1. They can appear white-on-black or use a charming color scheme, as illustrated in the figure.

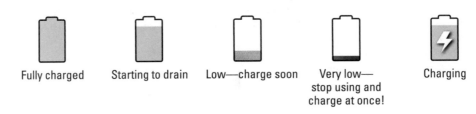

| Fully charged | Starting to drain | Low—charge soon | Very low—stop using and charge at once! | Charging |

Figure 22-1: Battery status icons.

You might also see an icon for a dead battery, but for some reason I can't get my Android tablet to turn on and display that icon.

- ✔ Heed those low-battery warnings! The tablet sounds a notification whenever the battery power gets low. Another notification sounds whenever the battery gets *very* low.

- ✔ When the battery level is too low, the Android tablet shuts itself off.

- ✔ The best way to deal with low battery power is to connect the tablet to a power source: Either plug it into a wall socket or connect it to a computer by using a USB cable. The tablet begins charging itself immediately; plus, you can use the device while it's charging.

- ✔ The tablet charges more efficiently when it's plugged into a wall socket rather than a computer.

- ✔ You don't have to fully charge the Android tablet to use it. When you have only 20 minutes to charge and you get only a 70 percent battery level, that's great. Well, it's not great, but it's far better than a lower battery level.

- ✔ Battery percentage values are best-guess estimates. Your Android tablet has a hearty battery that can last for hours. But when the battery meter gets low, the battery drains faster. So, if you get 8 hours of use from the tablet and the battery meter shows 20 percent remaining, those numbers don't imply that 20 percent equals 2 more hours of use. In practice, the amount of time you have left is much less than that. As a rule, when the battery percentage value gets low, the battery appears to drain faster.

Determining what is drawing power

An Android tablet is smart enough to know which of its features and apps use the most battery power. You can check it out for yourself on the battery usage screen, such as the one shown in Figure 22-2.

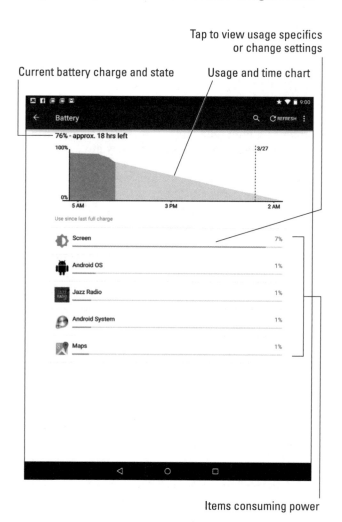

Tap to view usage specifics
or change settings

Current battery charge and state   Usage and time chart

Items consuming power

Figure 22-2: Things that drain the battery.

To view the battery usage screen on your tablet, open the Settings app and choose the Battery item. On a Samsung tablet, tap the General tab in the Settings app to locate the Battery item.

Tap an item in the list to view specific details. For some items, the details screen hosts a button that lets you adjust power settings or even disable the feature.

The number and variety of items shown on the battery usage screen depend on what you've been doing with your tablet between charges and how many different apps you've been using. Don't be surprised if an item doesn't show up in the list; not every app consumes a lot of battery power.

Extending battery life

A surefire way to make a battery last a good, long time is to never turn on the device in the first place. That's kind of impractical, so rather than let you use your Android tablet as a high-tech sushi tray, I offer a smattering of suggestions you can follow to help prolong tablet battery life:

Dim the screen: Refer to Figure 22-2 and you can see that the display (labeled Screen) draws quite a lot of battery power. Although a dim screen can be more difficult to see, especially outdoors, it definitely saves on battery life.

Adjust the screen brightness from the Settings app, or you can choose the Brightness Quick Action from the Quick Actions drawer. Also see Chapter 19 for information on setting the screen lock timeout.

Lower the volume: Consider lowering the volume for the various noises the Android tablet makes, especially notifications. Information on setting volume options is found in Chapter 19.

Disable the vibration options. The tablet's vibration is caused by a teensy motor. Though you don't see much battery savings by disabling the vibration options, it's better than no savings. To turn off vibration, see Chapter 19.

Turn off Bluetooth: When you're not using Bluetooth, turn it off. The fastest way to do that is to use the Bluetooth Quick Action. See Chapter 16 for information on Bluetooth.

 Many Android tablets come with battery-saving capabilities. These features are accessed either in the Settings app (Battery item) or by using a specific Battery Savings type of app. This feature automatically throttles certain battery-consuming items, including many in this list. It may kick in automatically when the battery gets low, or it might be something you must activate specifically.

If your tablet didn't come with such a feature, check for battery-saving apps at the Google Play Store. See Chapter 15.

Help and Troubleshooting

Wouldn't it be great if you could have an avuncular Mr. Wizard type available at a moment's notice? He could just walk in and, with a happy smile on his face and a reassuring hand on your shoulder, let you know what the problem is and how to fix it. Then he'd give you a cookie. Never mind that such a thing would be creepy — getting helpful advice is worth it.

Fixing random and annoying problems

Here are some typical problems you may encounter on your Android tablet and my suggestions for a solution:

General trouble

For just about any problem or minor quirk, consider restarting the tablet. If the tablet features a Restart action on the Device Options menu, use it. Otherwise, turn off the tablet, and then turn it on again. This procedure will most likely fix a majority of the annoying problems you encounter.

See Chapter 2 for basic tablet on/off instructions.

Connection woes

As you move about, the cellular signal can change. In fact, you may observe the status icon change from 4G LTE to 3G to even the dreaded 1X or — worse — nothing, depending on the strength and availability of the mobile data network.

My advice for random signal weirdness is to wait. Oftentimes, the signal comes back after a few minutes. If it doesn't, the mobile data network might be down, or you may just be in an area with lousy service. Consider changing your location.

For Wi-Fi connections, ensure that Wi-Fi is set up properly and working. This process usually involves pestering the person who configured the Wi-Fi router or, in a coffee shop, bothering the cheerful person with the tattoos and piercings who serves you coffee.

Perhaps the issue isn't with the tablet at all, but rather with the Wi-Fi network? Some networks have a "lease time" after which your tablet is disconnected. If so, follow the directions in Chapter 16 for turning off the tablet's Wi-Fi and then turn it on again. That often solves the issue.

Another problem I've heard about is that the Wi-Fi router doesn't recognize your Android tablet. In this case, the router might use older technology and it needs to be replaced. Especially if you have a Wi-Fi router over 5 years old, consider getting a newer router.

Music is playing and you want it to stop

It's awesome that your tablet continues to play music while you do other things. Getting the music to stop quickly, however, requires some skill. You can access the play controls for the Play Music app from a number of locations. They're found on the Lock screen, for example. You can also find them in the notifications drawer.

An app has run amok

Sometimes, apps that misbehave let you know. You see a warning on the screen announcing the app's stubborn disposition. When that happens, touch the Force Quit button to shut down the app. Then say, "Whew!"

To manually shut down an app, refer to Chapter 18.

You've reached your wit's end

When all else fails, you can do the drastic thing and perform a factory data reset on your Android tablet. Before committing to this step, you should contact support as described in the next section.

Refer to Chapter 20 for details on the factory data reset.

Finding help

Some tablets come supplied with the Help app. It may be called Help or Help Center or something similar, and it may not be the kind of avuncular, well-written assistance you get from this book, but it's better than nothing.

You may find the old, dratted manual lurking in eBook form, which doesn't make it any better. Look for it in the Play Books app.

A Guided Tour app or Tutorial app may also be available, which helps you understand how to work some of the tablet's specific and interesting features.

Getting support

Three sources are available for support for your Android tablet: the cellular provider, the tablet's manufacturer, and Google Play.

Cellular support

For LTE tablets, the first source of support is your cellular provider. Assuming that you're a current mobile-data subscriber, consider contacting the cellular provider for tablet issues. Table 22-1 lists contact information for U.S. cellular providers.

Table 22-1		U.S. Cellular Providers
Provider	*Toll-free Number*	*Website*
AT&T	800-331-0500	www.att.com/esupport
Sprint Nextel	800-211-4727	http://support.sprint.com/support
T-Mobile	800-866-2453	www.t-mobile.com/Contact.aspx
Verizon	800-922-0204	http://support.vzw.com/clc

Manufacturer support

The second source, or the only source if you have a Wi-Fi tablet, is the tablet manufacturer, such as Asus, Samsung, or LG. Information about support can be found in those random papers and pamphlets included in the box your tablet comes in. Remember how in Chapter 1 I tell you not to throw that stuff out? This is why.

Oh, and if you were suckered into a long-term service agreement at some Big Box store, you can try getting support from those people.

App support

For app issues, contact the developer. Follow these steps:

1. **Open the Play Store app.**
2. **Tap the Side Menu icon to display the navigation drawer.**
3. **Choose My Apps.**
4. **Tap the entry for the specific app, the one that's bothering you.**
5. **Choose the item Send Email.**

    Swipe the screen from button-to-top to scroll down the app's info screen and find the Send Email item. It's usually one of the last items on the screen.

Contacting the developer is no guarantee that you'll get a response.

Play Store support

For issues with the Play Store itself, contact Google at support.google.com/googleplay.

Information about my tablet

When contacting support, it helps to know your tablet's device ID and Android operating system version number. This information is found by opening the Settings app and choosing the About Tablet or About Device item. For a Samsung tablet, that item is found on the General tab.

The two items you should reference are the tablet's model number and Android version.

For convenience, and in case you can't get the tablet to turn on again in the future, you can jot down that information here:

Model number: _____

Android version: _____

Valuable Tablet Q&A

I love Q&A! Not only is it an effective way to express certain problems and solutions, but some of the questions might also cover things I've been wanting to ask.

"I can't turn the tablet on (or off)!"

Sometimes an Android tablet locks up. It's frustrating, but I've discovered that if you press and hold the Power/Lock key for about 8 seconds, the tablet turns either off or on, depending on which state it's in.

I've had a program lock my tablet tight when the 8-second Power/Lock key trick didn't work. In that case, I waited 12 minutes or so, just letting the tablet sit there and do nothing. Then I pressed and held the Power/Lock key for about 8 seconds, and it turned itself back on.

"The touchscreen doesn't work!"

A touchscreen requires a human finger for proper interaction. The tablet interprets the static potential between the human finger and the device to determine where the touchscreen is being touched.

You can use the touchscreen while wearing special touchscreen gloves. Yes, they actually make such things. But for regular gloves? Nope.

The touchscreen might fail also when the battery power is low or when the Android tablet has been physically damaged.

I've been informed that there's an Android app for cats. This implies that the touchscreen can also interpret a feline paw for proper interaction. Either that or the cat can hold a human finger in its mouth and manipulate the app that way. Because I don't have the app, I can't tell for certain.

"The screen is too dark!"

Android tablets feature a teensy light sensor on the front. The sensor is used to adjust the touchscreen's brightness based on the amount of ambient light at your location. If the sensor is covered, the screen can get very, very dark.

Ensure that you don't unintentionally block the light sensor. Avoid buying a case or screen protector that obscures the sensor.

The automatic brightness setting might also be vexing you. See Chapter 19 for information on setting screen brightness.

"The battery doesn't charge!"

Start from the source: Is the wall socket providing power? Is the cord plugged in? The cable may be damaged, so try another cable.

When charging from a USB port on a computer, ensure that the computer is turned on. Most computers don't provide USB power when they're turned off. Also, some USB ports may not supply enough power to charge the tablet. If possible, use a port on the computer console (the box) instead of a USB hub.

Some tablets may charge from a special cord, not the USB cable. Check to confirm that your tablet is able to take a charge from the USB cable.

"The tablet gets so hot that it turns itself off!"

Yikes! An overheating gadget can be a nasty problem. Judge how hot the tablet is by seeing whether you can hold it in your hand: When it's too hot to hold, it's *too* hot. If you're using the tablet to cook an egg, it's too hot.

Turn off your Android tablet and let the battery cool.

If the overheating problem continues, have the Android tablet looked at for potential repair. The battery might need to be replaced. As far as I can tell, there's no way to remove and replace the Android tablet battery by yourself.

Do not continue to use any gizmo that's too hot! The heat damages the electronics. It can also start a fire.

"My tablet doesn't do Landscape mode!"

Not every app takes advantage of the tablet's capability to reorient itself when you rotate the device between Portrait and Landscape modes — or even Upside-Down mode. For example, many games set their orientations one way and refuse to change, no matter how you hold the tablet. So, just because the app doesn't go into Horizontal or Vertical mode doesn't mean that anything is broken.

Confirm that the orientation lock isn't on: Check the Quick Settings. Ensure that the Rotation Lock or Screen Rotation item isn't turned on; if so, the screen doesn't reorient itself. Also, some eBook reader apps sport their own screen rotation lock feature. Tap the Action Overflow to determine whether it's enabled.

Part V
The Part of Tens

Enjoy an additional *Android Tablets For Dummies* Part of Tens chapter online at
www.dummies.com/extras/androidtablets.

In this part . . .

- Behold ten useful tips and tricks for getting the most from your Android tablet.
- Find out ten important things you shouldn't forget.

Ten Tips, Tricks, and Shortcuts

A *tip* is a small suggestion, a word of advice often spoken from bruising experience or knowledge passed along from someone with bruising experience. A *trick,* which is something not many know about, usually causes amazement or surprise. A *shortcut* is a quick way to get home, even though it crosses the old graveyard and you never quite know whether Old Man Witherspoon is the groundskeeper or a zombie.

I'd like to think that just about everything in this book is a tip, trick, or shortcut for using an Android tablet. Even so, I've distilled a list of items in this chapter that are definitely worthy of note.

Quickly Switch Apps

Android apps don't quit. Sure, some of them have a Quit or Sign Out command, but most apps lurk inside the tablet's memory while you do other things. The Android operating system may eventually kill off a stale app. Before that happens, you can deftly and quickly switch between all running apps.

The key to making the switch is to use the Recent navigation icon, found at the bottom of the touchscreen. Figure 23-1 illustrates two popular representations of the Recent navigation icon.

Android Lollipop   **Android Kitkat**

Figure 23-1: Incarnations of the Recent navigation icon.

After tapping the Recent navigation icon, choose an app from the list. Swipe the list up or down to peruse what's available. To dismiss the list, touch the Back icon or Home icon.

✔ On tablets that lack the Recent icon, long-press the Home navigation icon.

✔ To remove an app from the list of recent apps, swipe it left or right. This is effectively the same thing as quitting an app.

✔ Some tablets may feature a Task Manager. It's usually a more technical representation of the items you find on the list of recent apps, with the addition of internal apps and services.

✔ The list of recent apps is called the Overview, although everyone I know calls it the List of Recent Apps.

Install Apps from a Computer

You don't need to use an Android tablet to install apps. Using a computer, you can visit the Google Play website, browse for apps, and have that app installed remotely. It's kind of cool yet kind of scary at the same time. Here's how it works:

1. **Use a computer's web browser to visit the Google Play Store on the Internet:** `play.google.com/store`.

   Bookmark that site!

2. **If necessary, click the Sign In button to log in to your Google account.**

   Use the same Google account you used when setting up your Android tablet. You need to have access to that account so that Google can remotely update your various Android devices.

3. **Browse for something.**

   You can hunt down apps, books, music — the whole gamut. It works just like browsing the Play Store on your tablet.

4. **Click the Install button or Buy button.**

5. **Choose your Android tablet from the Choose a Device menu.**

If your tablet isn't listed, the app isn't compatible. That happens. Also, the tablet may be listed using its technical name, not the brand name you're used to.

6. **For a free app, click the Install button. For a paid app, click the Continue button, choose your payment source, and then click the Buy button.**

Installation proceeds.

As if by magic, the app is installed on your Android tablet — even though you used a computer to do it. Heck, the tablet need not even be within sight of you, and the app still installs remotely.

Shooting a Panorama

Most variations of the Camera app sport a panoramic shooting mode. The *panorama* is a wide shot — it works by panning the tablet across a scene. The Camera app then stitches together several images to build the panoramic image.

To shoot a panoramic shot, follow these steps in the Camera app:

1. **Choose the Camera app's Panorama mode.**

For the stock Android Camera app, swipe your finger inward from the left side of the screen. Tap the Panorama icon, shown in the margin, to switch the app into Panorama mode.

2. **Hold the tablet steady, and then touch the Shutter icon.**

3. **Pivot in one direction as shown on the screen, following along with the animation.**

Watch as the image is rendered and saved.

Panoramas work best for vistas, wide shots, or perhaps for a family gathering where not everyone likes each other.

Avoid Data Surcharges

An important issue for anyone using an LTE Android tablet is whether you're about to burst through your monthly data quota. Mobile data surcharges can pinch the wallet, but your Android tablet has a handy tool to help you avoid data overages. It's the Data Usage screen, shown in Figure 23-2.

Data Usage Cycle

Figure 23-2: Data usage (Wi-Fi tablet version).

To access the Data Usage screen, follow these steps:

1. **Open the Settings app.**

2. **Choose Data Usage.**

   On some Samsung tablets, you'll find the Data Usage item by choosing the Connections tab at the top of the Settings app screen.

The main screen is full of useful information and handy tools. The line chart (refer to Figure 23-2) informs you of your data usage over a specific period. You can touch the Data Usage Cycle action bar to set that timespan, for example, matching it up with your cellular provider's monthly billing cycle.

Figure 23-2 shows the Wi-Fi tablet's Data Usage screen. An LTE tablet's screen features a Cellular tab, which lists options, a mobile data graph, and those apps that access the mobile data network.

To help avoid data surcharges, slide the master control by the item Set Cellular Data Limit to the On position. You can then adjust the red and black sliders on the chart to create a warning and cutoff values: When the black line is crossed, a warning appears. When the red line is crossed, the tablet ceases using the mobile data network.

✔ My monthly data plan is capped at 10GB. I set the limits (on all my Android devices) to 8GB for the warning (black bar) and 9.5GB for the stop (red bar).

✔ Keep in mind that the data usage shown on your tablet may not reflect the same values tracked by the cellular provider.

✔ To review access for a specific app, scroll down and choose it from those shown on the Data Usage screen. Only apps that access the network appear.

✔ If you notice that the app is using more data than it should, tap the App Settings button. You may be able to adjust some settings to curtail unintended Internet access.

Share Mobile Data

It's marvelously convenient to have a cellular tablet and be able to use the Internet wherever you roam. If you're feeling benevolent, you can share that mobile data connection in one of two ways: create a mobile hotspot or tether the connection to a single device, such as a laptop computer.

To create a mobile hotspot, heed these steps:

1. **Turn off the tablet's Wi-Fi radio.**

   There's no point in creating a Wi-Fi hotspot where one is already available.

2. **If possible, connect your Android tablet to a power source.**

   Running a mobile hotspot draws a lot of power.

3. **Open the Settings app.**

   Some tablets may feature an app named Mobile Hotspot or 4G Hotspot. If so, open it instead.

4. **Tap the More item in the Wireless & Networks section.**

5. **Choose Tethering & Portable Hotspot.**

   The Tethering & Mobile Hotspot item might be found on the main Settings app screen. On some Samsung tablets, touch the Connections tab and then choose the command Tethering and Portable Hotspot.

   You may see text describing the process. If so, dismiss the text.

6. **Activate the Portable Wi-Fi Hotspot item.**

   The item might be titled Mobile Hotspot.

7. **Choose the item Set Up Wi-Fi Hotspot or Portable Wi-Fi Hotspot.**

   Give the hotspot a name, or SSID, and review, change, or assign a password. You may need to tap a Configure button to set up these items.

8. **Touch the Save button or OK button to set your changes.**

To deactivate the mobile hotspot, repeat these steps but deactivate the Portable Wi-Fi Hotspot item in Step 6.

A more direct way to share the mobile data network is to tether the tablet to a computer by using a USB cable. Follow these steps to set up Internet tethering:

1. **Connect the tablet to a computer or laptop by using the USB cable.**

2. **Open the Settings app.**

3. **Choose the More item in the Wireless & Networks section.**

   On Samsung tablets, touch the Connections tab and then choose Tethering.

4. **Activate USB Tethering.**

The other device should instantly recognize the Android tablet as a "modem" with Internet access. Further configuration may be required, which depends on the computer using the tethered connection. For example, you may have to accept the installation of new software when prompted by Windows.

To terminate your Internet tethering session, repeat Steps 2 through 4 to remove the check mark. You can then disconnect the USB cable.

- ✔ You can continue to use the tablet while it's sharing the mobile data connection.

- ✔ Some cellular providers limit your tablet's ability to create a mobile Wi-Fi hotspot unless you pay an extra fee.

- ✔ Sharing the mobile data network connection more rapidly consumes your cellular data quota. Be careful!

Make the Tablet Dream

Does your tablet lock, or does it fall asleep? I prefer to think that the tablet sleeps. That begs the question of whether or not it dreams.

Of course it does! You can even see the dreams, providing you activate the Daydream feature — and you keep the tablet connected to a power source. Heed these steps:

1. **Start the Settings app.**

2. **Choose Display and then Daydream.**

   The Display item is found on the Device tab on some Samsung tablets.

3. **Ensure that the Daydream master control is in the On position.**

4. **Choose which type of daydream you want displayed.**

   Clock is a popular item, though I'm fond of Colors.

   Some daydreams feature the Settings icon. Use it to customize how the daydream appears.

5. **Tap the Action Overflow and choose When to Daydream button.**

6. **Choose the Either option.**

The daydreaming begins when the screen would normally time-out and lock. So if you've set the tablet to lock after 1 minute of inactivity, it daydreams instead — as long as it's plugged in or docked.

✔ To disrupt the dream, swipe the screen.

✔ The tablet doesn't lock when it daydreams. To lock the tablet, press the Power/Lock key.

Add Spice to Dictation

I feel that too few people use dictation, despite how handy it can be. Anyway, if you've used dictation, you might notice that it occasionally censors some of the words you utter. Perhaps you're the kind of person who doesn't put up with that kind of s***.

Relax. You can lift the vocal censorship ban by following these steps:

1. **Start the Settings app.**

2. **Choose Language & Input.**

   On Samsung tablets, tap the General tab to locate the Language and Input item.

3. **Choose Google Voice Typing.**

4. **Disable the option Block Offensive Words.**

And just what are offensive words? I would think that *censorship* is an offensive word. But no, apparently only a few choice words fall into this category. I won't print them here, because the tablet's censor retains the initial letter and generally makes the foul language easy to guess. D***.

Add a Word to the Dictionary

Betcha didn't know that your tablet sports a dictionary. The dictionary keeps track of words you type — words that may not be recognized as being spelled properly.

Words unknown to the tablet are highlighted on the screen. Sometimes the word is shown in a different color or on a different background, and sometimes it's underlined. To add that word to the tablet's dictionary, long-press it. You see the Add Word to Dictionary action, which sticks the word in the tablet's dictionary.

To review or edit the tablet's dictionary, follow these steps:

1. **Start the Settings app.**

2. **Choose Language & Input.**

   Tap the General tab on your Samsung tablet to locate this item.

3. **Choose Personal Dictionary.**

   This action may not be obvious on some tablets: Try choosing the keyboard first, and then choose either the Dictionary or User Dictionary command.

With the dictionary visible, you can review words, edit them, remove them, or manually add new ones. To edit or delete a word, long-press it. To add a word, tap the Add icon.

Add Useful Widgets

Your tablet features a wide assortment of widgets with which to festoon the Home screen. They can be exceedingly handy, although you may not realize it because the sample widgets often included with the tablet are weak and unimpressive.

Good widgets to add include navigation, contact, eBook, and web page favorites. Adding any of these widgets starts out the same. Here are the brief directions, with more specifics offered in Chapter 18:

1. **Long-press the Home screen.**

2. **Choose Widgets.**

   Some tablets keep the widgets on a tab on the Apps drawer, so look for them there when the two preceding steps fail utterly.

3. **Drag a widget to the Home screen.**

4. **Complete the process.**

The process is specific for each type of widget suggestion in this section.

Navigation widget

The Navigation widget allows you to quickly summon directions to a specific location from wherever you happen to be.

To add a navigation shortcut, select the Navigation widget. After you plop the widget on the Home screen, select a travelling method and destination. You can type a contact name, an address, a business name, and so on. Add a shortcut name, which is a brief description to fit under the widget on the Home screen. Tap the Save button.

Tap the Navigation widget to use it. Instantly, the Maps app starts and enters Navigation mode, steering you from wherever you are to the location referenced by the widget.

Contact widget

For your most popular contacts, consider adding a contact widget: Choose Contact widget, and then select the specific contact from the tablet's address book. A widget representing the contact (with the contact's picture, if available) appears on the Home screen. Tapping the widget displays information about the contact, along with an email link, a phone number, a map location, and other details supplied for that contact.

eBook widget

When you're mired in the middle of that latest potboiler, put a Book shortcut on the Home screen: Choose the Book widget, and then select which eBooks in your digital library you want to access. Tap the widget to open the Play Books app and jump right into the book at the spot where you were last reading.

Web bookmark widget

For your favorite websites, consider adding a Home page widget. You can add the Bookmarks widget, found on the Widgets screen, but an easier shortcut is to open the web browser app, navigate to the page you desire, and then tap the Action Overflow and choose Add to Homescreen.

Take a Screen Shot

A *screen shot,* also called a *screen cap* (for *cap*ture), is a picture of your tablet's touchscreen. So if you see something interesting on the screen or you just want to take a quick pic of your tablet life, you take a screen shot.

The stock Android method of shooting the screen is to press and hold both the Volume Down and Power/Lock keys at the same time. Upon success, the touchscreen image reduces in size, you may hear a shutter sound, and the screen shot is saved.

- Screen shots are accessed through the Photos app. If your tablet uses the old Gallery app, you'll find screen shots in their own album.

- Some Samsung tablets use a Motion command to capture the screen: Hold your hand perpendicular to the tablet, like you're giving it a karate chop. Swipe the edge of your palm over the screen, right-to-left or left-to-right. Upon success, you hear a shutter sound.

- Internally, screen shots are stored in the Pictures/Screenshots folder. They're created in the PNG graphics file format.

Ten Things to Remember

*H*ave you ever tried to tie a string around your finger to remember something? I've not attempted that technique just yet. The main reason is that I keep forgetting to buy string and I have no way to remind myself.

For your Android tablet, some things are definitely worth remembering. From that long, long list, I've come up with ten good ones.

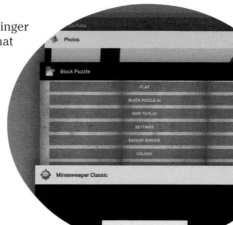

Dictate Text

Dictation is such a handy feature — don't forget to use it! You can dictate most text instead of typing it. Just tap the Microphone key on the keyboard — or anywhere you see the Microphone icon — and begin speaking. Your utterances are translated to text. In most cases, the translation is instantaneous.

 ✔ See Chapter 4 for more information on Android tablet dictation.

 ✔ Google Now doesn't require you to tap the Microphone icon. Instead, utter the phrase "OK Google" and it starts listening.

Change the Tablet's Orientation

Larger-format Android tablets have a natural horizontal orientation. Smaller tablets beg to be held vertically. You won't break any law by changing the tablet's orientation.

Apps such as Chrome and Gmail can look much better in the horizontal orientation, whereas apps such as Play Books and Play Music can look much better in the vertical orientation. The key to changing orientation is to rotate the tablet to view the app the way you like best. Rotate!

 ✔ Not every app changes its orientation. Some apps — specifically, games — appear in only one orientation: landscape or portrait.

 ✔ eBook reader apps have screen rotation settings that let you lock the orientation to the way you want, regardless of what the tablet is doing.

Work the Quick Settings

Many tablet controls are available at a single, handy location: the Quick Settings drawer. Pull it down to turn tablet features on or off, such as Wi-Fi, Bluetooth, screen orientation, and other On–Off settings. Using the Quick Settings drawer is far more expedient than visiting the Settings app.

 ✔ Some tablets feature a vast array of Quick Settings, only a handful of which appear at a time. Try swiping the Quick Settings left or right to see more.

 ✔ As a bonus, you may find a Settings app shortcut in the Quick Settings drawer.

Employ Keyboard Suggestions

Don't forget to take advantage of the predictive-text suggestions that appear above the onscreen keyboard while you're typing text. In fact, you don't even need to tap a suggestion; to replace your text with the highlighted suggestion, simply touch the onscreen keyboard's Space key. Zap! The word appears.

Refer to Chapter 4 for information on using the keyboard suggestions.

Avoid the Battery Hogs

Three items on an Android tablet suck down battery power faster than a massive alien fleet is defeated by a plucky antihero who just wants the girl:

- The display
- Navigation
- Wireless radios

The display is obviously a most necessary part of your Android tablet — but it's also a tremendous power hog. The Adaptive Brightness (also called Auto Brightness) setting is your best friend for saving power with the display. See Chapter 19.

Navigation is certainly handy, but the battery drains rapidly because the tablet's touchscreen is on the entire time and the speaker is dictating your directions. If possible, plug the tablet into the car's power socket when you're navigating.

Wireless radios include Wi-Fi networking, Bluetooth, and GPS. Though they do require extra power, they aren't power hogs, like navigation and the display. Still, when power is getting low, consider disabling those items.

See Chapter 22 for more information on managing the tablet's battery.

Unlock and Launch

Quite a few Android tablets feature special Lock screen icons. For example, you may see an icon representing the Camera app. Samsung tablets can sport several app icons on the Lock screen. To unlock and launch an app, swipe the icon across the screen. That app instantly runs.

- Depending on the screen lock that's installed, the app may run but the tablet won't be unlocked. To do anything other than run the app, you must work the screen lock.
- Samsung tablet lock-screen icons work only when the swipe lock is set.

Make Phone Calls

Yeah, I know: It's not a phone. Even Android tablets that use the mobile data network can't make phone calls. Why let that stop you?

Both the Hangouts and Skype apps let you place phone calls and video-chat with your friends. Boost your Skype account with some coinage and you can even dial into real phones. See Chapter 8 for details.

Check Your Schedule

The Calendar app reminds you of upcoming dates and generally keeps you on schedule. A great way to augment the calendar is to employ the Calendar widget on the Home screen.

The Calendar widget lists the current date and then a long list of upcoming appointments. It's a great way to check your schedule, especially when you use your tablet all the time. I recommend sticking the Calendar widget right on the main or center Home screen panel.

✔ See Chapter 18 for information on adding widgets to the Home screen; Chapter 14 covers the Calendar app.

✔ As long as I'm handing out tips, remember to specify location information when you set up an appointment in the Calendar app. Type the information just as though you were using the Maps app to search. You can then quickly navigate to your next appointment by touching the location item when you review the event.

Snap a Pic of That Contact

Here's something I always forget: Whenever you're near one of your contacts, take the person's picture. Sure, some people are bashful, but most folks are flattered. The idea is to build up the tablet's address book so that all your contacts have photos.

When taking a picture, be sure to show it to the person before you assign it to the contact. Let them decide whether it's good enough.

Use Google Now

Google is known worldwide for its searching capabilities and its popular website. By gum, the word *Google* is synonymous with searching. So please don't forget that your Android tablet, which uses the Google Android operating system, has a powerful search, nay, *knowledge* command. It's called Google Now.

✔ On most Android tablets, you access Google Now by swiping the screen from bottom to top. This trick may even work on the Lock screen.

✔ The Google Now app is titled *Google*.

✔ The Google Search widget provides a shortcut into Google Now.

✔ Review Chapter 14 for details on various Google Now commands.

✔ Beyond Google Now, you can take advantage of the various Search icons found in just about every app on an Android tablet. Use the Search icon to search for information, locations, people — you name it. It's handy.

Index

• J •

• K •

Notes

Notes

Notes

Notes

About the Author

Dan Gookin has been writing about technology for over 25 years. He combines his love of writing with his gizmo fascination to create books that are informative, entertaining, and not boring. Having written over 130 titles with 12 million copies in print translated into over 30 languages, Dan can attest that his method of crafting computer tomes seems to work.

Perhaps his most famous title is the original *DOS For Dummies,* published in 1991. It became the world's fastest-selling computer book, at one time moving more copies per week than the *New York Times* number-one bestseller (though, as a reference, it could not be listed on the *Times'* Best Sellers list). That book spawned the entire line of *For Dummies* books, which remains a publishing phenomenon to this day.

Dan's most popular titles include *PCs For Dummies, Word For Dummies, Laptops For Dummies,* and *Android Phones For Dummies*. He also maintains the vast and helpful website www.wambooli.com.

Dan holds a degree in Communications/Visual Arts from the University of California, San Diego. He lives in the Pacific Northwest, where he enjoys spending time with his sons playing video games indoors while they enjoy the gentle woods of Idaho.

Publisher's Acknowledgments

Acquisitions Editor: Katie Mohr

Senior Project Editor: Paul Levesque

Copy Editor: Rebecca Whitney

Editorial Assistant: Claire Brock

Sr. Editorial Assistant: Cherie Case

Project Coordinator: Kumar Chellapa

Cover Image: Yeko Photo Studio/Shutterstock, Kirill__M/Shutterstock, Feaspb/ Shutterstock, kentoh/iStockphoto

| le & Mac | Personal Finance | Mediterranean Diet | Diabetes For Dummies, |

le & Mac

For Dummies,
Edition
1-118-72306-7

ne For Dummies,
Edition
1-118-69083-3

s All-in-One
Dummies, 4th Edition
1-118-82210-4

Mavericks
Dummies
1-118-69188-5

ging & Social Media

book For Dummies,
Edition
1-118-63312-0

al Media Engagement
Dummies
1-118-53019-1

dPress For Dummies,
Edition
1-118-79161-5

ness

k Investing
Dummies, 4th Edition
1-118-37678-2

sting For Dummies,
Edition
0-470-90545-6

Personal Finance
For Dummies, 7th Edition
978-1-118-11785-9

QuickBooks 2014
For Dummies
978-1-118-72005-9

Small Business Marketing
Kit For Dummies,
3rd Edition
978-1-118-31183-7

Careers

Job Interviews
For Dummies, 4th Edition
978-1-118-11290-8

Job Searching with Social
Media For Dummies,
2nd Edition
978-1-118-67856-5

Personal Branding
For Dummies
978-1-118-11792-7

Resumes For Dummies,
6th Edition
978-0-470-87361-8

Starting an Etsy Business
For Dummies, 2nd Edition
978-1-118-59024-9

Diet & Nutrition

Belly Fat Diet For Dummies
978-1-118-34585-6

Mediterranean Diet
For Dummies
978-1-118-71525-3

Nutrition For Dummies,
5th Edition
978-0-470-93231-5

Digital Photography

Digital SLR Photography
All-in-One For Dummies,
2nd Edition
978-1-118-59082-9

Digital SLR Video &
Filmmaking For Dummies
978-1-118-36598-4

Photoshop Elements 12
For Dummies
978-1-118-72714-0

Gardening

Herb Gardening
For Dummies, 2nd Edition
978-0-470-61778-6

Gardening with Free-Range
Chickens For Dummies
978-1-118-54754-0

Health

Boosting Your Immunity
For Dummies
978-1-118-40200-9

Diabetes For Dummies,
4th Edition
978-1-118-29447-5

Living Paleo For Dummies
978-1-118-29405-5

Big Data

Big Data For Dummies
978-1-118-50422-2

Data Visualization
For Dummies
978-1-118-50289-1

Hadoop For Dummies
978-1-118-60755-8

**Language &
Foreign Language**

500 Spanish Verbs
For Dummies
978-1-118-02382-2

English Grammar
For Dummies, 2nd Edition
978-0-470-54664-2

French All-in-One
For Dummies
978-1-118-22815-9

German Essentials
For Dummies
978-1-118-18422-6

Italian For Dummies,
2nd Edition
978-1-118-00465-4

 Available in print and e-book formats.

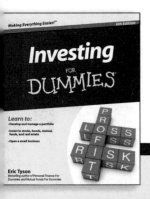 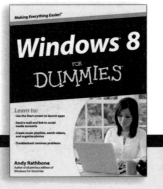  

Available wherever books are sold. **For more information or to order direct visit www.dummies.com**

Math & Science

Algebra I For Dummies,
2nd Edition
978-0-470-55964-2

Anatomy and Physiology
For Dummies, 2nd Edition
978-0-470-92326-9

Astronomy For Dummies,
3rd Edition
978-1-118-37697-3

Biology For Dummies,
2nd Edition
978-0-470-59875-7

Chemistry For Dummies,
2nd Edition
978-1-118-00730-3

1001 Algebra II Practice
Problems For Dummies
978-1-118-44662-1

Microsoft Office

Excel 2013 For Dummies
978-1-118-51012-4

Office 2013 All-in-One
For Dummies
978-1-118-51636-2

PowerPoint 2013
For Dummies
978-1-118-50253-2

Word 2013 For Dummies
978-1-118-49123-2

Music

Blues Harmonica
For Dummies
978-1-118-25269-7

Guitar For Dummies,
3rd Edition
978-1-118-11554-1

iPod & iTunes
For Dummies, 10th Edition
978-1-118-50864-0

Programming

Beginning Programming
with C For Dummies
978-1-118-73763-7

Excel VBA Programming
For Dummies, 3rd Edition
978-1-118-49037-2

Java For Dummies,
6th Edition
978-1-118-40780-6

Religion & Inspiration

The Bible For Dummies
978-0-7645-5296-0

Buddhism For Dummies,
2nd Edition
978-1-118-02379-2

Catholicism For Dummies,
2nd Edition
978-1-118-07778-8

Self-Help & Relationships

Beating Sugar Addiction
For Dummies
978-1-118-54645-1

Meditation For Dummies,
3rd Edition
978-1-118-29144-3

Seniors

Laptops For Seniors
For Dummies, 3rd Edition
978-1-118-71105-7

Computers For Seniors
For Dummies, 3rd Edition
978-1-118-11553-4

iPad For Seniors
For Dummies, 6th Edition
978-1-118-72826-0

Social Security
For Dummies
978-1-118-20573-0

Smartphones & Tablets

Android Phones
For Dummies, 2nd Edition
978-1-118-72030-1

Nexus Tablets
For Dummies
978-1-118-77243-0

Samsung Galaxy S 4
For Dummies
978-1-118-64222-1

Samsung Galaxy Tabs
For Dummies
978-1-118-77294-2

Test Prep

ACT For Dummies,
5th Edition
978-1-118-01259-8

ASVAB For Dummies,
3rd Edition
978-0-470-63760-9

GRE For Dummies,
7th Edition
978-0-470-88921-3

Officer Candidate Tests
For Dummies
978-0-470-59876-4

Physician's Assistant Ex
For Dummies
978-1-118-11556-5

Series 7 Exam For Dum
978-0-470-09932-2

Windows 8

Windows 8.1 All-in-One
For Dummies
978-1-118-82087-2

Windows 8.1 For Dumm
978-1-118-82121-3

Windows 8.1 For Dumm
Book + DVD Bundle
978-1-118-82107-7

 **Available in print and e-book formats.**

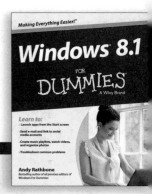

Available wherever books are sold. **For more information or to order direct visit www.dummies.com**

Take Dummies with you everywhere you go!

Whether you are excited about e-books, want more from the web, must have your mobile apps, or are swept up in social media, Dummies makes everything easier.

Visit Us

bit.ly/JE0O

Like Us

on.fb.me/1f1ThNu

Follow Us

bit.ly/ZDytkR

Watch Us

bit.ly/gbOQHn

Join Us

kd.in/1gurkMm

Pin Us

bit.ly/16caOLd

Circle Us

bit.ly/1aQTuDQ

Shop Us

bit.ly/4dEp9

For Dummies is the global leader in the reference category and one of the most trusted and highly regarded brands in the world. No longer just focused on books, customers now have access to the For Dummies content they need in the format they want. Let us help you develop a solution that will fit your brand and help you connect with your customers.

Advertising & Sponsorships

Connect with an engaged audience on a powerful multimedia site, and position your message alongside expert how-to content.

Targeted ads • Video • Email marketing • Microsites • Sweepstakes sponsorship

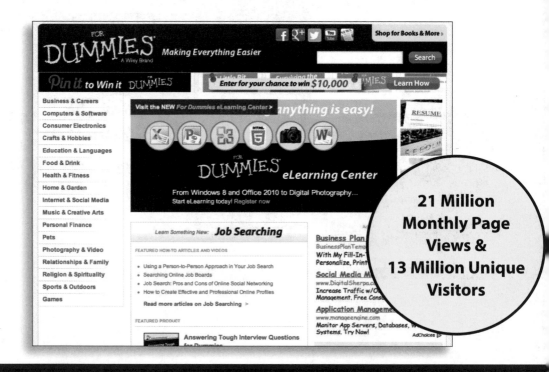

For Dummies is a registered trademark of John Wiley & Sons, Inc.

# of For Dummies

Custom Publishing

Reach a global audience in any language by creating a solution that will differentiate you from competitors, amplify your message, and encourage customers to make a buying decision.

Apps • Books • eBooks • Video • Audio • Webinars

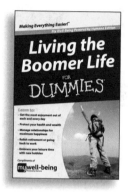

Brand Licensing & Content

Leverage the strength of the world's most popular reference brand to reach new audiences and channels of distribution.

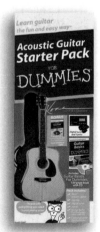

For more information, visit www.Dummies.com/biz

DUMMIES
A Wiley Brand

Dummies products make life easier

- DIY
- Consumer Electronics
- Crafts
- Software
- Cookware
- Hobbies
- Videos
- Music
- Games
- and More!

WITHDRAWN!

$26.99   8/31/15.

LONGWOOD PUBLIC LIBRARY
800 Middle Country Road
Middle Island, NY 11953
(631) 924-6400
longwoodlibrary.org

LIBRARY HOURS

Monday-Friday	9:30 a.m. - 9:00 p.m.
Saturday	9:30 a.m. - 5:00 p.m.
Sunday (Sept-June)	1:00 p.m. - 5:00 p.m.

For more info...   ...store by category.

For Dummies is a registered trademark of Joh...

FOR DUMMIE

A Wiley B...